For Jim Manning

Thanks for teaching me
Something about writing
and about life.

Michael R. Jaggs

1-6-2007

PASSION FOR REALITY

Passion for Reality

Paul Cabot and the

Boston Mutual Fund

Michael R. Yogg

To order additional copies of this book, contact:
Xlibris Corporation
1-888-795-4274
www.Xlibris.com
Orders@Xlibris.com
34382

Contents

TABLES

Photo Credits

Cover photo: Artwork by Bartek Malysa is reprinted with the permission of Harvard Magazine, The New York Times copyright © 1936, Harvard University Archives call # HUD 325.25 page 853, and State Street Research & Management Co. (now part of BlackRock Inc.)

Author photo and photo of Edward Leffler: reprinted with the permission of Putnam Investments.

Photo of Richard Paine: reprinted with the permission of State Street Research & Management Co. (now part of BlackRock Inc.)

Photo of Paul Cabot, Sidney Weinberg, and Sen. John F. Kennedy: reprinted with the permission of the Harvard University Archives call # HUP-SF Commencement 1959 (61).

Photo of George Bennett: reprinted with the permission of Mr. Bennett

All others from the personal collection of Paul C. Cabot III and reprinted with his permission.

In memory of
Howell J. Yogg and
Ellen C. Johnson Yogg

ACKNOWLEDGEMENTS

T his book builds upon the research and scholarship of others. While the endnotes make this clear, some contributors deserve special mention. Natalie Grow's PhD dissertation, "The 'Boston-Type Open-End Fund'— Development of a National Financial Institution: 1924-1940," placed Paul Cabot's activities in context and greatly enriched my understanding of the events of this period. Her bibliography of sources was an especially useful aid. But I only found these sources, and others, due to the resourcefulness of Paul Keane, a researcher (and something of a detective), working in the Washington, D.C. area.

While I heard all of the Paul Cabot stories from the source, I would not have remembered them all had not two talented interviewers, Rosario Tosiello and Jessica Holland, coaxed them out of Paul with tape recorders running. Ms. Holland did it twice: first for Goldman Sachs and a second time for the Columbia University Oral History Research Office Collection. The latter interview, available on tape at Columbia, is an absolute delight that captures Paul's personality better than any book could, and should be turned into a one-man play.

The best part of writing a book is the new friends one makes and the old friendships that are rekindled. The following contributed by supplying information, documents, photographs, advice, and, most important, encouragement: Bernard Bailyn, Frederick Ballou, Bob Beck, George Bennett, Peter Bennett, Francis H. Burr, Frederick C. Cabot, Paul Cabot, Jr., Paul Cabot, III, Wayne DeCesar of the National Archives & Records Administration, Charles Ellis, Charles Flather, Bill Frohlich, Bart Geer, Andrea Goldstein and her colleagues at the Harvard University Archives, Llewellyn Howland, Morton Keller, Phyllis Keller, Paula Kerrigan, Edward M. Lamont, Robert A. Lawrence, George Lewis, Marten Liander, Jacqueline Lynch, Frank Mandic and Larry Mills of the SEC Records Office, Paul Morgan, Robert H. Parks and his colleagues at the FDR Presidential Library, H. Bradlee Perry, George Putnam, Jr., William Saltonstall, John Schwartz and his colleagues at Goldman Sachs, John Thorndike, Peter Vermilye, Ike Williams, John Wood, Virginia "Chris" Cabot Wood, and last but not least, Joan Yogg.

Ken Lisotte of Emerson Consulting Inc. provided assistance at crucial points, most importantly by recommending Kathleen Victory Hannisian as my editor.

Introduction

"That Passion for Reality"

[He felt] hatred of all shams, scorn of all mummeries, a bitter merciless pleasure in the hard facts. And that passion for reality was beautiful in him . . . . He was a millionaire, and yet scrupulously simple . . .

from George Santayana, *The Last Puritan*[1]

How can I write objectively about someone I liked and admired? In the case of Paul Cabot, this question almost answers itself. He wouldn't have had it any other way. Paul is often associated with the phrase, "First, you've got to get the facts. Then you've got to face the facts," the quintessential expression of hardheaded rationalism, applied to the investment business. He faced the facts about stocks, business associates, and himself.

Why am I writing about Paul Cabot? To explain this I must go back to 1978. In that year I completed my PhD in history, but without prospects for a good academic job. I entered a six-week program that prepared humanities scholars for positions in business. And I went to work at Paul Cabot's State Street Research & Management Company. In 1984, the program sponsors asked me to contribute an essay to a book chronicling the experiences of its graduates. The essay traces the path that led to this book.

In that essay I compared the values of successful scholars and successful investors by drawing parallels between the thinking of Oscar Handlin, the historian, and that of Paul Cabot. The former was the dissertation advisor to my dissertation advisor, Bernard Bailyn; the latter founded the company I was then working for and hired, trained, and influenced the men who had hired, trained, and influenced me.

I defined a scholar as someone who studies evidence and can develop "an insight into its significance that contributes to the understanding of a broader range of issues." The scholar "discovers value that others have missed, either by

15

uncovering fresh evidence, or by looking with fresh insight into material previously studied by others. [He] sees something no one else has seen, understands its value, and knows how to make use of it." Similarly, the investor either uncovers fresh evidence about a company, perhaps from its customers, or studies the publicly available information with fresh insight. The key skills in these searches are the intellectual honesty to see the facts, rather than what confirms one's preconceived notions, and the creativity to understand their significance. Handlin identifies the key event as the discovery of facts in conflict with the scholar's original thesis. This "encounter with the evidence" pushes him toward a new version of the thesis. I concluded, "Encountering evidence in the world of scholarship and facing the facts of the investment world are very similar intellectual and emotional experiences."[2]

During a long and productive life, Paul Cabot (1898-1994) founded the first mutual fund and compiled an extraordinary investment record with it. He championed high standards of fiduciary responsibility when mutual funds were new and helped shape crucial legislation when the industry was under attack in the 1930s. And he shifted the bulk of the Harvard endowment from preferred stocks and bonds to common stocks in time for the post-World War II bull market, thereby setting an example for other colleges to follow. But I have written this book as much to capture who Paul Cabot was, his character, personality, and intellect, as to chronicle what he did.

Handlin uses the analogy of the puzzle to describe the work of the historian, who struggles to put the pieces in place but frequently comes upon "unexpected fragments," those stubborn facts in conflict with his original thesis.[3] While the facts of Paul's life are clear, how they fit together and contributed to the development of his personality is a puzzle, which this book describes but only partially solves. The pieces are these.

First of all, family: Paul saw his father as "the epitome of complete honesty and frankness" who instilled in his children "the necessity of trying to make something worthwhile of [their] lives and have regard for the well being" of others.[4] He was equally appreciative of his mother, who took responsibility for his religious training. Paul's children remember that their grandmother even supervised *their* religious training—"with a vengeance," according to one of them. While Paul was known more for his cigar smoking, whiskey drinking, and coarse language than for his religious faith, he adopted the rhetoric and the mindset of a Massachusetts preacher, some might say the prophet Jeremiah, when in the 1920s and 1930s he railed against the abuses of the investment trusts.

Second, the milieu of upper-class Boston: behind the conventions of Brahmin society laid a culture of rationalism and realism dating from when the Puritan settlers with their rigorous intellectualism encountered the harsh conditions of the New England wilderness. Their experience, as related by twentieth-century historians, transformed their culture over the course of more than a century into one that valued independence, shrewdness, and philanthropy—qualities that today are identified more as Yankee than as Puritan. This culture, along with commercial success and certain legal developments in Massachusetts, created the conditions for the growth of the money management profession in Boston in the nineteenth century. Paul possessed independence and shrewdness. Years before his birth, his family had achieved commercial success, social position, and the mastery of legal and financial affairs required of the Boston trustee. When Yale honored Paul with a doctor of laws degree in 1965, the citation praised "the bluntness of your speech and the soundness of your cold roast Boston eye for the Yankee Dollar." Paul was a product of place as well as of family.

Third, liberal education: Paul downplayed and underestimated the importance of all but the most practical, business-oriented portion of his schooling. He showed little interest in the study of literature, the core of an upper-class Boston education, but beneath the surface he absorbed certain values of classical and some modern writers, such as simplicity, clarity, and intellectual honesty. His choice of an undergraduate major, Mathematics, reflected a penchant for analytical rigor, which was most evident later on in business school and in his career.

Fourth, professional education: in business school he explored questions that really interested him. He became a top student and a scholar, and did research that, while never culminating in a completed doctoral dissertation, had an important impact on the history of American finance. Paul's hardheaded rationalism complemented the German Enlightenment empiricism of his advisor, Arthur Stone Dewing, who had begun his academic career studying philosophy.[5]

These four pieces of the puzzle all played important roles in Paul's business career and later life. While it is difficult, perhaps arbitrary, to separate them, a story about a decision he had to make shows them coming together. In 1932, Paul's company, State Street Research & Management, had the opportunity to purchase Lee, Higginson & Co., which went into liquidation after the suicide of Ivar Kreuger and the collapse of his Swedish Match Company. Paul wanted to consult his partner and cousin, Richard Paine, on the matter, but Paine was extremely ill and could not be disturbed. Because of his respect for his uncle and because father and son thought so much alike, he decided to consult Dick's father, Robert Treat Paine II, instead.

> **I remember trying to give him all the pros and cons of taking it over, . . . all the facts, . . . answering any questions he had . . . . And then I ended by asking him, have you any knowledge, Uncle Bob, of whether it is my judgment that we should or should not buy this company, because I wanted to try and just give you the facts without putting my personal opinion in them.**

Bob said that he did not know where Paul stood on the matter and proceeded to give him unbiased advice.[6]

In "Truth and Politics," Hannah Arendt identifies the deliberate confusion of fact and opinion as a form of lying. She then traces the disinterested pursuit of truth back to Homer.[7] Paul did not consciously trace intellectual honesty back to the Greeks, but he grew up with writers like Homer and Thucydides. While literature never captured his imagination, what Thucydides called "the simple way of looking at things, which is so much the mark of a noble nature," had an impact on his careers as mathematics major, business student, scholar, and investor.

Still, all of this does not explain Paul Cabot. As rich as his background was, it was not unique. Hundreds of his contemporaries had similar advantages and grew up more like John P. Marquand's fictional George Apley than Paul Cabot; that is, they lacked the insight and the force to question things and to change them. But Paul stands in sharp contrast to Marquand characters like Apley who said, "I am the sort of man I am because environment prevented my being anything else."[8] Paul adopted the highest ideals of Boston society—learning, leadership, service, honesty—but fused them onto a pragmatic, sometimes iconoclastic, personality. Marquand did not give Apley the courage or perspective to break through the limitations of his time and place the way Paul did. Instead, he relied on Apley's "biographer," Mr. Willing, to face the facts that Apley suppressed during his lifetime, though Marquand makes it clear that Apley shared some of Paul's honesty and would have lived more authentically had not the bonds of family and the conventions of society discouraged it.

Marquand wrote a novel in the form of a biography. George Santayana called *The Last Puritan* "a memoir in the form of a novel." They both created fictional characters and fictional biographers to present their views on Boston culture and society, among other subjects. But Paul's personality was much more powerful than those of Marquand's and Santayana's protagonists. He was born with a mental and emotional confidence that developed in the unique culture of Boston to produce an extraordinarily independent, forceful, and productive individual, more American than Bostonian or New Englander. To understand Paul and what he represented we must look to the specific, in his words, the realities and facts. These realities and facts begin on the next page.

Chapter I

Family, Education, and Army Service

> Dear Ma,
>
> I just received your letter advising me to quit. *Nothing doing.* I have
> been through half of this course & I'm going to finish it. It will take
> a stick of dynamite to get me out of here ... I hate this life .... so
> much that it makes me obstinate and pig-headed & come what may
> I'm going thru with it.[9]
>
> **Paul Cabot in a letter from the Army in 1918**

> That got me into studying these common stocks—other people must
> have been doing the same thing but I wasn't aware of it. At any rate
> I used to study the earnings and I still believe that the single most
> important fact, other than the honesty of the management, is the
> amount and direction of your earnings. So it got to me, and that's
> what I think started me in this sort of business—got me studying ...
> the companies and trying to determine what is the real value.[10]
>
> **Paul Cabot in 1971 reflecting on his Business School**
> **summer job in 1922**

C-R-A-C-K!
   Paul Cabot fired, pulled his ROTC rifle in from the window of
Persis Smith Hall, and gleefully surveyed the damage. Students were holding a
dance in the Quadrangle below.

> [The shot] had a terrific effect. All the little girls thought the Germans were out for them. They all rushed for shelter and there was terrible excitement.

It was a beautiful warm spring evening, May 29, 1918, at the end of Paul's freshman year. The next day he would leave Harvard for ROTC camp in Lancaster, Massachusetts, and, one month later, move on to the Army training camps at Plattsburg, New York. That day he had drilled with his unit at Fresh Pond under the direction of Lieutenant Andre Morize, later a Harvard Professor of French Literature, and other disabled French officers sent over to train Harvard students for war in Europe. Perhaps, in his mind, Paul was already in France, though with service in Massachusetts, New York, and Kentucky, Harvard was as close as he would get to the fighting. But whether it was the idea of going to war or the whiskey he was drinking, he thought nothing of shooting blanks into a group of Harvard students and their dates. Then he did it again.

> I let go another round. The door opened and the disciplinarian of the dormitory came in and caught me with the rifle with the smoke coming out of the barrel. Luckily my friends kicked the booze under the bed . . . . I knew I was in major trouble.

Paul tried to save his situation. He apologized to the "disciplinarian," Reginald Coggeshall, told him that he knew that what he had done was wrong, and explained that this was his last night at Harvard before going on active duty. Coggeshall, according to Paul, said that he would not report the incident, but he did. An unsigned memo in Paul's folder reads, in part,

> When the affair [the Freshman Jubilee] was nearly over, some one shot a rifle from Paul Cabot's window. Mr. Coggeshall was down below, and just as he looked up, he saw some one at the window drinking, then the rifle was thrust through the window, and another shot was fired. He went up immediately and found the room filled with fellows, all more or less under the influence of liquor. J. Otis '20 and Richard Saltonstall '20, who was in a sailor's uniform, were particularly ugly and disagreeable . . . . Then John Connolly, the yard policeman, came up. Otis and Saltonstall were rough in their attitude toward him.

Another memo reads,

Coggeshall says that before the dancing ended a Freshman came to him and complained that Cabot insisted on dancing with Freshman girl & that Cabot was drunk. Cabot's appearance and talk gave Coggeshall the impression that Cabot was drunk.

Shortly after Paul arrived at Plattsburg, he learned that Harvard planned to expel the entire group in his room that evening, including his future partner Dick Saltonstall and his future brother-in-law Sumner Roberts. Paul's family connections, however, saved him and his friends. His father, Henry Bromfield Cabot, interceded with *his* friend, Harvard President A. Lawrence Lowell, and, after being "admonished," Paul and his accomplices ended up graduating with their classes in 1920 and 1921. Dean E. R. Hay had written President Lowell on June 3rd, "I know that you will be personally interested in the matter, and if you wish to make any suggestions I shall be glad to have them." Paul's father wrote a thank you note to another dean.[11]

Paul later earned a reputation for honesty and integrity, and during the Depression was called upon to help rewrite the laws, in some ways the culture, governing the investment industry; but none of this was evident in 1918. On June 12th, writing in his own defense from the Plattsburgh training camp, he insisted,

In the first place I was not drunk and no one in my room was drunk .... I do not consider the disturbance was in the slightest way serious .... Thanking you for taking no action on the word of a watchman, reputed to be dishonest, I am sincerely yours, Paul C. Cabot [12]

At Paul's memorial service seventy-six years later, his son Frederick tried to capture the spirit of his father's mischief making, specifically the shooting incident, by quoting Yeats. "Not but in merriment begin a chase,/Nor but in merriment a quarrel."[13]

The Henry B. Cabot Family

Paul had known Harvard's President Lowell all of his life as perhaps the most brilliant and prominent of the many social and intellectual leaders of Boston who came frequently to Sunday lunch at the Cabot house on Heath Street in Brookline. The brother of poet Amy and astronomer Percival, Lowell came from what one could call a Renaissance family, equally accomplished in art, science, scholarship, and making money. President Lowell himself, according to Samuel Eliot Morison, had a mind of "Greek agility," meaning he was a quick learner and an enthusiastic teacher. Lowell was also a man of his time and place. Typical of many Progressives of his day, he worked on behalf of the Immigration Restriction League, supported the Massachusetts judicial system in its conviction of Sacco and Vanzetti, and opposed Louis Brandeis' appointment to the Supreme Court—on grounds of character.

Not only were Lowell and Henry Cabot friends, in 1893 they had worked together on the formation of The Boston Personal Property Trust, a precursor of the mutual fund, which had helped Harvard faculty members and staff invest in stocks. The trust differed from the modern mutual fund in that it was only valued four times a year; redemptions could only occur on those four dates; and even then, only if buyers for the redeemed shares could be found. The trust was later absorbed into the George Putnam Fund, one of the early mutual funds.[14]

Henry had built his house shortly after his marriage in 1892 on land that his father had bought in 1871. Today, at the beginning of the twenty-first century, six large luxury homes sit on that twenty-five acre parcel of land along a private road. But when Paul was a boy, at the beginning of the twentieth century, only three houses stood there: the house of his grandparents, Elizabeth Mason and Walter Channing Cabot; that of his aunt and uncle, Ruth Cabot and Robert Treat Paine II; and Paul's family's house. The twenty-five acres at the top of Heath Hill were all Cabot territory and Paul and his brothers and sisters and cousins had the complete run of the place. Paul's cousin and future partner Richard Paine, born in 1893, was the second oldest of nine Cabot grandchildren on the hill, while Paul was in the middle, fifth oldest of the nine.

Built to suit the family's needs, the Henry Cabot house was a very long rambling brick edifice, with the parents and the four brothers sleeping on the second floor. When the girls were born, Henry had a third story built for the boys, who moved up to make room for their sisters. The ground floor included a dining room and living rooms. The kitchen was below, adjacent to the cellar and connected to the dining room by a dumbwaiter. The Cabots generally had about five people serving as help, several of whom stayed with the family for over twenty-five years, one for almost eighty years.

Henry and Anna McMasters Codman Cabot, also known as Anne, were married at Trinity Church in Boston by the Reverend Phillips Brooks, who had been rector there for twenty-two years, but at that time was Episcopal Bishop of Massachusetts. The charismatic preacher, who had been a national figure since the Civil War, had been an important factor in drawing many upper-class Bostonians away from Unitarianism and to the Episcopal Church during the last third of the nineteenth century. Her grandchildren remember Anna, or Anne, Cabot migrating back and forth between the Episcopal and the Unitarian churches depending on the quality of the preaching. They saw her as an intellectual, very interested in the issues discussed in the sermons.

The Cabots moved to Brookline shortly after their marriage and their boys Henry Jr., Powell, Paul, and Charles were born in 1894, 1896, 1898, and 1900. Paul was almost five when his sister Anne was born in 1903 and almost nine when Susan, the youngest, arrived in 1907. Henry Senior was a lawyer, a trustee, and an investor, primarily in real estate but also in stocks. His real estate interests extended as far as Seattle. He also served as a director of the Edison Company (later Boston Edison), a director of the Boston-Lowell Railroad, and a trustee of six real estate trusts in Massachusetts, Minnesota, and Washington.[15]

Anna stayed at home with the children. In his early eighties, Paul looked back on

> an extremely happy household, and I think we all got along beautifully . . . . We were all very fond of one another. Of course we had our scraps every now and then . . . . There was always a lot of . . . good fun practical joking . . . . I and my younger brother always had a lot of guinea pigs that we kept down in the cellar, and much to my mother's annoyance we'd bring the guinea pigs up and take them to bed with us. You can imagine the result.[16]

Years later Paul remembered "an extremely happy household; and I think we all got along beautifully." Left to right: Paul, Anne Susan, Anne (mother), Charles, Powell, Henry Sr., Henry Jr.

For Paul, who was rambunctious in his nineties, a happy household would necessarily include scraps, practical joking, and guinea pigs in his bed.

According to Paul's sister Susan, the "scraps" didn't only involve the boys.

> [T]he first green peas had come from John Crockett's and they were
> absolutely yummy. They'd gone all the way around the table before
> they came to Charles. Anne, next to him was the last on the totem
> pole; and Charles took every last pea! Then, with a dimple and a
> twinkle he turned to her and said,
>
> "Did you want any?"
>
> At which, without a word, she turned and knocked his chair over
> backward. I can see him now, upside down with his legs in the air,
> absolute amazement on his face, and grinning like a Cheshire Cat.[17]

The "good fun practical joking" apparently increased when their grandmother, Elizabeth Cabot, was in charge. Paul remembered that "when our parents took a vacation from their four howling young men and their two little daughters," Grandma Cabot took on the "God-awful job" of looking after them. Elizabeth Cabot's diary notes,

> Get my exercise by walking the piazza [of her summer home]. 62
> times from one end east to west it makes a mile. I drop a bean [in a
> jar] & walk 30 times several times a day very fast.

But as Paul remembered it,

> She had a system how to measure the distance. She'd put stones in
> a little jug, indicating how far she'd walked; and of course we'd add
> stones and subtract stones and drive her nearly crazy.

When they had finished driving her crazy, they liked to scare her by blowing cigar smoke through chinks in the kitchen wall and make her think the house was on fire.[18]

Paul had a serious side too, even as a child. According to Susan, he never played with his sisters. "He was absolutely absorbed in his own interests and his own friends." On one occasion he and Sumner Roberts built a log cabin "museum" in the woods. It was supposed to be a secret but Paul couldn't keep from talking about it and, "We knew just where it was."[19]

Anne, Paul's mother, devoted her time to her family, friends, home, music, and church. She was a religious woman devoted to her children. As Paul remembered it, "It was her whole life." She listened to their prayers every evening and took them, and her husband, to church every Sunday. She studied homeopathic medicine, gardening, and the piano. It seems that she was at least as responsible for their Sunday luncheon guests and other aspects of their social life as was Henry. She was a woman of strong interests, but typical of her era and her social class, she pursued them at home and at church.

According to her daughter Susan, "Nowadays she would have been a doctor." She not only read the *New England Journal of Medicine*, she "digested" it. When the boys' friends at Harvard were sick, they came to her, rather than go to the Stillman Infirmary.[20]

Henry was an equally strong influence on his children, as Paul remembered it. When asked if a favorite uncle, Ellery Sedgwick, ever advised him on anything important in his life, Paul answered bluntly.

I looked to my father for advice.

My father was the epitome of complete honesty and frankness, which I hope we've inherited from him.

I think that my father instilled in us the necessity of trying to make something worthwhile of our lives and have a regard for the wellbeing of the nation, the state and the town we live in.[21]

Once, when a family friend asked Paul's sister-in-law, Olivia, Mrs. Henry B. Cabot Jr., to explain the worldly success of her husband and his brothers, her only answer was that whenever any of them faced a problem, they would consult with their father before making any decisions.[22]

But Henry also had a tender relationship with his children that Paul did not recall for the interviewer, perhaps because his father expressed it more easily toward his daughters, or perhaps because Paul just did not want to talk about it. Once, around 1920, when Henry was away from home on his birthday, Susan surprised him with a birthday telegram. She kept his response for the rest of her life.

"Your birthday telegram has just arrived, you dear, wicked Bedee; and I am as pleased with it as a child with a sugar plum," her father wrote to her. He went on to describe the telegram as sweeter than "sugar cane grown in the sunny south; or honey, even from Mt. Hermitos in the land of Hellos." He then quoted Falstaff to his daughter. "He hath given me drugs to make me love thee." Clearly father and daughter not only loved each other, but also had done a lot of reading together.

Henry wrote that he craves "understanding, sympathy and love," as a child does. "Middle-age folk feel sometimes as shy and awkward towards *infants* (emphasis in original) as you do towards the very old and infirm." Adults miss the friends from their youth, and this increases their longing to understand and be understood by the young. "We need your sympathy and to be allowed to share your life. That is why my sugar plum tastes so sweet." Not surprisingly, the *Boston Herald* noted upon his death in 1932, that Henry Cabot "was one of the most active townspeople in Brookline in child welfare work."[23]

Henry was both a serious man with a sense of duty and one brimming with sweetness and sentimentality. Both come through in another letter that Susan saved, this one written when she entered Smith College in 1925.

Henry opened, "We are going to miss you dreadfully and I hope you are going to miss us equally." He then asked why we, her parents, want her to attend college. He declared that happiness depends on having a real job, though not necessarily one outside the home, and from the satisfaction of having done it well. This requires young people to have long-term goals. "Many girls seem to suffer from not considering the possibility of some field of usefulness." Here Henry may have been reflecting the views of his mother, who campaigned for the admission of women to Harvard Medical School and for the rights of Radcliffe students in many areas. Since he viewed the home as "the most important factor and institution in our civilization," and since he saw running the home as "especially the woman's function," he was not opposed to women devoting their lives to their families. This job requires "the highest training of the head and heart, character and intelligence." To do it, Henry concluded,

> You must know, understand and love many kinds of persons. We hope this year in school may add to you some more of this wisdom and understanding by giving you a greater opportunity to love and know more different kind of folk than you would here in Brookline.

Naturally, Susan's recollections of their father emphasize his warmth, where Paul's reflect his sense of duty. To a family friend, she remarked,

> You would have adored him. In North Haven he used to read to us after supper. If he balked, we could always get him going by saying, "Father, how about starting a novel by Scott?" He was very partial to Sir Walter Scott; although he read other things such as the classics.[24]

It was Paul's recollections about his father's actions, more than his words, that gave him this feeling about Henry's sense of duty, though his regard for the well-being of others extended beyond town, state, and nation. In December of 1917, in the midst of World War I, a Belgian relief steamer struck a French steamship loaded with explosives in the harbor of Halifax, Nova Scotia, triggering a fire and soon after an explosion that demolished the French ship. The blast killed two thousand around the harbor, seriously injured another four thousand, and left six thousand homeless just before the first major snowstorm of the Canadian winter. Many of the homes still standing lost all of their windows and doors. Almost all the young men, six thousand in a city of fewer than fifty thousand, were away on active military duty.

According to Halifax historian Thomas H. Raddall, the Massachusetts Relief Commission, or what he termed "the ancient foe beyond the Bay of Fundy," provided the first and most crucial assistance. Henry Cabot was a key organizer and financial backer of the Commission, perhaps influenced by his close friend and the best man at his wedding, John F. Moors, who led the Red Cross contingent to Halifax. Massachusetts was "the ancient foe" because so many Haligonians traced their ancestry to Loyalists, or "Tories," who had fled New England during the American Revolution. Raddall described the "splendid heart and quick efficiency" of the Commission volunteers who sent food, clothing, medical supplies and personnel, trucks, drivers, gasoline, and other carefully selected supplies.[25] Today, nearly a century later, the city of Halifax still sends the city of Boston a Christmas tree every year as a token of its gratitude.

Henry and his peers had learned a lot about organizing relief efforts following the Salem, Massachusetts fire of June 1914. Paul recalled, "John F. Moors and my father . . . helped that community in every way they could." And like his fellow Brahmins, Henry worked for many charitable enterprises, everything from the Family Welfare Society, where he was Treasurer and a Director for many years, to the Town Tree Planting Committee. He also helped found the Country Day School and guided the fortunes of the local cemetery, a service organization for the benefit of soldiers at Fort Devens, and the town of Brookline, as a Town Meeting Representative. The Puritan-Yankee sense of civic duty was almost unmatched and Henry Bromfield Cabot was representative of his community in that respect.[26]

But in Henry, the serious element, his sense of duty, existed side-by-side with the warm, playful, personality that he showed to his family. It is possible that Paul responded to the soft side without quite acknowledging it, that he expressed his affection by praising his father's public virtues, even though it was his father's personality at home that he loved the most.

Early Education and the Army

Paul attended the Chestnut Hill School on Hammond Street in Newton, near his house, until age nine. He next went to the Country Day School, founded by his father among others, for eight years, graduating shortly before his eighteenth birthday. But his parents felt that he was too young, or immature, to go directly to Harvard from the Country Day School, not surprising for the parents of a young man who two years later would fire blanks into a college dance. So they sent him, accompanied by his friend Sumner Roberts, to El Rancho Bonito, also known as the Evans School, in Mesa, Arizona for a year.

Those who remember The Evans School sometimes refer to it as "The Bad Boys' School," since it was for privileged young men who, for one reason or another, were not ready for Harvard or Yale. They also tell about how the locals gained the upper hand on the wealthy Easterners (du Ponts, Heinzes, Pulitzers, Roosevelts, Vanderbilts, Lowells) by scaring them with mock holdups and Indian raids. Dick Saltonstall's older brother, Leverett, recalled that on his trip from the railroad station to the school, the driver suddenly slammed on the brakes and yelled, "My God, boys, it's a holdup! Get your hands up!" as two masked men aimed their weapons at them. Leverett proceeded to describe the "holdup," followed by their anxious journey to the school and an excited and sleepless night. The story ends with the return of all the boys' valuables at breakfast the next morning.[27]

Except in the field of mathematics, Paul was an indifferent student until he enrolled at the Harvard Business School. He had little interest in Latin, French, or German, and claimed never to have learned much about them. At the Evans School, he took a course designed to prepare him for freshman English at Harvard and failed it. Given the force and clarity of his prose later in life, as well as his perceptive readings of the character and ability of business associates, one must conclude that it was lack of interest, rather than lack of talent, that resulted in his uneven academic performance.

As an adult, while Paul thought intensely and creatively about a limited range of topics, generally related to business and finance, he virtually ignored the arts, literature, and most natural and social sciences. He simply could not be bothered with subjects that did not interest him. Music is a good example. Anna studied piano, required all of her children to do so, and played at family gatherings. Paul's oldest brother Henry was the most important Boston Symphony Orchestra volunteer of his generation, President of the Board of Trustees, and the individual most responsible for bringing conductor Charles Munch to Boston. Paul's father-in-law, the composer Frederick Converse, was Dean of the Faculty and Professor of Theory and Composition at the New England Conservatory. His cousin and partner, Richard Paine, was a Trustee of the Symphony and a lover of opera. Yet Paul had absolutely no interest in music. He remembered dinners with musicians like Munch, but nothing of the people or the conversation.

His aversion to music actually began many years before.

> I was made to go to music school, and I can remember there were seven or eight of us little kids and we were all to play the piano, the same tune at the same time, and I knew I would not play the right notes, so I just bounced my hands up and down the keyboard and never touched a key, and I got a prize because I didn't make any bad noise.

Paul appeared to have no strong interests early in life beyond having fun.

> **I knew a lot of things I didn't want to do. And I didn't really determine what I wanted to do until I was in Harvard Business School.**

But this was not unusual for that time. Paul did not have to earn his way to Harvard or to the Business School with a stellar academic record and a long list of extra-curricular achievements. He came from a Harvard family; they had money for tuition; and he was bright enough to pass the entrance exam. He could attend Harvard if and when he chose.

At every level of schooling, his most vivid memories were non-academic experiences filled with fun. When asked what stuck out in his mind about the Country Day School, he answered "getting there." The four brothers made the four-mile round trip by horse carriage.

> **But I most vividly remember the fun we had in winter when it was a sleigh, and we could pung . . . . That's standing on the runners of the sleigh . . . And then we'd tie our sleds—"Flexible Flyers" so-called at that time—back of the sleigh, and when we came to a hill, we'd coast down the hill ahead of the horse, [and] hook up to the sleigh when we got down to the bottom of the hill.**

> **Needless to say, we arrived at school covered with dirt and horse manure and snow.**

Young Paul striking a studious pose.

For Paul the Evans School was simply "the best fun I've ever had." H. David Evans had founded it to develop "self-reliance, independence, and initiative" in his students. To Evans, the West, "with its vision, distance, and colour, could kindle a boy's imagination, and leave him with that ethereal spark which might at any time burst into flame." Paul's recollections were more down to earth. After acknowledging his failure in English, he spoke enthusiastically about the school's pack trips, camping, shooting, and hunting,[28] all of which made a deep impression on him. A few years later he wrote his mother about a former forest ranger he had met in the army whose idyllic life of "riding all day through beautiful, impressive country" fascinated him so much that Paul was sure he could "never be a city businessman." Not an accurate prediction, but one suggestive of the love of the outdoors nourished by this school.[29]

When Paul arrived at Harvard in September of 1917, the campus resembled a military base. Samuel Eliot Morison recalled that from his previous teaching post, the war in Europe seemed as distant as the Wars of the Roses, so uninvolved were the students. At Harvard he felt like he was "on the outskirts of battle." Morison went on to describe the ambulance and hospital units that had gone over from the medical and dental schools and the scores of graduates enlisting in the Canadian and British expeditionary forces, the Foreign Legion, and the Lafayette flying squadron. A major force behind Harvard's enthusiasm for the Allies was President Lowell himself. He encouraged students to enroll in the ROTC; and the university arranged for General Leonard Wood to teach a course in Military Science. And it was Lowell who requested that the French government send a few disabled officers to train the Harvard cadets.[30]

Besides firing blanks into a student dance, Paul's crowning achievement freshman year was winning his freshman numerals in football, no small feat for a one-hundred-and-twenty-pound center. He was a substitute for all-American Charles Havemeyer. But by May he was on active duty in the army. Because the war ended six months later, he spent only nine months in uniform, and with Harvard's temporary shift to a trimester system, specifically to accommodate returning veterans, Paul and others were able to make up the time they had lost.

Paul began his military service as a pampered and provincial Bostonian. He and his friends purchased tickets for the club car on the train to Camp Zachary Taylor in Louisville. He paid others at Camp to take his kitchen duty. He continually begged his family for cigars and candy. "A box of fairly good cigars would be gratefully excepted [sic] . . . . I have no time to re-read any letters so forgive the spelling and grammar." He commented favorably on a few "bully" Harvard friends, and a few Yale friends of friends, that he ran into; but described most of his fellow soldiers as "hard" or "hard guys from the South." And a new Battery Commander was "an awful Jew." While Paul documented the charge of awful, the awkward juxtaposition would have embarrassed the worldly Paul Cabot of just a few years later. He claimed that "Except

for about two fellows this Batt[ery] is frightful. Not only the men but the officers."
He wondered how they received their commissions since they were "frightfully hard"
and uneducated, and as a result, "very poor teachers and very quick tempered."

He even took offense at a harmless, possibly admiring, remark made by an
officer.

> **Yesterday at inspection the officer asked me who discovered the
> Pacific.**
>
> **I replied, "Balboa, Sir."**
>
> **"Who discovered North America?"**
>
> **"Cabot, Sir."**
>
> **He snidely looked at my name, laughed & said, "You've been here
> quite a time haven't you." I stood at rigid attention.**

Paul wrote to his mother that "Everyone here is crazy to get out . . . . I can't tell
you how much I hate this life."[31]

Paul Cabot in 1919 wearing the bars of a 2nd Lieutenant

But in the army, Paul showed that his life would amount to more than just merriment. Ironically, he experienced a change of heart when the war ended on November 11. He had to choose whether to leave the army immediately or finish his officer training; and he decided to stay, one of only eighteen out of one hundred fifty to do so.[32] He wanted to earn a commission in the event there was another war; and some of his friends were staying. But he gave the most important reason for staying in a letter to his father on November 17th.

> **This is the hardest thing I have ever undertaken & something I dislike most intensely, something I have never done before & probably never will do again, hence it would be very good for me to go through with it.**[33]

He was going against the advice of some of the most prominent leaders of his world back home. On November 23rd he wrote,

> **Dear Ma,**
>
> **I got Pa's letter last Tuesday advising me to stay here. [Pa was then a member of the local draft board.] It certainly makes me feel better because that is what I decided to do in all events, in spite of the advice of so many older men including Mr. [Abbott Lawrence] Lowell, Bishop [William] Lawrence, Mr. [Thomas W.] Lamont, & others.**[34]

In deciding whether or not to spend an additional four months in the army, he had the advice of the President of Harvard, the Episcopal Bishop of Massachusetts who was also a Harvard Fellow, and the CEO of J.P. Morgan. It says something about the Cabots' social position and Paul's upbringing that he had so many prominent men concerned with his welfare. It would not be the last time Paul would ignore the advice of the powerful to follow his own judgment.

And it was a good thing he did. Toward the end of his ordeal he could write,

> **I wouldn't have missed this experience for the world mainly because of the many bully fellows I've met from different parts of the country.**[35]

This was the beginning of the end of his Boston provincialism.

Back to Harvard and on to Business School

But Paul lost sight of the serious side of life as a result of his return to Harvard College in April of 1919. Sophomore year was an important one, though again not for academic reasons.

> **In my sophomore year it goes without saying that I had the most fun out of ... [being] taken into a Final Club so-called, the Porcellian Club.**

Final Clubs accepted new members based on personality, accomplishments, and family connection; but in 1919 family was probably the most important factor. Richard Paine was a member, as was Paul's close friend Dick Saltonstall. But Paul's membership enabled him not only to mix with contemporaries, but to meet prominent alumni who came back for club dinners. While Porcellian Club member Theodore Roosevelt died shortly after Paul joined, Paul knew his sons Teddy and Kermit, and his son-in-law, House Speaker Nicholas Longworth, all club members who returned for alumni dinners. Paul no doubt developed a sense of ease, belonging, and even entitlement in getting to know the Roosevelts and others under informal circumstances.

"Informal circumstances" is perhaps an understatement. Of the many "improper stories," to use Paul's term, told by and about Nick Longworth, Paul felt only one was polite enough to be told in the presence of his female interviewer, in spite of her persistent questioning.

> **Nick Longworth was sitting at the table at the Porcellian Club, and he had a very bald head. One of the members came up and rubbed his head and said, "My God, Nick, that feels just like my wife's ass." Nick Longworth put his hand up and said, "So it does."**

Needless to say, club social events included a lot of drinking. Paul could

> **remember one time there was a dinner at the SK Club, ... and [President] Lowell came down to that dinner, which was a reasonably drunken affair. I can remember crawling under the ... table and coming up beside him, to say Hi to him. And he was very nice and pleasant about it all.**[36]

Or at least that is how Paul remembered it; but he almost certainly underestimated Lowell's displeasure. Lowell believed that man was a social animal and argued, in his Harvard inaugural address and elsewhere, that American colleges exist, in part, to develop man's powers as a social being. He supported the clubs, attended their dinners, and tolerated questionable behavior because he believed that the socializing and networking that club life encouraged enabled the country's elite to function more effectively. Paul demonstrated this many years later with the relaxed competence and confidence he demonstrated in a meeting with the second President Roosevelt, when legislation crucial to the mutual fund industry was taking shape. But Morison also recalls that President Lowell fretted over the large number of able students who were distracted by non-academic pursuits and assorted campus pranks and who treated the serious side of their education as if it was "an inconvenient ritual." He hated the catchphrase "C is the gentleman's grade," which had survived from the era of President Charles William Eliot (1869-1909).[37]

Lowell, a brilliant scholar who had known Paul from childhood, must have recognized him as a colossal underachiever who spent too much time engaging in pranks and not enough on his studies. Almost all of the grades on Paul's transcript were in the C+ to C- range. On May 30, 1918, the morning after the shooting, Paul took a government examination, which was considered evidence that indicated how drunk he had been. A dean wrote on the outside of the examination booklet that, "this is D+ or C-, not far from Cabot's average but less than his ability warrants."[38]

Still, it would be a mistake to exaggerate the drinking and the anti-intellectual atmosphere. The drinking took place mainly on Saturday nights. And the advantages of the Porcellian Club, according to Paul, included its convenient location, its excellent library, and rooms where members could study without disturbance. Paul served the club as "Librarian," a position of leadership and responsibility.

Paul finished his undergraduate career without further incident; but he had not developed any idea of what to do with his life. "There [were] a lot of things I didn't want to do [and] powerful few things that I did." He had even convinced himself that he had no aptitude for economics and wrote to a Harvard dean, "Last year I said I was going to concentrate in Economics . . . Finding that I have neither ability or [sic] interest in this field, I would like to change my concentration to English." Nonetheless, Paul's father, who viewed him as the "black sheep" among his children, suggested that he attend the Harvard Business School. Henry Jr. had already followed Henry Sr. to the law school and youngest brother Charles was soon to follow. But Paul, who at that age may have lacked the patience for law, decided that the business school might give him an idea about a career.[39]

A twenty-first century reader might conclude that the Harvard Business School was an obvious choice for the Harvard-educated son of a Boston trustee with a strong background in mathematics but no strong career orientation. Actually, nothing could be further from the truth. In the early twentieth century, the Harvard Business School was looked down upon as a trade school capitalizing on the Harvard name, not only by the college faculty but also by Boston society.[40]

As with so many pretensions, John P. Marquand captures this one perfectly with his fictional Boston trustee, George Apley. In the novel, Apley is outlining some of the family's history and its current situation to his children. An eighteenth-century Apley ancestor had angered his father by marrying into the Cabot family, at that time well below the Apleys in wealth and position. But in succeeding years the Cabots had prospered in trade, as indeed they had in real life, while the fictional Apleys had sunk into genteel poverty on their Sudbury farm. When George's grandfather came of age, he sought the help of his distant Cabot relations to secure a post at the Derby counting house in Salem. This led, by his eighteenth year, to a position as master of the Derby brig *Good Hope* and within a short time through shrewdness, daring, and good luck, to the making of his fortune. George then gratuitously added that "Somehow boys in this part of the world matured more quickly then in spite of there not being a Harvard Business School."

When George motored along the Charles River from Boston to Cambridge, he always kept his eyes to the right so as not to have to look at the business school, which he viewed as a "damnable example of materialism." He mocked an inscription on one of the buildings there that called business the "newest of the arts and the oldest of the professions," an inscription that appeared only in the novel. His retort, to himself, was that, "Certainly there is one profession that is older."[41]

President Lowell, while a professor in the government department, (actually *the* professor in the government department) joined in this skepticism toward business education. Lowell wrote, "General business is a pretty vague thing, for which it is probably impossible to give anything like a professional training."[42] Lowell graduated from the law school, as did Paul's father and uncle. And Lowell's nephew, George Putnam, who founded two formidable competitors to Paul Cabot's firm, Incorporated Investors in 1925 and Putnam Investments in 1937, followed Lowell to the Harvard Law School.[43] Today, in the early twenty-first century, most investment professionals have attended a business school, if not the business school at Harvard, and law school graduates are much less prominent in the profession.

So while Henry Cabot had not made the obvious suggestion, he had made a brilliant one. Once in the business school, Paul's attitude toward his studies changed dramatically.

> When I graduated from Harvard College in 1921, I went to the
> Business School and graduated second in my class [out of 196]. As
> a student I was a member of the *Business Review* . . . . I got an MBA
> with distinction . . . . It was strenuous and tough and you had to work,
> and I did work hard. Very hard. Much harder than I did in college . . .
> because I was interested in it.

Not only did Paul graduate second in his class; he was a frustrated and disappointed number two. His friend, Grant Keehn, who later became the head of both the First National Bank in New York and Equitable Insurance, "beat me the first year and I was bound I was going to beat him the second. He came out the second year one. I came out two again."[44]

Paul worked hard in business school because the subject interested him. Certainly the quantitative aspect of the material did. And he was a down-to-earth realist easily absorbed in the problems of the business world. The case method of instruction was introduced at Harvard Business School between 1920 and 1924, so Paul was exposed to it when it was fresh. And the organization of the curriculum around subjects like Marketing and Factory Management rather than around specialized, industry-specific training, which had been the school's practice before the war, improved course content. The introductory problem, a description of a complex business situation handed to students on their first day, was introduced with Paul's class in 1921. They were initially stumped by it, but over the course of their first year gradually gained the skills and knowledge needed to handle it easily.[45]

Paul was more of a scholar than he acknowledged later in life, perhaps more of a scholar than he realized. After completing his masters in business administration in 1923, he immediately began work on his doctorate, itself evidence of a seriousness of purpose. The Doctor of Commercial Science degree had only been introduced in 1922, so Paul was something of a pioneer. Previous doctoral candidates in business had studied jointly at the school and with the department of economics of the Graduate School of Arts and Sciences.[46]

Paul's advisor was an interesting choice, or coincidence. Arthur Stone Dewing had begun his academic career studying philosophy, before moving to finance. His most famous text, *The Financial Policy of Corporations* (1919), contained a fascinating discussion of valuation, one with a philosophical dimension. To Dewing, the study of business rested on an understanding of value. Man had long sought an ultimate measure from which all human experience might derive its relative importance. These ultimate measures have included God, the state, and even the theory of evolution, according to Dewing.

At times, he appeared to forget whom he was writing for. He asserted, without translation or explanation, that the greatest classic of reflective thinking began as follows: "Dass alle unserer Erkenntnis mit der Erfahrung anfange, daran is gar kein Zweifel." This, the opening sentence of Immanuel Kant's *Critique of Pure Reason*, can be translated, "There can be no doubt that all our cognition begins with experience." In experience, Dewing found a theory of value that linked two purposes, an end to be achieved and the sacrifice needed to achieve it. Value involves this tradeoff. When applied to economics, the tradeoff lies between an item's usefulness and restrictions on its availability.

There is generally more than one way to secure a useful thing or service, however. If one has a choice, the value of one way is limited by the cost of doing it the other way. This is its substitution value. But substitution value assumes a common measure of economic goods, like money, and a market in which to trade. Also, value is empirical and pragmatic, a composite of the judgments of many, not a fixed truth declared by God, science, or the state.[47]

This was truly business theory brought back to first principles. Dewing's approach no doubt appealed to Paul, not because he consciously thought in those terms, but because Dewing's ideas were the unconscious assumptions that lay behind Paul's thinking about markets and valuation. Paul began where Dewing left off. Comparing stocks on the basis of their price to earnings ratios (Dewing might call them restriction to usefulness ratios) implied a tradeoff. Subjective and ever-changing relative value required an empirical and pragmatic world, or stock market, not one guided by illusory, fixed signposts. So Paul had found a self-conscious exponent of German Enlightenment empiricism to advise him on his research. Perhaps the business school was not as materialistic as George Apley claimed, or perhaps it was materialistic in the philosophic sense more than in the commercial sense. But most likely, Paul recognized in Dewing's empiricism the academic equivalent of his own hardheaded realism. If so, Paul's motto—"First you've got to get the facts. Then you've got to face the facts."—had an academic as well as a business pedigree.

Dewing knew the Greek and Roman texts as well and used them, along with his tightly reasoned logical style, to make his points about business policy and finance. Even though Paul claimed not to like language study, the references probably struck a responsive chord because they were so familiar. For Paul and his classmates, the classics were always just beneath the surface, part of the common culture. Over a period of years, he had absorbed the classical virtues of simplicity, clarity, and intellectual honesty, and when he arrived at the business school, he encountered professors like Dewing who were using a congenial intellectual style to explore questions that really interested him.

Until 1927, when the business school moved to its current campus at Soldier's Field, student life was difficult. Classrooms and dormitories were spread all over the university, wherever space could be found. In his report for 1921-1922, Paul's first year, the dean concluded that "the living conditions of the men in the School are thoroughly unsatisfactory."[48] In 1924, a spokesman for the school complained that, "The only classrooms on which it has a first claim are two basement rooms, one of which had formerly been used as a boiler room and the other for dead storage."[49] Paul dealt with this by living with his family in Brookline. This led him to feel somewhat separated from his classmates on campus and he later regretted that he did not get to know them better. His best friend continued to be Sumner Roberts, who had been with him at the Country Day School, at the Evans School, and in his room in Smith Hall at Harvard when he fired the blank into the college dance. Roberts, who entered the medical school the same day Paul entered the business school, had a more difficult adjustment.

> I said to him, how was your first day at the Medical School? And he said, I don't think I can be a doctor. I said, good God, what happened? He said, we were all taken . . . to Massachusetts General Hospital and the famous Dr. John Warren stood up on stage, and . . . suddenly the curtain went up and here was a stiff with a meat hook in the back of his . . . neck . . . . Dr. Warren slapped it on the ass and it swung a little, and that's the last I remember. I passed out.

Roberts became a successful orthopedic surgeon, not a specialty for the faint of heart.[50]

When Paul began work on his Doctor of Commercial Science degree, a demanding course of study, he was also working at the First National Bank of Boston; and a short time later he was running his own business. He passed the written exam, which he remembered as being a difficult one. After about two years of study, he took the oral exam before eight professors and had an experience any graduate student could relate to. One of the professors asked him a question that Paul knew his panel disagreed on. He gave the questioner the answer he wanted to hear, though Paul personally disagreed with it, and winked at his best friend among the examiners, Professor of Statistics Albert Hettinger, because he and Hettinger agreed on that question and each knew what the other thought about it. What the 1920s called statistics, we today would call financial analysis. "He [Hettinger] knew exactly what I was doing and why. I passed the examination."[51]

While we do not know the question the panel disagreed on, we should hardly be surprised that Paul Cabot and Albert Hettinger agreed on investment matters. Both men became multi-millionaires on the basis of their expertise in fundamental research and valuation. Hettinger, who had a long association as analyst, director of research, and consultant to the Capital Group and predecessor companies, made perhaps a hundred million dollars in the stock markets over thirty years after retiring from the Harvard Business School in the 1960s.[52]

After passing all of the exams, Paul went on to write his thesis on equity securities valuation and also to do research on the British investment trusts, which he had studied while working for the First National Bank of Boston in London. He remembered working very hard on the dissertation; but just before he finished, his advisor, Dewing, unexpectedly announced that he was taking a sabbatical and transferred Paul to another professor, Paul's cousin, Philip Cabot.

> **He [Philip Cabot] took a look at my thesis and said, oh, you'd better do it all over. This way, that way, the other. I did it all over. Dewing came back. I'm re-transferred to Dewing. Dewing takes a look at it and says, oh, you've ruined it. I'd destroyed the original one foolishly. He said, you've got to do it all over. I said, to hell with it. I'm through.[53]**

Graduate students, who may have acted less decisively in similar situations, should know that Paul, at the time he quit his doctoral program, in 1926, was running a mutual fund in the middle of the greatest bull market that the country had experienced up to that time, and shortly thereafter he was advising Harvard Treasurer Charles Francis Adams on investments in the stock market.

He spent his first summer of business school in the credit department at the First National Bank of Boston, where he worked on collateral, or margin, loans, the department's "bread and butter" business. There he made an important discovery, one that only someone with his curiosity and self-confidence could make. Not yet twenty-three and with no real business experience, he decided that the bank's way of making these loans was completely wrong. Most were collateralized by stock, and the bank was simply lending eighty or ninety per cent of the value based on the last quotation, with no adjustment for valuation or liquidity.

> **Obviously, collateral is no good if you can't sell it . . . If you buy a stock in a small unknown company, that's one thing. If you're buying General Electric, it's quite another thing, and the quality of the securities is as important as the price of the securities . . . . I was able to point out that they were making great mistakes.**

Paul questioned everything; and he spoke up when he spotted an anomaly. Not only did he apparently have an impact on the bank's practices; he discovered his career. He found that he enjoyed studying common stocks and determining their "real value" by estimating their future earnings, which was, to Paul, "the single most important fact, other than the honesty of the management."

The following summer, after finishing his master's degree, he moved to England to work at the bank's office in London. The management there failed to impress him.

> **The head of the First National Bank of Boston's branch in London, was a horse's ass of the first order. He was terrible. He never allowed us kids to do anything. [He was] one of those fellows who thought that just because he'd been over there a year he was an Englishman . . . . The most responsible job I ever had was going out and getting him a box of cigars.**

This had its advantages, however, because it allowed Paul to spend much of his time studying the British investment trusts. While Paul was in London he met up with a friend and another future brother-in-law, Junius Morgan, the son of J.P. Morgan, Jr. (Jack Morgan). They both married daughters of the composer Frederick Converse, as did Sumner Roberts. Knowing Paul's interests, Morgan introduced him to a number of the principals of the British investment trusts, including Robert Fleming, who played a role in guiding his study. Paul remembered Fleming as polite and patient, and as having done ninety percent of the talking when they met. He later expressed a great sense of gratitude for the insights he had gained from these meetings.[54] While we do not know everything they discussed, Fleming surely described the business dealings of Junius's grandfather, J. P. Morgan Sr. (Pierpont Morgan). In the transfer of British capital to the American railroad industry in the nineteenth century, Fleming was arguably the most important British financier; J.P. Morgan certainly the most important American. Fleming probably told Paul, or gave him enough information to conclude, that Morgan's policy of keeping close tabs on the managements he funneled money to, visiting them frequently, sometimes withholding capital, sometimes encouraging mergers, was key to Morgan's, and Fleming's, success. It was for this reason that the biographer Ron Chernow describes Pierpont as "an arbiter as well as a financier of railroads."[55] When Paul and his partners founded their mutual fund, their policy of keeping close tabs on the managements whose companies they invested in was crucial to their success as well.

Paul's study of the investment trusts traced them back to the 1870's and focused on Fleming, who was the most important manager at that time. Fleming traveled from Scotland to New York as a young clerk in 1870 and immediately recognized the investment opportunities available in the U.S., particularly in the railroad industry. Perhaps his early appreciation of the potential in America was tied to his own provincial background. Not only did he hail from Scotland, but from Dundee, away from the metropolitan centers of Edinburgh and Glasgow. In 1873, near a low point in the economy and for securities prices, he headed a group that organized the Scottish-American Investment Trust. At that time, he could borrow in England, a capital-rich country, for as low as three per cent and purchase the first mortgage bonds of American railroads yielding six to eight percent. This highly lucrative activity expanded rapidly. By 1888, according to Paul's research, eighteen of these trusts, with a capitalization of 23 million British pounds, were listed on the London stock exchange; and by 1890 a "mania" was under way and the prices of these securities soared. Inevitably, boom was followed by bust and then by corruption. The money pouring into the trusts overwhelmed the potentially profitable investment opportunities of acceptable risk. And when the trusts ceased to fill an economic need, abuses arose.[56]

Paul did not undertake his research to uncover scandal. He was barely aware of it when he began. He studied the trusts because he wanted to replicate them in America and he needed to understand their successes and failures. But he found more scandal than he had bargained for, facts in conflict with his original thesis, and it made a strong impression on him. Because of his diligence and his passion on these issues, he became an expert not only on trusts, but also on their potential abuses. When these abuses began to appear in the United States in the late 1920s, he was among the first to identify them and the first to effectively publicize them, as we shall see in Chapter V. But first, we turn in Chapters II, III, and IV to Paul's activities during the first two decades of State Street Investment Corporation (SSIC) and the State Street Research & Management Company (SSRM).

Chapter II

The Twenties

> [Stocks] were just coming into fashion to be considered respectable moneymaking investments. Up to that time they were just considered wild speculation. People didn't buy common stocks, so that the whole trend was beginning which was perfect for the common stock investment company.[57]
>
> **Paul Cabot**

After about six months in London, nominally working for the First National Bank of Boston but actually studying the British investment trusts and researching his doctoral dissertation on equity valuation, Paul returned to Boston in late 1923.

> **When I got back . . . I was still very interested in stocks, common stocks. I wasn't a damn bit interested in bonds and money obligations.**

In spite of the strong language, Paul was not denigrating bonds and bond management as much as he was contrasting his interests with those of Robert Fleming and other British managers he had met in London.

> **[Their] investment trusts were very different and a very far cry from anything we started. What they basically did was borrow money in England at as low a rate as they could . . . . Then they'd turn around and lend it, mainly to American enterprises and mainly to American railroads . . . . Their whole game was to make money on the spread in money rates, to pyramid the thing, have a full equity ratio and make a spread that way.**

In other words Fleming had increased the profitability of the spread through leverage. Years later, his grandson, Ian Fleming, would honor his preferred financial instrument by naming one of the most famous characters in British fiction after it: Bond, James Bond.

While Paul had learned a lot from Fleming, he had his own idea of what an investment trust should look like, and he had no interest in following the British model. His arrival back in America coincided with the publication of Edgar L. Smith's *Common Stocks as Long-Term Investments*, which demonstrated the superiority of equity returns over bond returns, a difficult exercise for the years before the development of broad-based stock and bond indexes. Smith, a bond analyst, had attempted to prove that bonds had the higher return; but the facts forced a change in his argument.

He claimed, disingenuously, that his research had failed because it did not sustain his preconceived ideas. His findings did seem worthy of further examination, however. If they did not prove what he wanted them to prove, he would turn them loose and follow them wherever they led.

Smith based his conclusions on the period between 1866 and 1922. Dividing it into twelve sub-periods, he demonstrated that stocks were the superior investment in eleven of these, in times of both rising and falling inflation. He explained the superiority of stocks through the concept of "plowback," which today we would call retained earnings, that portion not distributed as dividends. Plowback operated like compound interest and, in his view, made stocks safer and more conservative than bonds, which suffered a loss of real value over the long term due to inflation.[58] In reality, stocks are safer than bonds only for those with an extremely long investment time horizon, if then. Nonetheless, modifications of this argument influenced Paul when he and his partners started their mutual fund in 1924 and again when he shifted the allocation of Harvard's endowment toward equities beginning in 1948.

By definition, Smith could have made his argument in any year, but the country was particularly receptive in 1924. The boom was well underway. The economy was both growing and maturing. Technological change, geographical expansion, and improved transportation contributed to the growing interconnectedness and complexity of the economy. Complexity favored the corporate form of organization, and due to growing economies of scale, corporations became larger and increasingly national. Additionally, technological innovation contributed to the development of mass production. Companies that could not mass-produce in an efficient manner could not compete against those that could. And the shift to mass production required large-scale financing. Corporations issued debt, but managements increasingly favored common equity, free of the fixed charges of interest or preferred dividends, during times when the public was receptive to their stock. And in the 1920s, the public was increasingly receptive to corporate stock issuance, especially in the "high-tech" industries like radio, automobiles, chemicals, and most of all, electric utilities.

Americans had gotten into the habit of investing during the Liberty Bond and Victory Loan drives of World War I. One fifth of the American population participated in the final Liberty Loan, whose securities were available in increments as small as fifty dollars. With the end of the war, government financing needs fell but corporate demand for funds rose, which kept interest rates high and sustained the public's interest in investing. Corporations' desire to diversify and strengthen their capital structures, together with measures taken to stabilize earnings and common stock dividends, increased the supply and the popularity of equities.[59]

By the mid-1920s investing in stocks had become a fad, if not yet a mania. This phenomenon raised a new problem: how could the average investor get competent and honest advice? The wealthy had access to recently founded Investment Counseling Firms as well as the lawyer-trustees, such as Paul Cabot's father, who had been serving friends and relatives since the nineteenth century. The upper-middle class had access to trust companies and the occasional well-informed stockbroker. But the average investor of modest means, and even the majority of brokers, faced a bewildering new world of investment opportunities and pitfalls.

As Professor Edward M. Campbell wrote in the *Harvard Business Review* of April 1924, the average investor faces the choice of either giving up all hope of becoming wealthy, or betting on stocks whose fluctuations were governed by factors he could not possibly master. In this he would be battling speculators who, even if they were honest, possessed far superior knowledge and resources. As a solution to this dilemma, Campbell proposed "investment corporations" along the lines of the British investment trusts to enable small investors to diversify their risk.[60] Charles Bennett came to a similar conclusion from the point of view of the small retail broker. He believed that stocks offered higher returns than bonds, though with more risk, but that he could minimize his clients' risk with a diversified portfolio under full-time professional management. Investment funds seemed a logical answer.[61]

It was at this time, Paul Cabot noted, that stocks were starting to be considered respectable investments, rather than rank speculation, "so that the whole trend was beginning which was perfect for the common stock investment company."[62]

State Street Investment Corporation

Paul left the First National Bank shortly after returning to Boston.

> **My first cousin, a fellow named Richard Paine, was at that time working for Lee, Higginson & Co .... in their credit department and my very close friend Richard Saltonstall worked in the credit department of the Merchant's National Bank .... We all were doing somewhat similar work and we were all interested in common stocks.**

Well the result was that we used to meet—this is now in the latter part of 1923 and the early part of 1924—once a week at the Old Parker House up here and yak about common stocks.[63]

Within a few months, these discussions led to the formation of a mutual investment company. In the early years, Richard, or Rich, Paine was the leader, and he became head of the fund, State Street Investment Corporation (SSIC), while Paul became President of State Street Research & Management Company (SSRM), which managed the assets of the fund and of other clients. They formed the management company in 1928 to better allocate expenses and fees among the clients. Rich, born in 1893, was four years older than Dick Saltonstall and five years older than his cousin, Paul. In 1924, when Paine was thirty-one, those four or five years counted for a lot, since he had held positions at Lee, Higginson & Co., the American Agricultural Company, and Scudder, Stevens, and Clark, while the younger men had had very little work experience in the business world.[64] Paul was aggressive at every stage in life, but it is easy to imagine him deferring to an older cousin, almost a brother, who had grown up with him on the family compound in Brookline.

Paul was almost as close to Dick as he was to his cousin. They were summer neighbors in Maine, as well as nearly the same age. A family story suggests the closeness of their friendship, as well as the privileged circumstances that all three of these men grew up in. One summer, while they were in college, they spent an inordinate amount of time sailing a boat belonging to Dick's father. The Saltonstalls were a disciplined family, Dick less so than his siblings, with set times for school work, piano practice, meals, and play. The older Saltonstall wanted Dick to make better use of his time; so he turned the boat over to a broker for sale. Paul bought it.[65]

Paul Cabot (far left) and Richard Saltonstall (far right), around 1930, relaxing in Maine.

Although Paul and Dick initially considered Rich to be the most able among the three, the older man lacked Paul's intensity, and over the next decade Paul gradually eclipsed his cousin. Paul first signed the annual report as President in 1934 while Rich had signed for the first ten years. For two years from 1937 to 1939, a period of turmoil on the investment and regulatory fronts, as well as on the world scene, Rich and his family cruised the Baltic, Adriatic, and Aegean Seas on his sixty-foot ketch. Meanwhile, Paul was busy lobbying politicians in Washington and running the company in Boston.

While Paul had intensity and drive, Rich had the investor's mind and emotional makeup *par excellence*. Generations of State Street professionals felt that they had learned the business from Paul, but Paul learned it from Rich as much as from anyone. When Paul described Richard Paine, he could have been describing himself.

> He was very open-minded and he studied realities and didn't let prejudices cloud his judgment. He was a remarkable investor, as was his father, my uncle . . . . He considered realities and not hopes and theories, and based his judgment on what he considered were sound facts.

> We owned a lot of John Deere stock . . . . We had bought it . . . at around forty, fifty dollars a share, and it had gone up, at the peak of the market . . . to a price of a hundred forty dollars a share, and at the bottom of the market it was selling at six dollars a share . . . . Paine . . . was convinced that John Deere was going to go busted, and so he decided to get what he could and he sold all the Deere stock that he owned personally at six dollars a share. I and another one of my partners [there were five at the time] had tried to persuade him that John Deere was not going to go busted. Believe it or not, the next morning he came in and said, I've been thinking it over and I agree with you that Deere isn't going to go busted. He turned around and bought it all back again at ten dollars a share. That was the bottom of the market, and it kept going up after that.

In Paul's mind, the important point was not who was right. It was Richard Paine's realism, flexibility, and open-mindedness.[66]

It was a few years later that SSRM had the opportunity to buy Lee, Higginson & Co. With Rich ill at the time, Paul sought the advice of his Uncle Bob Paine, advice that was based on the facts and an objective accounting of the pros and cons of the case, according to Paul. They followed his advice and did not buy the company.[67]

Cousin and partner Richard Paine.

In 1917, Rich interrupted his studies at Harvard to travel in Japan and China. When he returned to the U.S., all of his friends were serving the war effort, and he tried to enlist. Unable to do so because of poor eyesight, he joined the American Field Service and drove an ambulance for the French Army. He saw action at Argonne, Verdun, and Soissons and was decorated for valor; but in spite of the carnage he must have witnessed, when he talked about the war he dwelled on the French people and their culture, especially the food and wine. He later owned a house and a vineyard in France and had his own wine shipped home to Massachusetts every year. He no doubt had a taste for the finer things. While working in New York after graduation from Harvard, he frequently attended operas and concerts. In his twenty-fifth reunion class book, he identified his less formal interests as reading, meditating, listening to music, working around the house, playing tennis, and "drinking much wine with a few friends."[68] Paul, by way of contrast, had little time for meditating. His reading was purposeful; and when he drank, it was usually something stronger than wine.

Dick Saltonstall was a warm and charming man even, perhaps especially, in his eighties when this writer knew him. He too liked to recall those early luncheons at the Parker House and noted in his twenty-fifth reunion book that "after twenty years we are still lunching together and enjoying our trade."

At least one such meeting, actually fifty-five years later, started out less enjoyably for one young analyst. In those days, State Street (SSRM) served lunch for eight daily—Cabot, Saltonstall, CEO George Bennett, one or two other Managing Partners, and three or four more junior people, on a rotating basis. One day it was my turn and I accidentally arrived a few minutes early, only to find myself alone with the firm's two octogenarians. A little bit nervous and at a loss about what to say, I decided to show off my knowledge of Colonial American history and blurted out, "Mr. Cabot, I happen to know that your family got its start as pirates." During the Revolutionary War, members of the Cabot family did indeed make fortunes by taking out letters of marques and reprisal against British shipping. Paul said nothing for thirty seconds, which seemed at the time like thirty minutes. Then he shouted back, "Well . . . some people think we still are pirates." Paul didn't crack a smile, but Dick Saltonstall broke into laughter, to my great relief.

Cleveland Amory's *The Proper Bostonians* has a chapter titled "Customs but No Manners," which discusses the Cabot family among others. In one story, a young man from Philadelphia was visiting Godfrey Lowell Cabot. A bit uneasy, he asked him how it felt to be both a Lowell and a Cabot in Boston. Cabot said nothing for what must have seemed an eternity to the young man. Finally, unable to stand the tension, he blurted out, "I'm afraid that's a pretty silly question, Mr. Cabot." "Young man," Cabot answered, "It's the damnedest silliest question I've been asked in eighty years."

Dick saw the human side of every situation. While all three men worked tirelessly for charities and other non-profits, Dick put more of his heart into the effort. Paul made it sound like a chore, or at best a duty, that took him away from business, whereas Dick sounded more like he had genuine empathy for the recipients of his charity. When he got involved, he was "constantly reminded of the difficult problems and hardships of the low wage earner."[69]

Dick's empathy was not reserved for strangers. One nephew, whose father had died when he was about twenty, remembers Dick as attentive and protective toward him and his mother, Dick's sister. Indeed, he could be too protective. One time the nephew called Dick asking him if he should invest in Polaroid, whose technology had greatly impressed him. Dick felt that it was too speculative for the young man, who later found out that it apparently was not too speculative for State Street (SSRM), a major holder. At that time Polaroid had many great years ahead of it.[70]

Of the three partners, Paul was the most focused on business, except during World War II when he worked for the War Production Board in Washington as a dollar-a-year man. Richard Paine balanced his business involvement with interests in food, wine, music, and travel. Paul too had many interests, including sailing, shooting, tennis, and hunting. But while Paul took many vacations, he appeared to have a real need to work, even in his nineties, and his sailing and hunting trips often had a business connection. Of the three, Dick Saltonstall could most easily be called a Renaissance man. If Paul was the most passionate about business, Dick was the most passionate about his other interests, which included politics, farming, and, late in life, population issues. There was something almost Jeffersonian in Dick's interest in public service, his love of the agrarian life style, and his interest in problems facing future generations. And as Jefferson might well have done, he built a library for his home town of Sherborn.

Dick married Mary Bowditch Rogers, a direct descendant of another Renaissance man, Nathaniel Bowditch, well known as a mathematician, navigator, businessman, and Boston trustee, as well as the father, grandfather, and great-grandfather of many of the nineteenth and twentieth-century Boston trustees. Dick's entrée to politics was through his brother, Governor and U.S. Senator Leverett Saltonstall. He served as treasurer of every political campaign and became known as the man who said "No" to most of the numerous requests for money.[71]

From these campaigns Dick felt that he had gained an insight into human nature and an understanding of the functioning of democracy. Addressing his classmates, but perhaps thinking of his brother, he wrote of his respect for those who had entered politics and government service and of the need for "honest, clear-thinking, and open-minded" people in public office. Apparently, politics required the same kind of intellectual honesty as investing.

But when Dick started to mix his feelings about politics and rural life, it was his enthusiasm more than his considerable analytical ability that showed through in his prose. As a selectman, he "thoroughly enjoyed much valuable talk of a winter's evening around an overheated stove in an all-purpose room of a century-old town hall." This was not dialogue but written comments prepared for his Harvard class book. "Naturally I place my herd of Guernseys in the top flight in New England," he wrote, and then boasted about the cow that set a world record in milk production and the five-figure sum he was offered for a bull. As for the friends he made "in the cow game," he found them perhaps "a bit more sincere and more industrious" than those in politics. And with farming friends at "cow sales" he could relax and feel that he was in a different world, "for there is nothing to equal the importance of the Guernsey animal, which is first and foremost in the minds of all." In spite of many achievements in business and several corporate directorships, his class book reported that he was most proud of his position as President of Charlescote Farm. If not literally true, the statement shows where his heart was.

Not surprisingly, in 1966 when State Street (SSRM) moved from 140 Federal Street, an older office building with windows that opened, to a modern steel and glass skyscraper, Dick was uncomfortable. One day George Bennett, then Senior

Managing Partner, was conferring with a colleague when Dick rushed into his office. "Is it true that the windows in the new building won't open?" he asked. Dick got a specially made window that opened.

Dick's political, philanthropic, and other public service appeared to reflect the values of the Saltonstalls, a political family, as well as those of his mother's family the Brookses, whose wealth from maritime insurance and New Orleans and Chicago real estate may have engendered a sense of noblesse oblige in Dick and his siblings. Sir Richard Saltonstall had been an original member of the Massachusetts General Court of 1630, and the twentieth-century Dick Saltonstall had a great-grandfather, a grandfather, an uncle, a brother, and a nephew who were all active Massachusetts politicians.

In the 1960s, Dick became concerned about population growth and in 1963 endowed a chair at the Harvard School of Public Health. He later endowed a second. In his fiftieth reunion class book, he wrote at length of the religious and ethical issues surrounding population control and argued that the hunger and despair of so many around the world threatened the security of our nation.[72]

These three very different men founded a business that prospered in partnership form for sixty years and, in corporate form, for twenty-three more. While there have been many conflicts at State Street Research & Management Company, of which SSIC eventually became only a small part, there is no evidence of any serious conflicts among these three friends. Doubtless there were some disagreements, but they must not have been about core beliefs. Cabot, Paine, and Saltonstall were well matched in intelligence and ability. They had similar backgrounds and complementary personalities, but most important, a common set of values.

Cabot's personality was the brashest. One day his pocket watch, which he hung on a stand in his office at 140 Federal Street, was stolen. Paul summoned the building manager, Mr. Mackenzie, to his office and asked him who had cleaned his office. Mackenzie replied that he had just hired a new cleaning crew. Paul shot back, "Well they sure cleaned me out," and threatened to move the company if the watch were not returned immediately. The manager assembled the building staff and announced that every one of them would be looking for a new job if the watch were not returned. It soon reappeared. Paul may or may not have moved the company, but everyone believed him capable of it. The story is reminiscent of an incident involving John Codman, a nineteenth-century sea captain and a relative on Paul's mother's side. On the first day of a voyage, according to Cleveland Amory, the crew refused to scrub the deck, that particular job not being one of the duties enumerated in their labor agreement. Upon discovering this error in the contract, Codman ordered them to drop the anchor and hoist it repeatedly, duties permitted by the contract, until they took a broader view of their responsibilities.[73]

While Paul's personality must have produced some interesting encounters, the shared values of the three partners limited the conflict among them. Their ambition took the form of a passion for performance and integrity, never for growth and profitability for its own sake. More than their competitors, State Street put performance for existing clients above sales to new ones. Of course the three founding partners were, throughout their lives, among the largest clients, and putting clients first was in their own interest; but it was also very much in the tradition of the Boston trustee.

The Three Boston Funds of the 1920s

State Street did not arise in a vacuum; it reflected the social and business culture of Boston at that time. Other entrepreneurs were thinking along the same lines; and it is no coincidence that these others were also mostly Bostonians. Young, upper-class and wealthy, Harvard-educated Brahmins, along with one Midwesterner, founded Massachusetts Investors Trust (MIT) and Incorporated Investors (II) around the time that State Street (SSIC) began operations. But during the early years of the mutual fund industry, State Street best embodied the Boston investment culture.

Boston's leading families, including the Cabots, the family of Rich as well as Paul, and the Brookses, from which Dick's family inherited its money, had been extraordinarily successful in the years since the end of the eighteenth century. Early fortunes had been made in trade, especially the lucrative China trade, and succeeding generations had prospered in textiles and leather. These fortunes were later reinvested in Western railroads, real estate, and mining.

For religious and cultural reasons tied to Boston's Puritan and Yankee heritage, these families were more concerned with preserving fortunes for future generations than with consumption and the ostentatious show of wealth. Paul, for one, appeared to be more concerned with the ostentatious show of frugality. Fellow directors at J.P. Morgan once took up a collection to buy him some new shirts after he had appeared at too many directors' meetings with frayed collars and cuffs. [74]

This focus on future generations led many wealthy men to appoint trustees to handle their affairs in the event of their death. But unlike other cities, where trusteeship came under the control of corporate fiduciaries, in Boston it became an occupation of individual professionals, often lawyers. In fact, some law firms, over the course of the nineteenth century, gradually ceased doing legal work to focus solely on trust work. Today there are no lawyers at the former law firm Welch & Forbes, only trustees, money managers, and securities analysts.

But if social factors, especially the close-knit, inbred structure of Boston society, made the development of the institution of Boston trustee possible, it was a legal development unique to Massachusetts that made it nearly inevitable:

Justice Samuel Putnam's Prudent Man Rule of 1830. In *Harvard College v. Amory,* a case in which Harvard unsuccessfully argued that funds intended for the University and for Massachusetts General Hospital had been mismanaged, Justice Putnam held that

> **All that can be required of a trustee to invest, is, that he shall conduct himself faithfully and exercise a sound discretion. He is to observe how men of prudence, discretion and intelligence manage their own affairs, not in regard to speculation, but in regard to the permanent disposition of the funds, considering the probable income as well as the probable safety of capital to be invested . . . .**
>
> **These trustees are not to be made chargeable but for gross neglect and willful mismanagement.**[75]

In other words, the trustee was not liable unless he was guilty of "gross neglect and willful mismanagement." This decision set the bar to prove mismanagement high and gave Massachusetts's trustees broad discretion in how they could handle the funds in their care. Significantly, it allowed them to invest in common stocks when others were restricted to bonds. For example, a comparable ruling in New York in 1869 prevented trustees from investing in equities.[76] It was natural that when common stock investing became popular in the 1920s, descendants of the early Boston trustees were the first to come up with the idea of the equity mutual fund. And due to Boston's long experience with equities and reputation for prudence, the public had more confidence in Boston managers. In Paul's words,

> **There was a feeling on the investors' part that they didn't trust the New Yorkers quite as much as they did Boston because Boston had the reputation of the old Boston conservative trustee and New York had the reputation of the slick Wall Street fellows who take the shirt off your back. I think this Keystone moved from Philadelphia up here entirely for that reason. The atmosphere had the appearance at least of being better here than it was in those bigger cities.**[77]

Paul might have added that the George Putnam Fund, founded in 1937, was officially named the George Putnam Fund of Boston for just that reason.

Investment trusts had existed in England and Scotland since the 1830's; but two features were unique to the "Boston-type," "open-end" mutual fund. "Boston-type" referred to the capital structure of the fund. It issued one type of security, common stock, and all shareholders held an equal economic interest, as is the case with most mutual funds today. "Open-end" referred to the flexibility of the capital structure. The fund would issue new shares at net asset value if there were a demand for them. But it also agreed to redeem them at net asset value, or at a small discount, when shareholders wished to sell, also like most mutual funds today. The two features necessarily went together. An open-end fund would have to be Boston-type because no buyer of senior securities (bonds) would tolerate a structure that permitted holders of junior securities (equity shares) to liquidate. It would make the concept of senior security meaningless.

Paul explained the rationale behind the open-end structure as follows.

> **The banks were then and still are advertising and setting up personal revocable trusts .... If the individual didn't like the way the trust was going he could revoke it and go about his business. Well obviously this concept of a lot of shareholders going together and each individual shareholder having the right to revoke his part wasn't a very drastic change from the individual's revocable trust. Nonetheless I believe I have yet to hear of anyone else in the world who started it ahead of us.**[78]

Paul was correct that the Boston funds had been first; but it is not true that they had established a true revocable trust at inception. In this instance, Paul's memory oversimplified a complex and tentative evolution toward the "open-end" structure, an evolution similar to that which occurred at Massachusetts Investors Trust and Incorporated Investors. The original by-laws of SSIC allowed shareholders to offer stock back to the corporation but did not obligate the corporation to accept or redeem it. In fact, the corporation always did redeem it, but it reserved the legal right to refuse. When shares were offered to the general public at the beginning of 1927, the company declared its intention to buy back shares, but only its intention. In December of that year, however, the shareholders, including the three partners, did vote that the corporation would purchase any shares offered, at liquidating value less $2.00 per share (later reduced to $1.00) and with the possibility of a requirement of two months' written notice, which it however never enforced.[79] At about the same time, Scudder, Stevens, and Clark and Loomis Sayles granted the redemption privilege to investors in their pooled client funds.

Throughout the 1920s, the closed-end funds with debt and preferred stock in their capital structure dominated in the U.S., with over 98% of the assets. In Great Britain it was nearly 100%.[80] But the inherent leverage of the closed-end mutual funds with permanent debt led to disastrous performance for the holders of the more junior equity securities when the market crashed. Their performance and their well-publicized ethical lapses led to a discrediting of the closed-end concept and the ascendancy of the Boston-type, open-end fund after 1929. As Chapter V will make clear, Paul favored this structure because it was simpler to understand and less subject to abuse, and the fund always traded at net asset value. The disadvantage was—and still is—that portfolio managers often feel pressured to buy when stocks are popular and money is coming into their funds and feel forced to sell when stocks are out of favor and cheap. The boom of the 1920s and the bust of the 1930s illustrated this perfectly.

Partisans of State Street Investment Corporation and Massachusetts Investors Trust (MIT) have debated the question of who ran the first Boston-type, open-end fund for decades. State Street began operating early in 1924 but did not incorporate until July. Massachusetts Investors Trust incorporated in March but did not operate until July. Paul argued that State Street was first because while MIT was incorporated first, "they hadn't done a damned thing in operation."[81] Of more importance is the question of "First with what?" A 1925 MIT brochure is revealing on the subject of early practice.

> **The Trust, by complete diversification, both geographically and industrially, has eliminated the human element of prediction by adopting the mechanical Law of Averages as successfully demonstrated by insurance companies. The Trust's holdings of over 120 representative stocks cover about sixty different industries.**

MIT eliminated the human element in favor of the mechanical Law of Averages because, in fact, it had no research department for the first eight years of its operation. It was running what today is called an index fund.[82]

State Street's approach was totally different. Perhaps following the example of J.P. Morgan, who kept close tabs on his borrowers, the partners and other analysts visited companies before investing in them. They interviewed managements to obtain firsthand information and a sense of the managements' honesty, ability, and strategy. From this they developed forecasts of earnings, dividends, and capital requirements, and then used these forecasts to pick stocks. Their method, in short, was similar to that of a modern investment organization but without the appearance of precision afforded today by the computer. The key was that for a long time they were almost alone in doing this kind of research. State Street (SSIC), probably Paul, wrote in the 1926 annual report,

> **Your officers make many personal visits to those concerns in which they are interested, thereby obtaining a first-hand knowledge of the management as well as more detailed information than is usually included in the ordinary corporation report. This, we believe to be**

a service of very great importance and one which is not generally undertaken by those in charge of investment funds.[83]

Elsewhere, Paul remarked that analyst visits were so uncommon a practice that when an analyst did visit a company, the managers became quite talkative.

They were very interested in talking about their own companies, their lives. And to have somebody else interested in what they're doing, why, it stimulated them to talk about it.[84]

Table 1
Annual Investment Performance,
The Three Original Boston Funds and the S&P Index, 1924-1929[85]

	1924	1925	1926	1927	1928	1929	1925-1929 ann. rate	1926-1929 ann. rate
State Street Investment Corp.*	66.0%	80.7%	11.4%	52.7%	84.3%	-5.7%	39.8%	31.1%
Massachusetts Investors Trust**	7.8%	26.3%	10.9%	32.1%	28.7%	-8.4%	16.9%	14.6%
Incorporated Investors			10.2%	26.4%	56.2%	-4.3%	na	20.1%
Standard and Poor's Index		21.9%	5.7%	30.9%	37.9%	-11.9%	15.4%	13.9%

*For 1924, last 5 months only.

**For 1924, last 5 1/2 months only.

The difference in performance was what one would expect between managed and unmanaged funds in a highly inefficient market. State Street led the S&P by 59% in 1925 and never led by less than 5% in the 1920s. Its cumulative performance for the first five full calendar years (1925-1929) was 434% or 40% per year. MIT, with its "mechanical Law of Averages strategy" trailed at 17% per year, just beating the S&P at 15.4%. Incorporated Investors, for a slightly shorter period due to its later establishment, bested MIT by 5% per year but fell 11% per year behind State Street.

Paul summarized the performance of the first "seven and five twelfths years," through 1931, in the 1931 annual report. During this period, SSIC appreciated by 260%, while the Dow Jones Industrial Average had declined by 24%. State Street was so effective, due to stock selection and some degree of market timing (in the older sense of the word, of merely anticipating market moves) that an original stockholder in 1924 did as well as someone who had bought a representative list of stocks at inception, sold out at the peak in 1929, and kept the proceeds in cash up until 1931.[86] In other words, even around the time of the greatest stock market crash in history, these three young partners, through investment acumen primarily based on stock selection, were able to stay even with a hypothetical average investor who had anticipated the crash perfectly. While State Street's performance regressed toward the mean in later decades, it was not because the company's method or standards changed. It was because its stronger competitors, including the two other pioneer Boston funds, adapted its research methods; and the competition for ideas made the market more efficient.

Their success was not exclusively based on stock selection. State Street could and did move into and out of the market and it could and did borrow on margin to leverage its performance. An SEC report of 1933 notes the following about State Street.

> **The fact was that during this early period of its existence the issuer was a family trading pool. Detailed facts submitted at our request showed very active trading on the part of this pool on a far more speculative basis than could have been practiced, or was practiced, after this issuer became an investment trust of the usual type, offering its shares generally to the public.**[87]

The SEC called it a "family trading pool" because throughout 1924 and 1925, all of the shares belonged to the three partners and their close relatives; and even by the end of 1926, only ten percent belonged to outsiders, generally friends and acquaintances of the principals. In 1927, after the first sales effort, family ownership dropped to 62%, to 38% by 1928, and 23% on the eve of the crash, or about $6.7 million in a $29.1 million fund. Family ownership tended to increase during difficult periods in the market when outsiders were more likely to sell, and decrease during periods when sales were strong. When questioned by the SEC in 1936 about the significance of the still large position of his family in the stock, Paul answered that it implied "that I and members of my family, and associates were not only willing but desirous of having a very large proportion of our own money invested in our own venture."[88]

Table 2[89]
Investment of Partners and their Families in SSIC. Selected Years.
$ in millions. Year-end except for Sept. '29.

Year-end	1926	1927	1928	9/29*	1929	1930	1932	1935	1938
% Ownership	90	62	38	23	26	29	43	25	20
$ Ownership	1.2	2.1	4.6	6.7	4.5	3.4	3.2	10.6	7.7
Size of Fund	1.4	3.3	12.1	29.1	17.2	11.7	7.4	42.3	38.3
Shareholders	22	95	280	na	800	759	862	4154	na

Estimate

The 1937 Registration statement lists the top ten holders on October 20th of that year. The first five included the three founders, with 9% among them, Harvard with 4 ½ %, and Mayo Properties of Rochester, Minnesota with 3%. The next five—a fund trustee, two relatives of the founders, and two trust companies—owned 6 ½ % among them.[90]

An analysis of trading over the first four years and three months of the Fund's history does indicate extraordinary turnover, though public investors would probably have accepted this level of turnover if they had received these returns. A complete and quite beautiful hand-written record of all State Street Investment Corporation Transactions and other business dealings from July 29, 1924 to October 31, 1928 survived for many years in excellent condition in the State Street Research & Management Company library. The data for 1925 through 1928 shows the following.

Table 3[91]

Turnover Analysis: State Street Investment Corporation, 1925-1928

	Assets on January 1	Turnover (Sales)	Ratio Sales/Jan 1 Assets	Ratio Sales/ Ave Assets
1925	$165,796	$2,931,893	17.68	5.98
1926	$814,161	$3,580,009	4.40	3.31
1927	$1,351,607	$4,839,156	3.58	2.07
1928	$3,334,024	$8,257,783	2.48	1.40*

Data for 1928 is through October 31. Ratios for 1928 are annualized. *Estimate

(I have omitted August through December of 1924. The fund was new and positions were just being established.)

Because of the quadrupling of the fund's size in 1925, the ratio of turnover to beginning year assets, the traditional measure of turnover, is misleading; but even the ratio of turnover to average assets, 5.98, indicates an average holding period of about two months, twelve months divided by 5.98. For 1926 the average holding period, calculated in the same manner, is two to three months. For 1927 it is three to four months; and for the period in 1928 for which we have records, eight to nine months. Not surprisingly, the typical capital gain at the time of sale was modest; but modest gains taken several times in a single year can produce great performance. In contrast, the typical holding periods for the years 1933 through 1935 were 3.0, 3.1, and 2.4 years, respectively,[92] more typical of a modern mutual fund.

Importantly, active trading does not generate good performance unless the trader has a clear and correct rationale for his actions, a clear sense of value or whatever it is that drives stocks. And, as Paul pointed out in the 1936 annual report, turning over the portfolio is not necessarily speculative by nature.

> **It is often erroneously assumed that rapid changes in a portfolio indicate an undue amount of speculation. As a matter of fact, however, it is our belief that failure to make changes to conform with a rapidly changing situation would be considerably more speculative, and that alertness, ability and willingness to make changes contribute much to safety of principal.**[93]

Leveraging works both ways, as does market timing. State Street bought low and sold high, which sounds simple enough until you recall that this required them to find counter parties that would sell low and buy high. State Street was playing in more games than were its competitors, but the important point is that it was winning all of them. The question remains, how did a small group of investors achieve returns of 434% in a market that was up less than 200%?

The answers are research, analysis, valuation, and luck. While the country in the 1920s was obsessed with the ups and downs of the stock market, few investors looked at the real companies behind the pieces of paper, and fewer still went to the trouble of boarding a train to visit managements. In many instances, the analyst from State Street must have been the only one to visit a company in a given year. The fewer the number of investors doing first-hand primary research, the more valuable it became. This research was analyzed and translated into financial forecasts. And State Street was among the first to forecast earnings and value stocks by using the ratio of price to earnings, in addition to the more traditional dividend yield. Additionally, when State Street interviewed managements, they certainly asked about plans to issue equity and debt, since that would affect the supply and price of stock as well as the company's earnings, earnings per share, and dividends per share. Capital invested, how that capital was raised, return on capital, and the proportion of earnings paid out as dividends have been the classic concerns of investors ever since. When Paul invested, he was thinking "of the honesty, integrity, ability of management and the probability or possibility of increasing earnings and increasing dividends." His instinct to focus on the earning power of a company was something he had inherited from his father, who "may not have called it price/earnings, but he certainly knew about and studied the prospects of the companies in which he invested,"[94] according to Paul.

Anecdotes from the 1920s

State Street, however, did not always operate in classic textbook fashion. While not reflected in official documents, the idea at times appeared to be "make money any way you can." Paul recalled that his Uncle Bob Paine was

> A hell of an able investor . . . [who] . . . had an amazing nose for what was good. The old man did his brokerage through Jackson & Curtis . . . . We had a friend in J&C who'd tell us what Paine's father—my uncle—was doing. Say he was buying American Gas and Electric [now called American Electric Power.] Our friend would tell us. So I'd study up on the company. Then I'd go to the old man and say, "You know. Uncle, I've found an interesting stock. It's American Gas and Electric." "Is that so?" my uncle would say. "Yes I like it too. In fact, I like it a lot. I don't think it'll just go up 20 percent or something like that: I think it's going to double, and here's why." So we'd know the goddamn thing was okay. [95]

Amazingly, the "old man" never caught on. Or maybe it was Paul who never caught on. In any event, such ideas were not developed in the classic manner; and there was an element of luck involved, even if the luck was just in having an uncle "with an amazing nose for what was good." Paul did "study up" on the company; and for Paul, who was extraordinarily thorough, this meant reading every available piece of information. But when the stock actually did double, in a little over a year, it was Bob Paine, more than the young partners, who deserved the credit.

According to the SSIC Record Book, the partners bought 2500 shares of American Gas and Electric in eight lots in January of 1927, paying between $68 and $75 per share and an average price of about $72. They added 1500 shares in February at about the same price and 1000 in May at just below $84. In November they sold 1100 shares at $122 and change, the following January 500 at $119 and change, in February 580 at $124, 1000 at $139 in March, 500 at $146 in April, and 1500 at $162 and change in May. They sold more than they bought because of stock dividends. [96] Even though the idea came from Richard's father, the partners appeared to have a forecast and a valuation discipline that told them when to buy and when to sell. All the purchases were below 84 and all the sales went at above 119. They almost doubled their money in little more than a year.

Kraft Cheese, managed without parental or avuncular guidance, was a more typical example of how the partners worked. State Street bought 1000 shares in February 1925 at just below 50 dollars and 1500 in March at 63 dollars and change. But they turned around in May and sold at a small profit, and sold out most of their position by July. Significantly, the record book indicates that Paul received $100 for travel to Chicago in May. While there, he surely visited Kraft, which for a while represented over 15% of the portfolio.[97]

Actually, most of State Street's research on Kraft and many other companies was so good that the modern Securities and Exchange Commission would declare it in violation of Regulation FD, which requires simultaneous disclosure of material information to all investors and potential investors on an equal basis. This is just one way in which the rules governing the use of proprietary or "inside" information have been changed, mostly tightened up, over the years. Practices that were commonplace in the 1920s would be illegal today.

> We [Cabot and Saltonstall] used to go out, oh, once a month, I'd say, to Chicago and talk to Mr. J.L. Kraft . . . . He and his brothers . . . . were the first to make pasteurized cheese, and then market that. I thought the taste was god awful, but the general public seemed to like it.

> We had a great friend in Philadelphia named Trimble, who ran a brokerage house there, an investment house, and we asked him to go on the Kraft Board to represent us. Which he did. One time I was out in Chicago . . . with Jim Trimble. Trimble was a great big fellow, about six foot six, and we were in our room up in the Blackstone Hotel having a scotch and soda and smoking cigars, when in walked Mr. J.L. Kraft, who didn't believe in either smoking or drinking. I think he was a little shocked to see us drinking and smoking. He said, "I have just arranged to make a sizeable loan . . . from Halsey Stuart & Company" . . . .

> Jim Trimble was lying—he was about seven feet tall—he was lying on the bed, came together like a jackknife and said, "What? Those sons of bitches?" We later learned that . . . he had, for a few million dollars . . . agreed to . . . give approximately [a quarter] of the company away in the form of warrants on these bonds. Those bonds that came out at par were in a few weeks or months selling at around a hundred and eighty per cent of par value, giving, in substance, a quarter of the company away with it.

> [Kraft] had no sense whatever about finance and money matters. He was a merchandiser and that's as far as he went. He was a very good

merchandiser and he built a very big and successful company, but he knew nothing about finance.[98]

State Street was out of the stock at a profit before the market caught on.

While some today might question the propriety of the sale, a few years later in 1933 the Supreme Judicial Court of Massachusetts, in *Goodwin v. Agassiz,* ruled that an insider was required to disclose material inside information only in cases where he engaged in a private face-to-face transaction. Chief Justice Arthur Prentice Rugg wrote

Fiduciary obligations of Directors ought not to be made so onerous that men of experience and ability will be deterred from accepting such office . . . .

Law in its sanctions is not coextensive with morality. It cannot undertake to put all parties to every contract on an equality as to knowledge, experience, skill, and shrewdness.

In other words, if you possessed superior information, you probably deserved it. The SEC did not seek to ensure equal access to information for all investors until the 1960s.[99]

Not all firsthand research provided helpful insights. In April of 1927 State Street bought 2000 shares of International Nickel, later known as Inco, at about $54.[100] In this case, they had uncharacteristically taken a position without first visiting the company. A few days later Dick Saltonstall traveled to Sudbury, Ontario to visit management and its nickel mine. He returned to Boston and reported to his partners that there was nothing out there but this huge pit and that he couldn't see much value in it. Paul and Richard agreed that it was unlikely to amount to much and they sold at a small loss. International Nickel became the most profitable mining company in North America as well as a constituent of the Dow Jones Industrial Average.

By the late 1920s, the optimism generated by the new technologies of mass production and electrification had spread to all sectors of the economy. Optimism became euphoria and the bull market accelerated into a mania. As in manias before and since, the frenzied buying of securities reduced the cost of capital to issuers and led to over-investment, especially in the "high tech" sectors of that day. The technology-led nature of the mania resembled the experience of the early 1870s, which had centered on the new railroad networks, and that of the late 1990s, which centered on information and telecommunications technology, including the overbuilding of the fiber-optic network along those same railroad rights of way.[101]

As the months passed and the mania spread throughout the economy, judgment and historical perspective became increasingly important. Even Paul, who had studied the financial history of the late nineteenth century, did not foresee the stock market crash, and underestimated it once it began; but he did sense a rise in the overall risk level. In the 1927 annual report, State Street warned that

> **Only a reckless optimist could assume that the past four years might be taken as a fair indication of the future course of stock prices over a similar period.**

> **The successful handling of funds during the year 1928 will require a greater display of intelligence and more thorough investigation and patient research than has been necessary in the past . . . .**

> **A successful investment trust must be able not merely to accept profits in a rising market, but also to curtail losses in a period when securities are declining. The latter phase has not demanded much attention as yet, and when it does it may be found surprisingly difficult to accomplish.** [102]

CHAPTER III

THE CRASH, THE DEPRESSION, AND STATE STREET'S RESPONSE

It was an exciting and frightening experience. As the books say, down on Wall Street all the brokers were jumping out of the windows and killing themselves. *But we were young and not particularly frightened.*[103]

Paul Cabot

As it turned out, the State Street partners were over a year early in their warning. The S&P gained nearly 44% in 1928, the best showing of the decade. Yet during the early weeks of the year, at the time when Paul and his partners were writing the 1927 annual report, quoted at the end of the previous chapter, they fretted over the speculation in the market—evidenced by the high trading volume and high levels of margin debt—in spite of an economy that had been faltering since the previous summer. The fact that they themselves had participated in the speculation did not lessen their concerns about it. The market of 1927 was sustained not by the economy, but by the accommodative policy of the Federal Reserve Board and the "jawboning" of Treasury Secretary Andrew Mellon, President Calvin Coolidge, and others. State Street began warning its shareholders of "the relatively high prices at which common stocks have been selling" in its quarterly letters beginning in July 1927.[104]

The Stock Market Crash

But the partners did not act as worried as their warnings suggested they should have. They virtually eliminated their margin debt in the spring of 1928 but remained fully invested, primarily in aggressive industrial stocks that could

---

be expected to outperform in a strong market but underperform in a correction. They believed that the market was too high, but they did not want to miss out on any rallies, which they expected. Thus they faced the classic investor's dilemma, the choice between value and momentum—what to do when you believe that the market is too high, but is about to go even higher? When the economy and the stock market did take off that spring, however, they were well-positioned. The Dow Jones Industrial Average (for which, unlike the S&P, there is a record of daily prices from the 1920s) crossed the 200 mark on March 9, after stalling for several months, and advanced sharply thereafter. But State Street's 1928 performance, up over 84%, nearly doubled the rate of gain of the averages, largely due to aggressive and correct stock selection. If they had taken a more defensive stance, the partners would surely have lagged the bull market. They were clearly worried; they temporarily put 20% of the fund in cash in March of 1928, and by April were describing the market as "dangerously high."[105] But they thought they could ride it higher and get out before any correction. This activity, basically a form of speculation, put their entire enterprise at risk; but for the most part, due to timing and stock selection, it worked, for them at least. From the end of March, and for the following eighteen months, their portfolio outpaced the market, which itself soared in spite of a reversal in policy at the Federal Reserve Board, which had finally become concerned about the speculation and began selling government securities and pushing up the discount rate.

Table 4[106]

SSIC Margin Debt at Quarter End, 1927-1930 (in thousands of dollars)

	1927-I	1927-II	1927-III	1927-IV	1928-I	1928-II	1928-III	1928-IV
Margin Debt	461	300	834	856	35	0	0	303
Net Assets	1,675	2,098	2,702	3,373	4,664	5,924	7,439	12,201
Margin Debt %	28%	14%	31%	25%	1%	0%	0%	2%

	1929-I	1929-II	1929-III	1929-IV	1930-I	1930-II	1930-III	1930-IV
Margin Debt	0	1,508	840	925*	409	24	2	0
Net Assets	17,134	21,260	29,099	17,398	22,269	17,648	14,821	11,869
Margin Debt %	0%	7%	3%	5%	2%	0%	0%	0%

*Note: SSIC had $5 million in margin debt at one point during the fourth quarter of 1929, but less than $1 million at the end of the quarter

The State Street partners continued their research at the individual industry and company level and even hired additional analysts, but their top-down, macro strategy appeared to have been to ride the momentum of the market, in spite of their private and public fears. In June of 1928, not for the last time, they were almost tripped up by this strategy.

The month began with the Industrial Average holding at around 220. But meanwhile, on the San Francisco Exchange, a handful of stocks of companies associated with the Giannini family broke down and a panic ensued, which rapidly spread east. By June 12th, the average in New York had fallen nearly 9%, back down to about 200. More worrisome, on the 12th the exchange recorded its first five-million-share trading day, and newspaper headlines announced the end of the bull market. At least some key opinion makers were getting very jittery. But on the next day, June 13th, the averages recovered somewhat. And on June 14th, Herbert Hoover received the Republican nomination for President, and the rally continued through Hoover's election victory in November. Interestingly, State Street did not even mention the market correction in their second quarter letter. For the third quarter, they wrote that they had no debts, and 9% of the funds in cash and call loans, which they described as "a most conservative position."[107]

In early December, another panic shook the Street. The average fell by about 13% from 296 on November 28th to 257 on December 8th. But once again, it was short-lived. By the close of 1928, the market had risen to 300, and State Street was again using margin debt.

Yet many experienced investors felt that the Fed had boxed itself in with its accommodative policy in 1927. What if it took a crash to end the speculation? The longer the Fed delayed before tightening decisively, the more dangerous, it was thought, that tightening would be. Not only Wall Street but also Main Street America and the Treasury would feel the impact. So when the Fed did respond, it did so less decisively than it might have.

In early 1929 it attempted to cool the fires on Wall Street, without overly burdening the rest of the economy. On February 2, it prohibited the use of the resources of the Federal Reserve Banks for speculative purposes. In other words, member banks could not make margin loans. This produced a flurry of calls on those loans, a sharp increase in the interest rate charged on margin debt, and a market decline, this one from 320 to 296.

But by late March some banks, fearing the consequences of a complete cessation of margin lending, made money available to speculators, albeit at very high rates, and the pressure eased. Margin buyers had to pay up, but they could still borrow; and with returns to lenders higher than what was available elsewhere, banks and other corporations found ways to circumvent the Federal Reserve System. Speculation continued and the stock market resumed its climb, with the Industrial Average topping out on September 3rd at 381.

Between early September and late October the market followed a volatile downward course. But it always seemed to regain at least some measure of balance, perhaps because investors had learned over the past two years to view "corrections" as "buying opportunities." After falling to 325 on October 4th, down 15% from the peak, it rallied back to above 350 on the 10th and 11th, only to fall 15%, back below 300, by October 26th, the Saturday before the crash. This was in spite of a desperate rescue attempt by some Wall Street bankers on the preceding Thursday.

Early that afternoon, Thomas W. Lamont, head of J.P. Morgan, held a meeting with five other leading bankers at which they decided, on behalf of their institutions, to contribute to a fund (the exact size of which is in dispute) to attempt to bring order to the market. By carefully supporting the prices of a few leading blue chip stocks, they succeeded in this, not only steadying the market, but igniting a brief rally. But stocks retreated in the last hour of trading. Another rout had been avoided, but the averages were down again that day; trading volume set a new record, almost 13 million shares; and the ticker ran over four hours late, finally recording the last sale just after 7PM.

The market moved narrowly on Friday and Saturday, though volume continued frightfully heavy, and stocks began to fall right before Saturday's close. On Monday, Saturday's decline accelerated. And on Tuesday, October 29th, everything unraveled. The selling panic became a stampede as volume surged to 16.4 million shares. The Dow, which had closed at just under 300 on Saturday, closed at 230 on Tuesday.

A chorus of reassuring statements and symbolic actions propped the market up on Wednesday and during a shortened Thursday session. The authorities closed the exchange on Friday and Saturday so that brokers and investors could get their books in order.[108] The appearance of order returned, but things would never be the same. The 1920s had ended.

The State Street partners had played the 1928 market very well. At times they bought on margin; at other times, when they thought the market was too high, they raised cash. In retrospect, one could argue that stock prices were inflated at that time and that all investors who were long equities had a flawed sense of valuation. But at least the partners were in tune with their market. They sold when it got ahead of itself; and they bought when they saw a short-term opportunity, even if they worried about the overall level of valuation and the long-term outlook.

In 1929 they turned cautious, just in time. They sold heavily over the summer to reduce their margin debt and to raise cash, but with an eye toward buying stocks back at lower prices later on; so they were defensively positioned by the time of the market peak on September 3rd and through the crash in October, but not because they truly appreciated what was happening. While their sense of valuation and their sense of history led them to expect a correction, they were not ready for a Crash; and they had no idea that the consequences of the Crash would take a decade to fully play out. They sensed danger; but they also seem to have been confused and uncertain of what to expect.

For this reason, they took it all somewhat casually. Unlike Paul's close friend, Sidney Weinberg of Goldman Sachs in New York, who had strong memories of that day and stayed at work for a week after the Crash without going home once, Paul himself, at least in his early eighties, had no strong recollection of October 29th. As he explained it,

> **New York was the center of finance in the United States; [the Crash] would be felt far greater than in Boston, and I think that most of the financial interests in Boston were much more conservative and conservatively run than many of the institutions in New York. So that in a panic such as that, why, the less conservative ones got hurt the most.**[109]

Of course SSIC was not conservatively run, just conservatively positioned on October 29th.

But the conservatism did not last. Barely a month later, they were back at it, confirming the fact that they did not fully comprehend the situation. They made the classic mistake of young investors, and quite a few older ones. They reflexively bought too early, on the "dip," because stocks, while still high, were so much lower than they had been two to four weeks before. They even borrowed five million dollars, an amount equal to 20% of the assets of the fund, to leverage their purchases "at prices which appeared attractive at that time, but which afterwards proved to be considerably above the final low points." As Paul said many years later, "We were young and not particularly frightened," perhaps not as frightened as they should have been.[110] When a sharp though short-lived recovery occurred in December of 1929, they took the opportunity to get out of many of their positions and 80% of their debt. In the 1929 annual report, they concluded that while stocks were cheaper than they had been at any time during the past two years, the current business recession could develop into a depression, "which might run for a year or two." Should that occur, stocks would offer few opportunities for profitable investment. They maintained a large cash position and invested primarily in what we today would call defensive or recession-resistant sectors—utility and food stocks for example—until the U.S. went off the gold standard in 1933.[111]

State Street's experience with Chain Store Fund illustrates their misplaced confidence in 1929, but also their ability to adjust to changing realities when things turned against them. As its name implies, this was a fund formed to invest in chain stores, most of which were unlisted and nearly all of which were too small and illiquid for SSIC to invest in individually. It was a mutual fund specializing in one industry; and at that time there were no impediments to one mutual fund buying the shares of another.

Childs, Jeffries & Company established the fund with the sale of 100,000 shares (of an originally planned 200,000-share offering) at $25, one month before the crash. State Street bought 12,000 shares a few days later at $25.50, for a total investment of $306,000. They did so primarily because of their respect for the ability and performance record of Paul Childs, the sponsoring firm's principal, and also because they thought that these businesses were inexpensive relative to other investments. We know this through a memo written to the SEC years later by one of the newer partners, Bill Morton; but he was clearly representing Paul Cabot's point of view on this, as well as his own.

The market collapse prevented the issuance of the second 100,000 shares and dried up trading for the existing shares. Fortunately, it also prevented Chain Store Fund from fully investing even the smaller amount of money it had raised. When they had invested about half, a dispute broke out about whether to continue, or to conserve cash, with State Street arguing the latter. At this point, early 1930, Bill Morton joined the Board; they could hardly refuse him a seat with State Street owning twelve percent of the stock. Once on the Board, Morton argued,

> **we were in for bad times, that what remained in cash should be kept in cash, and that *we should face the realities of the situation* and realize that a fund of this size was too small to justify the existence of the organization which was set up in contemplation of a fund twice as large. (emphasis added)**

Morton initially lost this argument; so he went to the other shareholders and with them, eventually—in July of the following year—forced the payment of an $11 per share special dividend, thus returning to investors almost half of their original investment. He then attempted to force the sale of the other assets, and in early 1933, after numerous attempts, managed to sell them to a group led by the fund managers in exchange for debentures collateralized by the assets being sold. The debentures, valued at $2.50 per share, were declared as a liquidating dividend, along with $1.50 in cash. But State Street could only sell the debentures at a price equivalent to $1.52 per share, validating Morton's judgment of three years earlier that the business outlook was poor. In the end, State Street salvaged $164,000 of its $306,000 investment.[112]

What is notable about this episode is that State Street was flexible enough to continually reevaluate their decisions, and when they made a bad one, to reverse course before it was too late. They were alert, pragmatic, and open-minded, which reduced the cost of sometimes being wrong.

They decided that, for a while at least, research would be less important than common sense. Writing in the 1930 annual report and reflecting on the events since the crash, they concluded that

[A]ll common stock investors lost, irrespective of the care with which their investments were made or supervised. No amount of research work could have prevented such losses unless it was decided that no equities should be used.

One has only to review the utterances of leading economists, research organizations, and businessmen during the past eighteen months to discover how small is the amount of real knowledge and understanding concerning problems of major economic importance. In spite of all the research work that has been done on such problems, it appears that *common sense still remains the intelligent investor's most reliable and useful asset.*[113]

The Sales Campaign

As of the end of September 1929, the management company, State Street Research & Management, handled investment portfolios of over $50 million: $29 million for SSIC, $5 million for Mohawk Investment Company, a smaller, more conservative fund; $15 million for two Shawmut Bank Trusts; and $5 million for various private clients. But in the early 1930s, the open-end funds shrank with the capitalization of the stock market and, in State Street's case, even more. SSIC suffered especially hard because it did not maintain an active sales effort and therefore had no effective way to counteract the decline in assets caused not only by the fall in securities prices but also by the redemptions of its shareholders. In testimony before the SEC, Paul minimized the connection between the redemption feature and the establishment of a sales arm, but he did not appear to convince the commissioners.[114]

Yet the funds lost more than assets; they also lost prestige and reputation. Paul wrote, as the market neared its low point,

In 1929 all investment trusts were considered good and in 1931 they were all bad. It is the hope of most of us who are in the business that some time in the not-too-distant future it will be recognized that there is as much difference in this field as regards to quality, scope, and purpose as is true in such fields as law and medicine.[115]

Paul frequently compared his profession to law, and even more often to medicine; and it was this sense that he was in a profession at least as much as in a business that determined his attitude toward sales, and especially advertising. Advertising and active selling by doctors and lawyers were considered unethical in the 1930s, and it would have been equally distasteful to this son of a Boston trustee who saw himself and his partners as the modern embodiments of nineteenth-century trustees. But by 1932 things had taken a serious turn. In a little over three years, from September 30, 1929 to December 31, 1932, the assets of SSIC dropped by 75% from $29 million to less than $7.5 million. The net asset value per share dropped 70%, with the remainder of the decline resulting from net redemptions. The other assets managed by State Street Research dropped almost proportionately.

And revenues to the management company dropped even more. In order to avoid cutting the dividend, and perhaps to discourage redemptions, they cut the management fee in half to half a percent. These events reduced the revenue to management from SSIC, their major source of income, from the $213,000 they had received in 1929 to just $36,000 by 1932, which may not have covered their expenses and salaries, which had totaled about $27,000 in 1927, when assets were much less. However, revenue did recover to nearly a quarter of a million dollars by 1936.[116]

The natural reaction to this triple setback—depressed share price, fewer shares, lower fees—was to try to boost the income and assets of the fund. They considered reducing the large cash position of SSIC in the hope that a more fully invested fund would produce more current income and, possibly, capital gains. But the market appeared to be so fragile before Roosevelt took the U.S. off the gold standard that the partners were unwilling to place too much of their shareholders' funds in equities. As they wrote in the 1931 annual report, "In view of the uncertain political and economic conditions which exist throughout the world, only an extremely conservative attitude towards all types of investment is warranted."[117]

Their next move was to cut the dividend. This was a difficult step because the management company was barely breaking even; it could not pay a significant profit to the partners, and SSIC dividends therefore accounted for much of the partners' personal income. In addition, most of their shareholders needed the money even more than they did. State Street followed a more liberal policy than its competitors in that it paid not only dividend and interest income to shareholders but realized capital gains as well. This enabled the partners to maintain a generous $3.00 per share payout through the end of 1931. In the annual report of that year, they had told the shareholders that they hoped to maintain the dividend unless business failed to show "any improvement during the coming year."[118]

Importantly, until 1933, State Street (SSIC) had two classes of stock. Class A, owned only by the founders and their families, held all of the voting rights. Class B stock, sold to the public, was equivalent in financial and economic terms, but without the vote. By the early thirties, however, State Street was far from the private firm it had been in the mid-twenties. The holdings of the founders had fallen from 100% in 1925 to a range of 25% to 43% during the first half of the following decade. And times were changing. The founders believed that they were the best stewards of shareholder wealth and could be trusted with complete control. Yet they must have wondered whether even their shareholders would passively accept the actions of management indefinitely.[119]

By 1932, realized losses had eliminated the fund's capital surplus and there were no more gains left to take. Their way out of this situation was extraordinary—to amend the Articles of Incorporation so that they could use paid-in capital, funds generated by the sale of shares, to pay the dividend.[120] This was a radical step that shows the lengths to which Cabot and his partners would go to avoid eliminating the dividend. In the quarterly report for the winter of 1932, they wrote

> On February 19, 1932, *in order to permit a continuance of the dividend,* it was voted to transfer $10,000,000 from capital to surplus and from this surplus to set up a reserve amounting to the difference between the cost and the market value of securities as of December 31, 1931.[121]

This action was not without consequences, however. Illinois, Ohio, and Maine later suspended the sale of State Street shares, as did Minnesota, and even Massachusetts for a brief period.[122]

Years later, after Paul became Treasurer of Harvard, he developed a reputation for conservatism and probity. He sharply criticized younger men, notably Mc George Bundy of Harvard and later of the Ford Foundation, for urging, even pressuring, colleges and other non-profits to spend capital gains, realized and unrealized, in support of their operating budgets. There is a great deal to be said for Paul's point of view on this issue, as we will see in Chapter VI; but it should be remembered that when Paul was young, and when the financial system was in much greater crisis than it has ever been since, he pursued a policy with his mutual fund that was arguably more aggressive than anything his opponents later urged on Harvard and other colleges.

But State Street had to cut the dividend nevertheless—to $2.50 in 1932, $1.70 in 1933, and $1.60 in 1934—even with the paid-in capital account which contributed 40% of the funds for the dividend in 1932 and 100% in the years 1933 through 1935. The partners wrote hopefully that they had made every effort "to improve the quality and extend the scope of the work performed by" State Street Research & Management,[123] but the fund was no longer large enough to support a first-class research effort and an active sales campaign was the only answer to State Street's dilemma.

The partners had spent very little time and effort on sales during the 1920s. They believed that they and their clients would fare best if they concentrated on investing and let their record sell the fund. They were also very cautious, one might say overly so, about investing client money in an unproven venture. Before starting State Street in 1924, Paul and his partners, as he recalled,

> **went around and discussed this whole venture with ... the most intelligent, and brightest financiers in the country at the time. People like Mr. Charles Francis Adams, ... Treasurer of Harvard, Neil Rantoul who was head of F.S. Moseley and was one of the astutest old guys I ever knew. Mr. J.P. Morgan [Jr.] who was at that time my brother-in-law's father, and other members of the J.P. Morgan & Co. like Mr. Russell Leffingwell ....**

> **The comments I got were extremely interesting. The first comment was, "A company? Your propose to start a company whose stockholders can liquidate it whenever they have a notion to?" I said, yes. They said it's insane, and then they went on to say, even if it weren't insane, this is the worst time ... possible to start a common stock fund. This would be terrible.**

> **Actually, to go back and use hindsight you'd find that time [1924] was just about the best time you could have picked.**

They began selling to the general public in 1927 and ended up with 95 shareholders. By 1929, they had eight hundred. They had no sales force or selling commission; they just sold it to anyone who showed up at their offices.[124]

In 1928 they could still write

> **At no time have we undertaken any sort of selling campaign, believing that good results must eventually attract the investor, and realizing that such results can be most effectively attained through the concentration of effort on the main problem: i.e., selection and supervision of securities best suited to meet the needs of the company.[125]**

In other words, build a better mousetrap and the world will beat a path to your door. The strategy worked, at least in good times. In some years in the 1920s, State Street outsold its two Boston open-end competitors, even without a sales effort. In time it became the favorite fund of the relatively sophisticated investor. While management fees were higher, for a while, and the investor had to make an effort to seek it out, the higher fees paid for better, first-hand research and better investment performance. The choice of State Street was an easy one for those who "did their homework" and, not surprisingly, the average State Street shareholder held a larger investment in the fund than did his counterparts at Massachusetts Investors Trust or Incorporated Investors. As Paul later noted, "Up to 1932 we didn't spend five cents for selling stock. Just got it around that if somebody wanted to come in and buy stock, he could."[126]

The selling documents were the annual reports, which I believe Paul wrote, particularly that of 1926, released in January 1927 when the fund was first opened to the public. This report argued the superiority of common stocks as a long-term investment, explained the decision to use debt to increase leverage, justified moving into and out of the market as conditions changed, held out the goal of at least 10% annual return, and outlined a research effort that balanced macroeconomic, industry, and individual company analysis. After the stock market crash, Paul and his partners claimed to have de-emphasized macroeconomic research and market timing and to be putting more effort into the study of individual companies.[127] The professional staff by then included Steven Heard an insurance and financial company analyst, and William C. Morton, who wrote the Chain Store Fund memo and later became an internationally-recognized expert on the oil industry. But their strategy in the early thirties incorporated market timing, and a *Registration Statement* from the late thirties gave equal emphasis to general economic conditions, industries, and individual companies, stating:

> **There are times when the investor's best interests are served by having a substantial portion of his funds in cash or cash equivalents and other times when the fund should be largely invested in common stocks.**[128]

State Street could be aggressive in the way they used their investment performance record to win business. A letter that accompanied the 1931 annual report read as follows.

> **Boston, Mass.**
> **February 3, 1932**
>
> **Dear Sir:**
>
> **We have recently had occasion to make a comparison of the three largest New England investment funds of a mutual nature which have been operating for a sufficient length of time to make their records**

significant. The results of this comparison, which may be of interest to you, are given below.

Very truly yours,
STATE STREET INVESTMENT CORP.[129]

COMPARISON OF PERFORMANCE

(Adjustments made for Stock and Cash Dividends)

	State Street Invest Corp Organized July 1924	Massachusetts Investors Trust Organized July 1924	Incorporated Investors Organized Nov. 1926
Percent Gain from date of Organization to Dec. 31, 1929	603%	76%	90%
Percent Loss from Dec 31, 1929 to Dec. 31, 1931	49%	61%	62%
Percent Gain or Loss from date of Organization to Dec. 31, 1931	260%	31%	28%
Total Cash Dividends from Organization	$ 19.50	$ 14.18	$ 6.73
Original Investment	$ 12.50	$ 23.55	$ 24.60
Percent Return on Original Investment	156%	60%	27%

By "Per cent Return on Original Investment," State Street meant total cash dividends divided by original investment, not total return in the modern sense. Contrary to the above, Incorporated Investors was in fact organized in November of 1925.

Paul remembered the following in reaction to this letter.

> [Massachusetts Investors Trust President] Griswold used to come around and say to me I think it's very unfair to put our figures in there. Won't you please not do so? I said to hell with you, we're going to put them in and pass them out. We used to show them because they were out peddling their stock like hell. They were just a regular sales organization.[130]

While State Street's record looked good next to that of MIT and the other open-end funds, it looked far better next to the closed-end funds. State Street used limited leverage, or debt, and this hurt them at times, but the closed-end funds, accounting for $7.10 billion of the $7.25 billion of managed funds invested in the U.S. at the market peak, had a great deal of debt, and therefore leverage, embedded in their capital structures.[131] This helped performance in the rising market of the 1920s but nearly wiped them out in 1929. The collapse of many of these highly leveraged, closed-end funds, combined with their well-publicized ethical and even legal abuses, sharply limited their position as competitors to the Boston-type funds, which were less leveraged, if at all, and honestly and, for the most part, ably run. [132]

In the 1932 third quarter report, the partners disclosed that they had "decided to encourage brokers to sell the stock."[133] It says something about the fund business in Boston that when Dick Saltonstall sought advice on whom to hire to run the sales campaign, he asked a competitor, William A. Parker of Incorporated Investors, for suggestions. However, this was less surprising in view of the fact that the competitor's sister, Olivia, was married to Paul's brother, Henry. Parker's recommendation was a man who had already left his mark on Massachusetts Investors Trust and Incorporated Investors, Edward G. Leffler.[134]

Edward G. Leffler. One securities dealer compared his sales presentation to "getting religion at a camp meeting."

Leffler was born in Milwaukee in 1892 to Swedish immigrants. Even as a boy he was a natural salesman. In grade school he sold the *Saturday Evening Post* door-to-door and, after graduation from Gustavus Adolphus College, sold almost anything—shoes, books, pots and pans. While at college he became active in the temperance movement and developed a reputation as an effective speaker, a salesman really, on behalf of prohibition. He was so good that he was later hired by the National Prohibition Party to speak on behalf of the movement in Kansas. This led to a position selling bonds for temperance hotels in Kansas, his first job as a securities salesman.

This experience ended badly when the hotels went bankrupt. Leffler took it personally when his customers, many of whom were his friends, lost money. He later made it up to them, replacing the bonds with the shares of Incorporated Investors. He worked for six more years as a securities salesman but never achieved significant success and never felt good about the products he was selling.[135]

In a "confidential memo," Leffler explained that even "the highest types" of security firms "would in the course of events, hand me securities to sell to my clients which would turn out to be unsatisfactory." Yet he concluded, "when an investor attempts to buy equities without professional aid . . . such a program will almost inevitably be a failure." Like Paul, he even studied the British investment trusts, "but found their structure not quite suitable." The solution to his quandary turned out to be the Boston mutual fund.

> [T]he solution lay in employing a full-time professional management, pool[ing] the funds of many investors so that proper diversification could be had, and costs kept within tolerable limits. I also wished to introduce a provision that investors could present their shares and receive liquidating values at any time.[136]

In 1924, an article in the *Federal Reserve Bulletin* introduced him to the idea of the investment trust. Once familiar with the idea, his personality and values led him to the Boston funds. Leffler's instincts were egalitarian and democratic, in the tradition of the Midwestern, Scandinavian political Progressives. Funds offering a single class of security appeared, to Leffler, to be more democratic than funds with various levels of senior and junior securities—bonds, preferred, and common. The redemption feature was also democratic because those dissatisfied with performance could liquidate at minimal cost.

Leffler was an ideal salesman for the Boston mutual fund product because he genuinely cared about his customers. He wanted to sell only products he could believe in, and the Boston-type open-end fund was just such a product. One dealer wrote that, "He was an excellent salesman in the best sense of the word—honest, clear speaking, resourceful, clear thinking." Another was taken by his "evangelical zeal." To William Parker, Leffler spoke "with the conviction of a prophet who had had a visitation from God." Paul described him as a "super-duper salesman." Then he added, "I like him." This writer cannot name another prohibitionist that Paul liked.

Leffler's passion on this subject led him, along with two Boston brokers, to set up the Massachusetts Investors Trust at just about the same time that Paul and his partners were setting up SSIC.[137] But Leffler soon decided that he did not like the direction MIT was taking, ironically because of its overemphasis on sales. Also, he did not like the portfolio. He objected to the extreme diversification and the emphasis on income stocks over growth stocks. MIT received a percentage of portfolio income rather than a percentage of assets, as was the case with the other two funds. He departed within the year to set up a new sales company, Leffler & Co., with Parker and John T. Nightingale, which did however sell MIT's shares, among others.

But they quickly found that sophisticated Boston investors, their target market, were not interested in a portfolio with as many as 120 names, too many for the managers to understand thoroughly, even if they had tried. Another problem was that MIT did not have any principals with the name recognition of a Cabot or a Saltonstall. Bostonians were most comfortable placing their money with men whose names they associated with the old Boston trustees. At least partially for this reason, Merrill Griswold was asked to become a trustee at MIT in 1925.

But the addition of Griswold to the board did not resolve all of Leffler's objections to the management at MIT, and by 1925 Leffler, Parker, and Nightingale decided to form another investment company. They required additional funds for start-up expenses and formed a partnership with George Putnam, who invested $5,000 in the new enterprise. A scion of both the Putnam and Lowell families, Putnam, along with the money, contributed the name recognition and the investment expertise that they needed. They named the new company Incorporated Investors and changed the name of the sales company to Parker, Putnam & Nightingale, with Parker, Putnam, Nightingale, and Leffler as the officers and directors. Unlike at MIT, the sales organization for Incorporated Investors was subsidiary to the money management operation so the investors controlled how their product was to be marketed.[138]

Incorporated Investors typically owned 25 to 35 stocks, a small enough number so that, like the principals at State Street, they could understand the business dynamics and key stock price drivers of every one.[139] Their overall approach was closer to that of SSIC than to that of MIT, as the 1928 report to shareholders makes clear.

> **The policy of Incorporated Investors in buying into the great money-earners for long-term investing, will in the long run prove of greater benefit to the stockholders than a method of investing their money which is dependent for success upon guessing temporary movements.**[140]

(When Putnam Investments, the second investment firm founded by George Putnam, acquired his first investment firm in 1964, the fund changed its name to Putnam Investors Fund; but the strategy of "buying into the great money-earners for long term investing" continues.)

With their expertise and with the old New England families represented in management, Incorporated Investors was also able to sell itself as the twentieth-century embodiment of the old Boston trustees. And by distributing through regional securities firms all over the U.S., they were able to market this concept nationally. But the key to the marketing effort was the one non-New Englander among them, Edward Leffler, whose style contrasted markedly with that of the Boston trustee. One Wells-Dickey broker, while calling Leffler's sales approach "very low key," also observed that he had "an evangelistic zeal for investment management," and sold the idea with enthusiasm. He even compared a sales presentation by Leffler to "getting religion at a camp meeting."[141]

After the meeting, Wells-Dickey acquired the exclusive right to sell Incorporated Investors shares in the Ninth Federal Reserve District, centered in Minneapolis. By 1928, Incorporated Investors had a relationship with a retail distributor in virtually every region of the country. But the entire sales effort, $30 million sold through brokers and the regulatory approvals, or what he called "the Blue Sky burden," rested on Leffler's shoulders. The intense, personal one-on-one selling, literally coast-to-coast, took its toll. By the spring of 1929, six months before the crash, Leffler retired to Florida at the age of 37, on account of his "spiritual and physical exhaustion," but comforted by a $245,000 severance payment, which he used to purchase a villa and a new Packard.

Within eighteen months, Leffler had tired of retirement and set up a small sales office at 140 Federal Street in Boston, where State Street just happened to be located. It is likely that Parker recommended Leffler to Saltonstall with Leffler's knowledge and approval. Certainly, as Natalie Grow points out, Leffler's need for something to do and State Street's need for a dynamic salesman coincided. They came to an agreement in November 1932 similar to the one Leffler had had with Incorporated Investors. They set the selling commission at 6% and reduced the cost of redemption from $2 to $1 per share. Leffler lined up 38 securities dealers in 11 states to sell the shares; and State Street reserved for itself the right to sell in New England and New York City. [142] But the primary concern of the State Street partners was that they not be distracted by the sales effort. They wrote investors,

> **So far as it is possible, it is our intention to turn over the active selling and the commissions therefrom to dealers and others, thereby leaving us free to devote, as heretofore, our entire time and effort to research and the study of the problems of investment.**[143]

The sales effort started slowly because of the need for regulatory approval in each state in which the fund was to be sold.[144] Leffler again had to make the rounds of the state regulators. Investor confidence was at an all-time low in 1932. And because the State Street partners were among those who lacked confidence, cash accounted for over 60% of the fund's assets. Investors are always reluctant to pay a management fee to hold cash.

But on April 19th of 1933, the U.S. went off the gold standard, optimism returned to Wall Street, and State Street returned to the equity market. This was not exactly a surprise to the partners. Two months before, in the 1932 annual report, they had written shareholders that:

> **In the present chaotic conditions of the world very drastic and possibly very rapid changes may become necessary. For example, if one or more of the inflationary schemes now being considered in Washington should become effective, it might be necessary and desirable to make a very rapid transfer from dollar obligations such as our treasury certificates and cash, which have become increasingly valuable during the depression, to equities and possibly commodities. We have been and are studying this aspect of the problem in detail and it is our hope and belief that we can render services to our shareholders in this respect that they could not perform for themselves.[145]**

When the President made his move, Paul was vacationing in Florida and his partners telephoned him. Paul urged them to "Buy all you can." Paine agreed and they did just that. But that day was apparently so chaotic that it took nearly a year to properly account for all of the transactions.[146]

Less than two months later, however, in mid-June, State Street sent out "a special interim report" covering the events of April and May. As the partners pointed out, there had been "very drastic and rapid changes in the economic situation which have caused equally rapid changes in [their] investment policy." And they reminded their shareholders that they had warned them of this possibility. The interim report noted that the SSIC equity position, which had been 43% on March 31, 1933 before the U.S. abandoned the gold standard, had risen to 88% by May 31. It would be 96% by year-end.

They also used the interim report to announce that Mohawk Investment Company shareholders were being offered the opportunity to merge into State Street (SSIC). And they announced, "in accordance with the spirit of the times," that State Street's Class B stockholders would henceforth receive voting rights and that the corporation would have only one class of stock.[147] While this was truly "in accordance with the spirit of the times," it is also likely that they had to give all shareholders the vote to gain approval for the merger from the Mohawk shareholders.

Mohawk differed from State Street in two important respects. Its borrowing powers were sharply limited and, under normal conditions, it was supposed to remain nearly fully invested. After the market crash, neither fund did much borrowing. And with financial conditions far from normal, neither fund was fully invested. As the portfolios became nearly identical, the case for a merger, which the partners explained to the shareholders in a letter, became obvious. It would save on costs. The Mohawk investors would "become participants in a larger and better known fund with a longer record." And they would own the same fund that the partners and their families had channeled almost all of their own wealth into.[148] The merger closed on July 17, 1933.

In its investigation of the Mutual Fund Industry, the SEC tried to prove that the sales effort had prompted the shift out of cash, since an equity fund with more than 50% in cash was a difficult sell. But Leffler, who was grilled on this question, never conceded this point. He told the SEC that, "If I lost a sale because of it [the cash position], I would rather lose a sale."[149] It is clear that Cabot and his partners had been planning to move out of cash for a while and it seems very unlikely that they would have risked investors' money, including their own, to aid the sales effort. In fact, while the equity position rose to 98% by March 1934, it fell to 72% by June, which must have made the task of selling the fund harder.[150]

But when the market took off in April 1933, the sales campaign did as well. The partners had both a good investment record and good name recognition. And they were willing to make small changes in their operations to increase investor appeal. They limited their borrowing to 25% of net assets, another move which fit the mood of the times. They began publishing their portfolio in detail quarterly, instead of just listing the stocks owned. And they added four, high-profile outside directors. [151]

In the end the sales effort, from the standpoint of the partners, succeeded too well. It continued only until June 1935, at which time they decided that the fund was growing so rapidly ($18 million in sales in 31 months) that they could not invest the cash profitably.[152] While they slightly trailed their two major Boston rivals in sales, they took in almost $10 million in the last three quarters of 1933 after selling less than $400 thousand of shares in 1932. Sales by share count, as outlined in the February 1942 Prospectus, were as follows.

Table 5
SSIC Sales of Treasury and New Shares, and Shares Outstanding[153]

	Sales of Treas Shs	Sales of New Shs	Shares Outstanding	
Jun 30, 1931 thru June 30, 1933	53,770	0	215,196	
Jul 1, 1933 thru Dec 31, 1935	36,103	224,476	439,672	
1933, Shares for Mohawk acquisition		37,498	477,170	
Jan 1, 1936 thru Jan 30, 1937	27,690	22,820	499,990	thru subscription warrants
Nov 2, 1938		10	500,000	

Investing what at the time seemed like a massive amount of money was only one of their objections to the sales effort. Management never quite trusted the sales force, though Leffler, by all accounts, was scrupulously honest. In the 1932 annual report, management wrote:

> **It is very definitely our desire to sell our shares soundly and conservatively. We would very greatly appreciate any information which will aid us in accomplishing this result, and prevent excessive and unwarranted statements and assertions.**[154]

Perhaps most importantly, they resented the time that sales, both the filing of reports and meeting with prospects, took from research and money management, as do investors today. They wrote in the 1934 Report that "Barring a major decline in stock prices . . . it is our intention to cease the active selling of our stock in the relatively near future," which they did.[155]

For a while afterward, they sold shares to individuals who came to their office, but only when they had on hand treasury stock that had been sold back to them by other investors. Investors sold back 124,625 shares between 1927 and 1935, roughly one quarter of shares outstanding. But by the end of 1935, the fund had reached what the partners believed was a nearly unmanageable $42 million, and all sales ceased. Several funds have since exceeded $42 *billion*; but the partners had exceeded their goals. Between December 1932 and December 1935, assets grew six-fold; the price per share more than doubled; shares outstanding almost tripled; and the number of shareholders increased almost five-fold to 4,150. The sales effort had given State Street the assets and revenue it needed to support the research and management effort,[156] but Paul and the others still resented the time devoted to selling.

> **We always said that if we had been actively selling our stock, we couldn't have been 60% in cash in 1932 . . . The appendage [sales] eventually begins to wag the dog . . . . The times we decided to sell we kept it a long way from us. And we did it for the shortest possible time we could.**[157]

Investment Performance through 1940

During the 1930s, State Street built upon the investment record that they had established during the 1920s. We have already discussed the extraordinary performance of SSIC relative to its competitors and the S&P Index during that earlier decade. (See Table 1 in Chapter II for a summary.) This margin of outperformance continued in the early 1930s, in part due to State Street's accurate analysis of deflation, inflation, and the significance of Roosevelt's move off of the gold standard in April 1933. But its performance advantage shrank during the latter 1930s as competitors strengthened their research departments. Much of State Street's performance resulted from market timing, putting money in defensive stocks and in cash in anticipation of deflation, and moving toward cyclical stocks when a stronger economy and inflation appeared likely. In contrast, Incorporated Investors was closer to what we today would call a growth stock fund, and MIT owned more income and value stocks.

Table 6[158]
Investment Performance: State Street Investment Corporation,
Massachusetts Investors Trust, Incorporated Investors, and S&P

	1930	1931	1932	1933	1934	1935	1936	1937	1938	1939	1940
SSIC	-23.7%	-27.7%	2.4%	57.1%	2.7%	39.3%	45.8%	-32.0%	17.5%	1.8%	-10.5%
MIT	-26.3%	-43.3%	-3.3%	31.4%	11.2%	32.9%	29.7%	-32.5%	24.0%	-1.7%	-9.2%
II	-28.3%	-44.2%	-15.3%	47.4%	2.7%	33.0%	43.7%	-34.4%	25.0%	-8.7%	-11.4%
S&P	-24.9%	-43.3%	-8.2%	54.0%	-1.4%	47.7%	33.9%	-35.0%	31.1%	-0.4%	-9.8%

	1930 -1940 (Annualized)	Fund Origin-1940	(Annualized)
State Street Investment Corp.	2.7%	from 7/31/24	16.5%
Massachusetts Investors Trust	-2.5%	from 7/15/24	3.6%
Incorporated Investors	-3.9%	from 1/1/26	2.0%
S&P	-1.0%	from 1/1/26	4.0%

For the first three years of the decade, through December 31, 1932, State Street's strategy, one that incorporated both market timing and stock selection, saved its investors money; but its fund still dropped by 17.3% per year, compared to the S&P Index's drop at a 26.9% rate. MIT slightly outperformed the market, falling at a 26.0% annual rate. Incorporated Investor's more aggressive stance caused them to underperform, dropping 30.3% per year. All calculations are presented on a total return basis that includes dividends, as well as capital appreciation and depreciation, and management fees. Over the next four years, a period that included State Street's defensive positioning followed by its move into equities after April 19, 1933, SSIC again led the pack, but by a smaller margin. State Street was up 34.6% per year, 3% ahead of the S&P at 31.6%. Incorporated Investors rose 30.4% per year while MIT, as would be expected in a bull market, trailed with a rise of 26% per year. Over the next four years however, 1937-1940,

MIT fared the best. Its 7% annual decline closely tracked the S&P, which was down 6.5% per year. State Street fell at a 7.7% rate, while Incorporated Investors fell by 9.8% per year.

When the decades of the twenties and the thirties are combined, one can see how consistently superior stock selection and some attention to macro factors compound over time. For its first sixteen years and five months, until the end of 1940, State Street's annual rate of appreciation was 16.5 %. The comparable number for Massachusetts Investors Trust was 3.6%. Incorporated Investors appreciated at a 2.0% rate for its first fifteen years, ending in 1940, though this number is not precisely comparable because of that company's later starting date.[159]

Over the next four years, Paul's concerns would center on the war, especially during nearly three years of active civilian service in Washington, as we shall see in Chapter V. But by the end of the 1940s, he would be working on behalf of Harvard University as well as State Street shareholders, and Harvard would be leading the parade of university endowments into the stock market in time for the post-war bull market, which is covered in Chapter VI. But next, we turn in Chapter IV to Paul's immersion in the politics of the New Deal, specifically the Revenue Act of 1936 and the Investment Company Act of 1940.

CHAPTER IV

THE REVENUE ACT AND
THE INVESTMENT COMPANY ACT

We went in to see the President and I was tremendously impressed. I
gave him my speech "A." He pulled just one sheet out of his drawer and
it had the whole summarized tax bill that was up for consideration. I
told him what we wanted and why. And he understood what it was all
about better than anybody—mind you I was prejudiced against the
guy—he understood it better and quicker and asked more intelligent
questions about it than anybody I had talked to in Washington.[160]

Paul Cabot

Sometime in the late spring of 1936, President Franklin D. Roosevelt sat
alone in his White House study reading analyses of the bill that would
become the Revenue Act of that year. The issue had been a contentious one
since the President's Budget Message on March 3rd, with various factions of the
House, Senate, and Treasury battling over questions of tax equity and efficacy.
But since January 6th, when the Supreme Court had ruled the Agricultural
Adjustment Act unconstitutional, thereby invalidating a tax that had generated
$500 million in annual revenue, Roosevelt had believed a tax increase to be
necessary, even if it hurt his reelection chances.

One of those analyses, a May 11 private memo to the President from Marriner
Eccles, the Chairman of the Federal Reserve Board and former special assistant to
Treasury Secretary Morgenthau, made the case for the taxation of undistributed
earnings of corporations, which in his judgment was "highly desirable from
the fiscal, economic, social, and monetary points of view." "Existing great
accumulations of cash in the hands of large corporations," he wrote, were "obstacles
to recovery" because they kept funds out of the hands of consumers. They were

unjust because they enabled shareholders to accumulate wealth, in the form of retained earnings, nearly tax-free. Yet they deprived middle-class shareholders of the dividends they needed, and the government of the tax revenue it needed. Another of those papers was a longer Eccles memo on the same subject, written for a broader audience. A third was a short outline, a little over a page, which contained "the whole summarized tax bill that was up for consideration."

At one point, the President rolled a piece of paper into his typewriter and typed a note to his companion and secretary, Missy LeHand.

MISSY:

Put in middle drawer of my desk in office.

F.D.R.

The note and the three memos remained in the middle drawer of his desk for nearly two years until, on February 11, 1938, they were removed to a central file and eventually to the Roosevelt Presidential Library at Hyde Park, New York.[161]

The Revenue Act of 1936

A meeting that Paul, along with two Boston competitors, had with Roosevelt on June 3rd, 1936 contributed to the passage of legislation crucial to the fortunes of the Boston funds. It enabled them to avoid a tax, actually part of a triple-tax, on mutual fund dividends, which would have stopped the infant industry "dead in its tracks." One of these competitors was MIT's Merrill Griswold. In the 1920s and early 1930s, Cabot and Griswold had competed aggressively, even acrimoniously. During the middle and later thirties, although the competition continued, external threats—regulation, taxation, an SEC investigation, and the Depression—brought them together as allies in a battle against these developments that threatened their business.

The stock market crash and Depression were financial and psychological events, as these terms suggest. But while not primarily criminal in nature, they were exacerbated by lax ethics and some malfeasance; and the public, which was suffering the consequences, wanted the individuals responsible brought to justice. They demanded investigations into causes, in particular anything that smacked of misconduct, and they demanded legislation to prevent its recurrence. Much of this legislation affected the Boston open-end funds only indirectly. The Securities Act of 1933 imposed reporting and filing requirements on issuers of new securities, the filing of a Registration Statement with the SEC and the offering of a Prospectus to prospective buyers. This was burdensome for the open-end funds because they were continually issuing shares; but it did not affect the way they did business since the funds had generally disclosed their operations quite fully. The Securities Exchange Act of 1934 regulated trading on national exchanges and created the Securities and Exchange Commission. Since the Boston funds were investors on the exchanges, they were among those whom the act was designed to protect; so beyond the required reports and testimony, they were not seriously affected as long as they obeyed the laws and regulations.

There were, however, two series of events of great significance for the mutual fund industry; and the principals of the Boston Funds were deeply involved in both. The first of these was the Revenue Act of 1936. The second was the chain of events, including the Public Utility Holding Company Act of 1935 and the SEC investigation of the mutual fund industry of 1935-1939, which culminated in the Investment Company Act of 1940.

In June 1935, President Roosevelt proposed a tax bill that included, among other provisions, an increase in the corporate tax rate and a reduction in the deduction (from 100% to 90%) that corporations received for dividends received from other domestic corporations. This latter provision was particularly threatening to mutual funds because it meant that dividends received from stocks in their portfolios, or at least 10% of them, were taxable, and holders of mutual fund shares were subject to triple taxation—first when the corporation made the profit; second when the mutual fund received its share of the profit in the form of the dividend; and third when the mutual fund shareholder received the dividend from his fund. The deduction limited the liability, but the tax could have established a precedent that corporate dividends paid to a fund were taxable to the fund.[162]

The middle-class investor, who owned shares through a mutual fund, would be at a disadvantage relative to the upper-class investor who owned them directly and could afford to hire a private investment advisor. In 1937, 83% of the shareholders of SSIC owned 100 or fewer shares, an investment of less than $7,000. They accounted for 25% of the total value of the fund, compared to 34% owned by the top 52 shareholders (1.2%) owning more than 1,000 shares each.[163] The mutual fund manager would have been at a severe disadvantage had corporate dividends paid to a fund become taxable to the fund, since a third level of taxation could in many cases erase any value added by the manager.

Fortunately, Roosevelt was aware of this potential problem and his 1935 tax message included the following.

> **Bona fide investment trusts that submit to public regulation and perform the function of permitting small investors to obtain the benefit of diversification of risk may well be exempted from this tax.**[164]

Merrill Griswold later dubbed this the "conduit theory" because it viewed the mutual fund as a vehicle through which small investors could own a diversified portfolio, assuming all the risks and rewards and paying all the taxes, while the fund itself had no tax liability as long as it retained none or almost none of the income. As the 1936 State Street annual report explained,

> **This permits the grouping together of many individuals of limited means who are seeking expert advice and diversity through the medium of an investment company without subjecting them to double [actually triple] taxation and leaves them in substantially the same position relative to Federal taxes as if they were investing independently.**[165]

Nonetheless, in August 1935 the tax bill passed with an increase in the corporate tax rate from 13¾ % to 15% and a reduction in the deduction for dividends received from domestic corporations from 100% to 90%, without any explicit exemption for *bona fide* investment trusts. This was a significant, though temporary, setback to the mutual fund industry.

In the Budget Message for the following year, delivered March 3rd, 1936, Roosevelt presented a Revenue Act that reduced the dividend deduction from 90% to 85% and, at the prompting of Treasury, proposed a tax on undistributed profits, or retained earnings. It was this tax that Marriner Eccles argued, was "highly desirable from the fiscal, economic, social, and monetary points of view."

Shortly thereafter, a senior partner of a leading Boston investment bank approached the three pioneer Boston mutual funds to join in the fight against the tax. But Griswold, with Roosevelt's 1935 reference to *bona fide* investment trusts in mind, concluded that a tax on undistributed profits might mean that if a fund distributed all of its income and capital gains, it would have no tax liability. He spoke to Paul Cabot on this and Paul agreed immediately. Rather than oppose the undistributed profits tax, they would persuade the government to adopt it for the funds. They reasoned that under this law, only income paid out as dividends would be taxable, and that only by the shareholders receiving the dividends, not the fund company itself. Griswold and Cabot enlisted the support of Tudor Gardiner, a former governor of Maine with excellent political connections who had bought George Putnam Sr.'s interest in Incorporated Investors. Later in March 1936, they embarked on their lobbying campaign.[166]

The three went to work on Treasury, the Department of Internal Revenue, and Congress, especially one of the Massachusetts Senators, David I. Walsh, a Democrat from Worcester who was a member of the Senate Finance Committee. Though of working-class background, Walsh had a close relationship with Charles Francis Adams, the State Street Director who had been Secretary of the Navy when Walsh was a member of the Senate Naval Affairs Committee. The Bostonians explained their situation to Walsh at a dinner party, arranged for that purpose, at Adams' home.[167] And they continued their lobbying in Washington.

> **We did most of our work through the late Senator David I. Walsh. We'd get him every night, fill him full of cocktails and give him speech "A" which was this is a conduit and all you do is you put your money in, it's just as though you directly owned those things because you get all of the gain if there is a gain and all of the income and you've got to pay full taxes and therefore it's unfair to tax the conduit as such.[168]**

This was the crux of their argument. The wealthy, with their financial advisors, paid tax at two levels, when the corporation made its profit and when the shareholder received his dividend. It was unfair for the middle-class mutual fund holder to be forced to pay a third time, when his fund took possession of the dividend.

Paul had previewed this argument with Chairman Landis, a former Dean of Harvard Law School, before the opening of the SEC investigation into the funds in August 1935, but Landis declined to become involved ahead of the investigation and merely asked Paul to keep him informed of developments. Paul periodically briefed him, along with Tommy Gammach, an old friend who was then working as an assistant to Landis, [169] and had an interesting reaction to the Chairman.

> **He thanked us for the information and didn't register whether he was for or against. It was only through Gammach that we learned he was opposed to it . . . .**
>
> **Later, to our dismay, [we] learned through Gammach that he was trying to knife us and prevent this. But nonetheless we did succeed.[170]**

Probably Landis was opposed, but not forcefully or vocally. Natalie Grow believed that Landis feared the funds would take any tax break as a government imprimatur, and based on her exhaustive reading of all of the mutual fund quarterly and annual reports from these years, believed that his fear was justified.[171] But there is no reason why Paul should have felt that Landis had "knifed" them.

Certainly the Boston fund managers thought that they had Landis in their camp when, on March 16th, 1936, Griswold wrote President Roosevelt urging the administration to solicit the views of the SEC "as to how the interests of the shareholders of investment trusts can best be reconciled under the new law with the interests of the Government." Perhaps they thought that their case was so strong that no one who truly understood the issues would oppose them. The President's personal secretary, Mr. Gaston, replied to Griswold that Treasury Secretary Morgenthau had directed his subordinates to study all of the available reports and suggestions.

On March 20th, Revenue Bill H.R. 12395 was introduced in the House.[172] Four days later, Paul met with three officials of Internal Revenue on the subject; later that day with L.H. Parker, Chief of Staff of the Joint (House-Senate) Committee on Internal Revenue Taxation; and on the following day with Guy T. Helvering, Commissioner of Internal Revenue. The purpose, according to Paul's letter requesting these meetings, was "to present to you certain ideas relative to future taxation which have been brought about by the President's recent message." In other words, he was making the same arguments (Speech "A") again and again, to different interested parties.

The feedback he received at these meetings led Cabot, along with Griswold, to draw up a series of suggestions on the treatment of mutual fund taxation, suggestions which dealt with some issues they had not previously addressed. It likened the mutual fund to a partnership. It calculated the effective tax rate on capital gains for typical investors under various scenarios, and pointed out the special importance of realized gains for mutual funds, in contrast to other corporations, because it is through them that the funds realize nearly all their profits. It countered the idea that the payment to shareholders of all capital gains would deplete the funds available for future investment. A convenient, tax-efficient dividend and capital gains reinvestment plan, or in State Street's (SSIC's) case, the issuance of subscription warrants, [173] would keep money in the funds of those managers who had earned the confidence of their shareholders. And perhaps most important, it quoted Secretary Morgenthau supporting their overall position. The Secretary told the Senate in April,

> **It will be well to bear in mind at all times that this is purely and simply a proposal to put all taxes on business profits essentially on the same equitable basis; to give no advantages and to impose no penalties upon corporation stockholders that are not given to and imposed upon the individual taxpayer.**[174]

By early May Paul had called on Bill Morton to help him in Washington, and during the second week of that month, Morton and Griswold held a series of meetings with L.H. Parker, various Senators on the Finance Committee, and at least three administration officials, including Herman Oliphant, General Counsel at Treasury. Also that week, Senator Walsh introduced Cabot's and Griswold's "Suggestions Regarding Treatment of Mutual Investment Trusts," supplemented by a clarifying memorandum, before the Senate Finance Committee.[175]

This clarifying memorandum,[176] initially prepared for a meeting in Senator Walsh's office on May 26th with Arthur Kent, Chief Counsel to the Bureau of Internal Revenue, and his associate Mr. Lusk, dealt with the conduit theory and whether it should be reserved for open-end funds. That it was so reserved became so controversial, particularly among the closed-end funds, that hearings were held during deliberations over the Investment Company Act of 1940 to determine how a provision so favorable to the open-end funds had become law. Did Paul Cabot and his associates exert too much influence in the drafting of the 1936 tax bill? The evidence suggests that they did. When the closed-end funds finally realized what was going on, they sent a lawyer to see Cabot and Griswold at The Hay Adams Hotel, their headquarters in Washington. The two Bostonians, realizing what the lawyer was there for, got him drunk, in Cabot's account, or got him involved in a card game, in another version of the story. Whichever is true, and possibly both are, the closed-end funds were denied an effective spokesman to oppose the Boston funds' proposals.[177]

Paul's memo generously urged the application of the conduit theory to all investment trusts but, somewhat disingenuously, suggested wording that could be used to restrict the proposed tax benefits to open-end, Boston-type funds, "were this [restriction] deemed to be advisable." Paul did not argue for special treatment for his type of fund but suggested wording to anyone who wanted to give it to him anyway.

> **You will note that in the specific suggestions the definition of an investment trust is broad and does not limit the category to "mutual investment corporations." Were this deemed to be advisable, we would add the following to the definition as submitted: "Provided further, that it shall apply only to corporations *each shareholder of which, upon reasonable notice and under reasonable conditions, is entitled to withdraw his shares of the corporation property or its equivalent in cash.*[178]**

In other words, it shall apply only to open-end funds. Within two days of the meeting on May 26th, Kent of Internal Revenue placed amendments before the Executive Session of the Senate Finance Committee exempting fixed trusts, whose lobbyist had also been active, and mutual investment companies paying out their dividends to shareholders from taxes. It defined a mutual investment company as one where the fund was diversified in terms of holdings (no more than 10% of the securities in any one corporation), in terms of ownership (no more than 10% of the fund owned by any one individual), and where

> *each stockholder of which, upon reasonable notice and under reasonable conditions, is entitled to withdraw his shares of the corporate property or its equivalent in cash.*

This is almost the exact wording of Paul's memo. (Compare italicized portions.)[179]

On May 28th the amendments were referred back to Internal Revenue for refining and clarification. But by the next day, Senator Robert La Follette Jr. of Wisconsin, the son of the Progressive Republican leader of the same name, was checking back through the especially damaging report of a subcommittee of the Committee on Banking and Currency, the Pecora Committee Report (recording committee proceedings of 1932 and 1933). There he came upon descriptions of the abuses of the investment trusts, specifically the closed-end companies, abuses that Paul had complained and warned about in the 1920s. When La Follette spoke against the trusts on account of these abuses, Walsh interrupted him to point out that his amendment would benefit only five trusts and that these five had not committed any of the offenses that so concerned La Follette. He then asked,

Would it not be in the public interest, decidedly in the interest of those poor who go into these investment trusts, to require them to distribute every dollar that they take in, and furthermore to be in a position to give them cash when they want to get it out? [180]

In the debate that followed, Walsh was occasionally confused, including on the number of trusts. But he stuck to two ideas that were essentially correct: that the open-end funds benefited what he called "those poor," at least poor relative to some other investors; and that the Boston Brahmins, whose interests he was representing, the friends of his friend Charles Francis Adams, really were, as a group, more worthy of trust than the closed-end fund managers who had been exposed by the Pecora Committee Report. The fact that Paul Cabot and his Boston peers had escaped censure and that Paul had projected his rectitude through a widely-read magazine article and several speeches did make a difference. If all the trusts had been lumped together, it is unlikely that the open-end funds would have received their exemption from taxes on the dividends distributed to shareholders, at least not in 1936. As it was, they faced difficulties enough.

To get through to a U.S. Congress that did not fully understand their concerns and a Treasury that had much greater issues with the bill, Cabot, Griswold, and Gardiner felt they had to meet with President Roosevelt in person. Allan Forbes, President of State Street Trust Company, where Charles Francis Adams was the non-executive Chairman of the Board, wired Roosevelt that he "would appreciate it awfully much if you would see . . . three particular fiends of mine . . . on a matter of importance." M.H. McIntyre, Assistant Secretary to the President, recommended that the President not see them, "at least until we know what they want to talk about," but Roosevelt overruled him and agreed to see the trio on June 3rd.[181] As Merrill Griswold remembered the meeting,

We had no sooner entered the President's office than the telephone rang and Mr. Roosevelt proceeded to talk for the entire ten minutes, without our being able to utter a word, whereupon Mr. McIntire came in to "throw us out." Paul Cabot saved the day. He said, and these are his exact words, "Mr. President, this is a damned outrage. It is true we were promised only ten minutes but you wasted the entire ten minutes talking to that man on the telephone." At this Mr. Roosevelt laughed, and said, "all right boys you can have another ten minutes."[182]

As Paul remembered it,

Tudor Gardiner . . . had been Governor of Maine so Franklin D. knew him personally. They hated each other, certainly Gardner hated Roosevelt and Griswold and Gardiner hated each other. Gardiner would say that slick crooked attorney Griswold, and Griswold would say to me that dumb cluck ex-governor Gardiner. I was sort of the middle man and I had to do all of the talking, because they both fought so and we had to get along . . . .

We went in to see the President. And I was tremendously impressed. I gave him my speech "A." He pulled just one sheet out of his drawer, and it had the whole summarized tax bill that was up for consideration. I told him what we wanted and why. And he understood what it was all about better than anybody—mind you I was prejudiced against the guy—he understood it better and quicker and asked more intelligent questions about it than anybody I had talked to in Washington and I was amazed.

Then he said, I'm all for you, I agree with you, what can I do to help you. Well I said, Mr. President we've been having great difficulty with the Treasury Department. They have been very difficult and won't listen to our story and I think they're opposed to us. He said, you go see [Herman] Oliphant [General Counsel at the Treasury Department] and I'll have somebody call him up and tell him you're coming around . . . . And, oh boy, was Oliphant nice to us then . . . [183]

The summary that Roosevelt pulled out of his drawer actually said nothing about the application of the undistributed profits tax to investment trusts, which was not a concern of many Washington insiders at that time. The President apparently understood the significance of the investment trust related issues unaided by notes, though Secretary Morgenthau, who was sympathetic to the funds' situation, had met with him two hours earlier and probably had briefed him on what to expect from the three visitors from Boston. The summary outlined a rate schedule, including the continuation of the corporate tax, an exemption for the first $15,000 of undistributed profits, and a progressive tax schedule based on the percentage of income retained, that topped out at 50% on the income retained in excess of 50% of net income. In other words, if a corporation made $10 million, paid out $3 million in dividends, and retained $7 million, $2 million would be taxed at the top rate and $5 million would be taxed at lower rates or be exempt. The summary also described exemptions for corporations in bankruptcy or other forms of financial distress. And it calculated the revenue realized at $640 million, which was $140 million more than the projected loss in Agricultural Adjustment Act revenues.[184]

Paul felt that the President was supportive of the mutual funds' cause and the three Bostonians thanked him, in a note, for agreeing to intercede on their behalf with a key Congressman. They also left a draft of a proposed amendment to the Revenue Bill that suited their purposes. The same day, June 3rd, an amendment to the Revenue Bill was agreed upon by the Senate Finance Committee, which, they pointed out in the note to the President, "differs somewhat from the draft we left with you, [but] solves the problem and is satisfactory to us."[185]

On June 5th, certain technical amendments were added and Walsh presented it on the floor of the Senate. On June 12th, Milton Katz, executive assistant to the Chairman of the SEC, met with the Boston group and wrote a memo to Chairman Landis, Chief Counsel Schenker, and Research Director Gourrich that reflected the views of the trio from Boston.[186] On June 18th, after versions had passed both houses, it went to the House-Senate Conference Committee. The Senators and Congressmen quizzed the three Bostonians about what they wanted and why, and at the crucial moment, Merrill Griswold was able to give the legislators the exact wording needed. Paul recalled,

> **This was where Griswold was damned good. They asked us a lot of questions about what we wanted, why we wanted it, so forth and so on, and we told them. Then they said, "Have you got words, specific words, that you can put into the law to body this thing?" Well I turned to Griswold, who was a lawyer, and I said, "Griswold, what are the words?" I didn't know he had them, and by God he reeled them right off.**

But after a moment's reflection, Paul saw something in the wording that he did not like.

I got outside the door and I suddenly realized that the words Griswold put in—I don't think he did this intentionally . . . were such that Massachusetts Investors and Incorporated Investors would get the immediate tax benefit but it would take us another year to change things around to qualify. All this just because of a couple of little words in there and this was going to cost my shareholders several million dollars. Oh I had a fit.

So I said boy I've got to get this thing fixed. I started to go back in through the door. Well the bouncer says you can't come in here so I said by God I'm going to wait outside until I get in. A little Senator came out from New Jersey, I forget what his name was now [William H. Smathers]. I told him the story. He says, I'll fix you right up, come right in with me, he took me in, I gave them the right words, I changed it, I was in, everything was fine.[187]

The bill passed into law on June 20th.

The final victory was in the Senate. We appeared before the Senate Finance Committee and David I. Walsh was a member of the . . . Committee . . . . We appeared also before the House, Ways and Means Committee . . . . Well we had lost the thing in the House, and actually David I. Walsh was the one who won it in the Senate but my God, how did we win it. He reported out the committee to the full floor of the Senate. We were up in the gallery listening to his speech. Well practically nobody knew what an investment trust was and these fellows couldn't care less. The amount of revenue they got out of taxing them was peanuts anyhow. Anyway, David I. Walsh gets up and he says, to our horror, these things are just like a savings bank. He says we don't tax a savings bank. You put your money in, you take your money out any time you want . . . . We had tried to explain to him that you take it out at the market value, not at the face value of what you put it in. We gave him that every night for three months and he never could get it through his head . . . . Well it didn't bother him a bit, it went sailing through.[188]

Open-end, Boston-type mutual funds were not required to pay taxes on dividends and capital gains as long as substantially all of this income was passed on to the shareholders of the funds, who would then also take on the tax liability; closed-end funds did not gain this privilege until 1942. The only significant requirements were that substantially all of the income was investment income, that substantially all of it be distributed as taxable income, that holdings be diversified (no more than five percent invested in the securities of any one corporation and no more that ten percent ownership of any corporation), and that no more than thirty percent of the income be derived from short-term capital gains, to discourage speculation. The mutual funds made every effort to keep dividends and capital gains distributions under their management either through the issuance of warrants or by persuading the shareholders to reinvest their distributions in new shares created to fill this need. The Boston funds got exactly what they wanted; or as Paul put it years later, "God I practically wrote the law."[189]

A related incident gives another view of the way Paul operated in Washington during this period. He and Griswold had gotten word that legislative action harmful to the interests of the investment banking industry was being considered in the Congress, and he generously alerted the president of the bankers' trade association. The president asked Cabot and Griswold to contact the association's lawyers, Haywalt and Haywalt, and the two consented to meet at their law offices on one of the hottest days of the summer of 1936. Cabot and Griswold arrived at 10 AM on the appointed morning, waited in the heat for forty-five minutes, said "to hell with this," and left word for the lawyers to contact them at the Hay Adams Hotel.

Their hotel room was no cooler; in fact it was so hot that they stripped down to where they were wearing nothing but bath towels, and began playing poker. As Paul told the story,

> **So we sat there, bare ass, towels over our parts, when guess who walks in unannounced? Haywalt and Haywalt. Both of them! God, they must have been hot; because they were wearing morning coats and striped pants!**
>
> **It was worth the price of admission to see the look on their faces when they came into that room.**[190]

The SEC Investigation

For the Boston fund managers, the Revenue Act of 1936 signaled only the end of the beginning of their struggles over securities legislation and regulation in the 1930s. The Great Depression and the New Deal had brought committed, sometimes highly ideological public servants to Washington. The Roosevelt administration included a great number of intelligent, motivated men and women who felt that they were on a mission to use government power to ameliorate the suffering brought on by the Great Depression, to mend the flaws in our economy and our polity that had contributed to it, and to punish those responsible. Among the New Deal agencies, probably none exemplified this spirit more than the Securities and Exchange Commission. And among SEC officials, probably none was more representative of this spirit than Chief Counsel David Schenker.

The Public Utility Holding Company Act of 1935, while it came about as a result of the financial abuses in the utility industry, directed the SEC to conduct a wide-ranging investigation of investment trusts and investment companies in support of Congress in its effort to protect investors, an effort that culminated in passage of the Investment Company Act of 1940. The investigation, originally scheduled to be completed by January 1, 1937, stretched out over 56 months, three times the intended time span, and took place under three different SEC chairmen and numerous changes in staff. By the time the investigation wound down in 1939, Congress was focusing more on the Second World War than on the abuses of the investment trusts. But David Schenker kept the inquiry on track, even when Congressional interest waned and attendance at hearings fell to two or three legislators. Schenker was a tough but reasonable investigator and a man with a good sense of humor, just the kind of man whom Paul could be expected to like.

> There were certain examiners that I had a high regard for, who were very careful, but very fair and honest. There were others who weren't that way. But on the whole I would say that . . . the thing was conducted fairly and honestly . . . . One of the chief examiners was a man named Schenker, Dave Schenker, and he was very good. He was completely fair. He was completely honest, but you couldn't fool him if you tried. He was very good at it.[191]

> I got very fond of him. Most of the others thought he was a bastard but I thought he was a good guy. Bright as hell.[192]

A clue to Schenker's personality is revealed in this anecdote. Harry Heller, an associate counsel at the time, recalled that after working one night until 2 A.M. he stopped to write a personal letter. Schenker passing by his desk asked, "What? On government time?"[193] But Paul was the exception in remembering the SEC investigation fondly. Indeed it appears that he enjoyed the experience, which others viewed with distaste.

The SEC organized committees to help prepare separate questionnaires for the different segments of the industry. Cabot, Griswold, and William A. Parker comprised the open-end fund committee. But having a hand in formulating the questions did not guarantee that they would enjoy answering them, especially on the witness stand. Several who testified complained of harsh treatment or of being pressured to criticize the actions of competitors. Parker described his experience as a "private inquisition." He compared the SEC examiners to people who would catch a butterfly to pull off its wings and claimed that, on one occasion, when he was testifying until 3 A.M., he asked to say something by way of clarification off the record and was refused. Whether or not the story is precisely true, it does represent how some industry representatives felt about the examiners.[194]

Parker did recall one advantage he held over his interrogators. They didn't speak English. He was referring, somewhat chauvinistically, to the Austrian-born Paul Gourrich, the SEC's director of research, who had lost a fortune in the crash and was described by a colleague as a "very able man—but not a happy man by nature or experience." Parker interpreted Gourrich's heavily accented speech for the recording secretary until he became fed up with the entire proceeding.[195]

Paul's experience was different. In the 1935 annual report, he had welcomed the investigation which he believed, correctly as it turned out, would expose the same abuses that he had pointed out in the twenties and demonstrate the advantages of the simplicity of the Boston-type, open-end fund.[196] But while he welcomed the SEC investigation, saw the need for it, and claimed to have fun during his testimony, he also questioned the tactics of the SEC staff.

> **Their game was to bring out all of the awful things that were going on or had gone on in the industry. This was . . . four or five years after the industry began to pick up again, and . . . there were a lot of abuses creeping in, and if you want to read a chamber of horrors you get the testimony before that . . . committee. I had to testify down there for about three days. Had pretty good fun doing it. One fellow I remember . . . did they get a list of horrors on [him.] The man got more and more embarrassed and he finally said will you excuse me a minute, I've got to go to the men's room. He didn't go to the men's room; he went straight to South America.[197]**

Perhaps because Paul was questioned in September 1936, much of his testimony amounted to an *ex post facto* defense of the Revenue Act of 1936. In his prepared comments, he repeated the rationale for the act, arguing its fairness to the investor of moderate means. He also invoked Roosevelt's support for the act and for the conduit theory.[198] While the act was, by then, law, he was clearly trying to shore up support for it within the SEC, explaining what he thought was Congress's reasoning in including the provisions and the wording that they did.

In brief, he defended provisions that restricted the act to investment companies, that excluded rapid traders or speculators, and that insured that nearly all dividends were passed on to shareholders so that the income would appear on individuals' tax returns and the government would get the tax revenue it needed. But most important to Paul, the act was restricted to those funds whose "shareholders [were] upon reasonable notice entitled to redemption of their stock."[199]

In the 1930s, when many questioned the efficacy of capitalism, Paul had a late-twentieth century businessman's faith in the market. He felt that the right of redemption was more important than the right to vote because the manager of a redeemable fund could not stay in business without satisfying his customers. In theory, he was even opposed to giving shareholders the vote, though he did not consider the issue worth fighting for. He told the SEC that his shareholders

> **have the vote entirely, and it is my frank opinion that it doesn't do them one earthly bit of good.**
>
> **[The redemption privilege] gives each one of those stockholders, if he just doesn't like the color of my eyes, and if we do anything that doesn't appeal to him, [the right to withdraw his funds.] [H]e can get out immediately, for example, if our expenses are too high . . .**
>
> **The Congress of the United States and the Securities and Exchange Commission can sit here the rest of their lives, but they can't legislate honesty and ability. This redeemable feature, however, means that unless the management is honest and capable, the stockholders will take the immediate and most effective move, and they will withdraw their funds from the supervision of that company.**[200]

The SEC worried about the redeemable funds' need for continual selling and that a sudden outflow of funds would make the investment process unstable. Paul countered that pressure to sell put pressure on management to perform, that management could follow its own best investment instincts knowing those who disagreed could easily leave, that the requirement to own liquid stocks to be ready for redemptions probably improved the quality of the portfolio, and that, in any event, SSIC had sold a significant number of shares in only three of their first twelve years.[201]

At one point a questioner attempted to discredit the bill on the grounds that the open-end funds had exerted too much influence and had gotten exactly what they had wanted. The following exchange ensued.

Question:	**Doesn't this [Revenue Act of 1936], . . . merely result from an embodiment of your investment philosophy?**
Cabot:	**Congress and the President make the laws, I don't . . . . It so happens that the law they have made here conforms**

> with my notions . . . as to what should be done, very
> closely. And I can't say that about all laws.

The questioner countered that Paul only favored the act because of the tax breaks granted to his type of fund, which elicited the following.

Cabot:　　　There is nothing in the world that can prevent any one
of the other trusts from conforming to this law. We
had to do a variety of things to conform to the law, and
there is no reason in the world that others cannot do
likewise.[202]

The most significant action that State Street took to conform to the law was to limit holdings in the securities of a single corporation to five percent of the fund. This forced them into selling two large positions in stocks that they had a lot of confidence in; and the sales, according to Paul, hurt performance. Paul preferred safety through superior knowledge of a relatively small number of holdings to safety through diversification, and declared,

> I thought it was a shame to have to reduce. In the conduct of
> investment trusts I am a great believer, not in the theory of don't put
> all your eggs in one basket, but know good and well in what basket
> you are putting yours eggs into. [203]

Paul did encounter tough questioning from the SEC on conflict of interest matters. State Street Research & Management Company managed two trusts for the Shawmut Bank. Paul was asked what would happen if he had to sell a 20,000-share block of Chrysler, 10,000 for State Street and 10,000 for Shawmut. Common practice at the time of this writing is to sell the shares of all clients proportionately, but Paul answered,

> In our contracts with the Shawmut Bank it is clearly and definitely
> stated that if there is any question, State Street Investment
> Corporation comes first

In other words, trades did not have to be executed simultaneously as long as the procedures were known to all parties and were fully disclosed in writing. He went on to explain that while it might sound like this would hurt the performance of the Shawmut trusts, in fact that did not turn out to be the case because State Street so often sold before the peak in a stock. He did concede that it did cause a possible conflict of interest.[204]

The SEC also questioned him on his receipt of directors' fees, in the form of options, from the National Investors Corporation, on whose board he served. National Investors, founded in Detroit in the 1920s, was one of very few firms doing research similar to State Street's at that time, in the late twenties. The questioner from the SEC objected to the fact that State Street's research facilities were serving the interests of National Investors while Paul was pocketing the fees. Paul answered that he had only joined that board to learn about the problems facing other mutual funds and to improve State Street's operations, probably true but a dubious rationale nonetheless. He suggested further that it would be mutually beneficial to cooperate with anybody doing similar securities research toward similar business ends.

Paul described a meeting of Shawmut trustees in 1928 at which a Mr. Thayer brought in a piece of promotional material from National Investors. After some discussion, the trustees decided to have Thayer and Cabot negotiate, and possibly invest, with National Investors. They ended up putting in $110,000. National Investors then asked Paul, along with Walter Bucklin, Shawmut's President, to go on their board. But Paul refused unless he received the same compensation (stock options) that other directors had received. National Investors did not meet his requirement, apparently because there were not enough options to go around, and accepted Thayer on the board in Paul's stead. Several months later, Thayer resigned; National Investors then took options away from other directors in order to meet Paul's price; and on January 11, 1929, he joined the board.[205]

Paul's actions would be challenged in today's environment (2006); but they were legal then. He had hired a lawyer to keep him out of trouble; his actions were consistent; and they were clearly spelled out in a letter that he had written to the bank that sponsored National Investors. On January 11, 1929, he had written to Mr. John Grier that,

> **I am only assuming those responsibilities and duties that normally fall to the lot of any Director and that as such I am not expected to sell or recommend for purchase the various securities that may be issued from time to time . . . .**

> **My first duty is to my own companies and trusts and secondly to the present two funds of the National Shawmut Bank [and only thirdly to National Investors.]**

> **We here [at State Street] are not to be put in the position of undertaking investigations and services purely upon the desire or**

request of the National Investors . . . . We might be only too glad
to study and examine situations that you might suggest, but . . . this
shall be entirely voluntary.[206]

Everything was clearly spelled out in advance. Nonetheless, there were two
problems with this. There was an appearance of a conflict of interest; and Paul
made a great deal of money at National Investors when the options performed
beyond expectations. To make matters worse, his attitude toward all of this was
flippant, perhaps even foolish, as the following exchange shows.

Question:	This is an example whereby through your position with State Street, you were enabled to get the special benefits that came to the inside group in this National Investors picture . . .
Cabot:	I don't think that State Street had a great deal to do with it. It was because of my position in the community, I guess, and because of my particular associations.
Question:	As you look over the past picture, in which there was a conflict of interest, would you get into such a situation again?
Cabot:	I would love to, yes. How much money did you say I got?
Question:	$334,000.
Cabot:	I think that it would be fine.
Question:	You don't recognize that there is any conflict of interest?
Cabot:	I most certainly did recognize that there was a conflict of interest, and that is why I retained counsel to guide me through it all.[207]

Paul's defense was that he was selected for his ability as a stock analyst,
not his association with State Street; that he made the money unexpectedly;
and that he joined boards only to increase his effectiveness at State Street. The

first is believable, or at least difficult to refute. The second is likewise plausible, though it is perhaps telling that he held out for the options before joining the board and probably saw the potential there. The third is the least defensible, and surprisingly drew the least comment from the Commission. Should mutual funds, or business corporations, accept directors whose main motivation for joining is to gain experience to be used elsewhere? In other words, should directors be more interested in educating themselves than in representing the interests of shareholders? This question came up a second time when the SEC questioned him about his board membership at Eastern Gas & Fuel.

The questioner pointed out that State Street had bought some stock for $205,000 and that it was currently worth $24,000. He wanted to know, in effect, whether Paul's responsibilities as a director at Eastern, and possibly their desire to keep their stock price up, had influenced State Street's purchase. Paul denied any connection.

Cabot:	**It was a very poor investment .... It is only fair to say that it was a very insignificant one relative to the size of the whole fund .... By virtue of the fact of being a trustee of that corporation, I was obviously in a good deal more intimate acquaintance with what was going on, than I might have been .... As to inside information, it shows that it isn't very helpful .... I thought that [the condition of the company] looked pretty good. I was wrong ....**
Question:	**Do you feel that as a Director you couldn't go about selling the shares of the company with as much freedom as though you weren't a Director?**
Cabot:	**No I did not. I felt that my first duty was to the State Street Investment Corporation.**[208]

This was the best possible answer under the circumstances and no doubt true because Paul's own money was in SSIC; but directors who serve a corporation part-time should not, as a consequence, be only partly committed to the shareholders. While selling an overvalued stock may not necessarily be considered a disservice to shareholders, money managers who serve on boards of public companies had and have difficulty avoiding at least the appearance of a conflict. In accepting outside directorships, Paul put himself at risk and was lucky to escape without having his conduct censured.

He closed his testimony with a set of recommendations for the Commission to make to Congress. As an expert on industry abuses, Paul's recommendations received wide coverage in the national press, and he took advantage of this to publicize his views. He stressed the importance of honesty and ability. He noted that the proposals he wished to put forward would not necessarily benefit State Street and could in fact limit management prerogatives, but were designed to benefit "the whole investment trust movement." The public nonetheless needed protection from historic and potential abuses and this consideration justified limited curtailment of the industry's autonomy.

Paul made five specific proposals. First, he urged that the SEC adapt standardized accounting for financial statements. Examples would be the way in which funds calculated the sales load and their treatment of capital gains. He further urged that the funds make public all of these statements, including all reports to the SEC. Paul did not agree, however, under questioning, that his directors' fees from the National Shawmut Bank were any business of SSIC stockholders. Third, he conceded that there should be limitations on the right of investment trusts to borrow money, provided that these limitations were not stricter than those placed on individuals. Fourth, Paul suggested that legislation separating investment banks or "banking houses" from commercial banks and investment trusts would, on balance, be advisable. He particularly feared that investment banks would dump unmarketable securities on their investment trust affiliates, thus favoring the relatively more powerful and sophisticated investment banking clients over individual investors. He also worried that trust managers would "churn" the mutual funds to generate commission dollars for the brokerage arms of the investment banks. Paul did acknowledge a contrary argument. Most trusts run by investment banks were competently run and investment bankers constituted a very high proportion of those qualified to do such work. But he came down on the side of more restrictive legislation nonetheless. A fifth proposal dealt with small technical improvements to the Revenue Act of 1936.[209]

He also opposed several of the proposals under consideration, including periodic examinations of investment trusts, as expensive and unnecessary. He pointed to the failure of national bank examination in 1932 and argued that standardized accounting, strictly enforced, would be more effective. He opposed the separation of a mutual fund from its distributing agency with the argument that a fund should exercise control over its sales agents. He opposed limits on selling commissions and management fees as well as requirements for or limits to diversification. This was the manager's, not the government's job. He opposed limits on "trading" or portfolio turnover, on short-selling, and on a fund's right to participate in new underwritings. And he opposed legislation requiring all shareholders to have voting rights, again arguing that the right of redemption was more important.

> In our case we saw little objection to giving our people the voting right [in 1933], but had we been forced to do so, in the early days of our career, I think that it would have worked greatly to the detriment of our stockholders, and certainly greatly increased their costs.

There were, according to Paul, several occasions when they had to get shareholder approval quickly or forfeit money. As an example, he cited situations, from the mid-twenties, when they needed rapid shareholder approval to comply with certain Massachusetts tax regulations.[210] Actually, a voting requirement in 1936 would have been an advantage to State Street since they had already granted the vote and imposing such a requirement would have been a barrier to entry by new competitors. While Paul's positions were debatable, they followed a consistent pattern. He tended to favor freedom and discretion for managers; but he also wanted to protect the relatively weak and less sophisticated investor when there was a significant danger of abuse.

Paul's activities in Washington during this period were not restricted to the witness stand. His son Frederick recalled that after a busy day,

> Dad repaired to a nearby bar. He wanted a Planter's Punch, and because the bartender didn't know how to mix it, he got permission from the proprietress to mix one himself. His explanation to her was that he was a visiting planter from St. Kitts, in town to seek an increase in his sugar quota. He mixed several Planter's Punches, and shared these with other customers, of course sampling them himself.
>
> At closing time the proprietress wisely called a cab to take him home, and as he made the best of his way into the cab's back seat she leaned in the window and said to him, "St. Kitts, my ass! I'm from Malden, and I know a Boston accent when I hear one."[211]

The Investment Company Act of 1940[212]

After cooperating with the SEC investigation for four and one-half years, the mutual fund executives expected to exert significant influence over the Commission's legislative proposals. At the very least, they had hoped to see the SEC's draft before it was submitted to Congress. Instead, they were taken by surprise. There was no advance briefing; the proposed bill was more onerous than the industry had anticipated; and in its draft the SEC gave itself an unprecedented degree of discretion in administering what would become the Investment Company Act. According to Paul, the SEC wanted "a bill that would burn down the barn to kill the rats."[213] He was particularly concerned by what he considered to be government micro-management of the industry, including limitations on fund size and regulations that would discourage qualified candidates from serving as directors.

Unlike the earlier securities legislation, which had dealt primarily with disclosure, the 1940 Act focused on regulation. SEC Commissioner Healy, who opened the testimony at the hearings for the Act, charged that "the most pessimistic prophets of the dire consequences to the investors of unregulated investment trusts have been justified," and he blasted the industry for its shocking record of malfeasance.[214] The solution, according to Healy, was

> **a group of expert investment trust managers who do not make their profits originating and distributing trust securities, styled principally for their sales appeal, but from wise, careful management of the funds entrusted to them.**[215]

The SEC Commissioners were anxious to protect the mutual fund investor from the distorting impact of sales. Products designed for their appeal to the market did not, and do not, necessarily make the best investments. On this issue, Paul Cabot, with his longstanding disdain for sales, stood with the SEC one hundred percent.

But on many major issues under consideration, he had strong philosophic differences with the Commission. These did not directly threaten State Street's business franchise, at least not nearly as much as they threatened that of its competitors. Indeed, he might have supported the Commission's proposals on the grounds that they would have helped State Street by handicapping the competition. But he opposed them on grounds of principle. He testified as an informed, involved, and respected observer, but at the same time a relatively disinterested one.

For this reason Paul was given the task of speaking on issues affecting the entire open-end fund industry, while other industry representatives testified about issues of special concern to them. His testimony was the most generic and comprehensive among the industry witnesses, and arguably the most objective. His positions sometimes favored and sometimes disfavored the interests of State Street Investment Corporation, a point that was not lost on the legislators whose task it was to turn the Commission's findings and recommendations into law.

A task force of about ten industry executives, including Cabot, Griswold, Gardner, and William A. Parker, convened at the Hay Adams Hotel in the early spring of 1940. Paul remembered,

> **I personally was working with an industry committee of Boston and New York [people] . . . . This made it a little more awkward but . . . we could handle it because the ten of us ran the show. We immediately came back and admitted that these abuses existed; couldn't deny it; there they were; and then got up legislation, legal language, that we thought would cure the abuse without burning down the barn.[216]**

The open-end fund group took an especially conciliatory approach, conceding that abuses had been committed, but by others. While Paul later blasted the SEC proposal, his initial public reaction was only that he did "not think that the present bill is the soundest approach to the problem." This was as diplomatic as Paul Cabot ever got. Parker recalled that the "New York group" representing closed-end funds tended to resent "Boston's holier-than-thou attitude." But the groups worked together to shape the legislation and to this end spent weeks testifying before the committees and cajoling legislators. They met together nightly to plot strategy and to decide which industry representative would be most effective testifying on whatever issue was being debated the next day. As a result, their presentations were informative, tactful, and effective.[217]

The hearings began on April 2nd. The SEC opening presentation, which included descriptions of numerous scandals, was followed by the closed-end group's rebuttal, which amounted to the argument that although these abuses actually occurred, they were unrepresentative of the industry as a whole. Massachusetts Investors Trust testified first for the open-end funds. By many measures, including size and sales, they were the most important player in the industry at that time; and their spokesmen argued that the organization and operation of the open-end fund naturally favored and protected the shareholder. Paul followed, on April 16th, with a presentation that included nine criticisms of the SEC draft proposal and fourteen suggestions to improve it.

He opened by noting that while State Street was an open-end fund, it had been closed to net new investment since 1935, except for subscription rights offered to existing shareholders. Paul's intention here, no doubt, was to emphasize the fact that State Street no longer needed sales to prosper. The subscription rights held the monies that would otherwise have left the fund as dividends and capital gains; and redeemed shares easily found buyers without any sales effort. In fact, so great was the reputation of management, Paul implied, that the redeemed shares sold at a premium to net asset value. Paul conceded the SEC witnesses' case that horrible abuses had occurred; but used this as an opportunity to showcase the record of his own company. He briefly touched on State Street's investment performance; then submitted for the record the 1939 annual report, which included performance calculations.[218]

He next quoted from a 1929 *Atlantic Monthly* article he had written on what to do about the abuses that he had uncovered at that time. His answers were publicity and education. In the twenties Paul believed, and here seemed still to be arguing, that an informed public could look out for its own interests. But the SEC and the Congress had moved beyond that position. Virtually everyone wanted stricter regulation. Perhaps this argument was just an exercise in self-promotion. He used it as an excuse to get his extremely prescient 1929 article submitted for the record as well. He then conceded that regulation was required after all, just not the SEC's draft proposal. He opposed the SEC draft even though

> **We [at State Street] are in a fortunate position with respect to the specific provisions of the bill which is before you, in that except in one instance we are not affected by it, insofar as I can judge. I do not mean to imply by this, of course, that we will not be affected by any or all of the innumerable rules, regulations, and orders that the bill in its present form authorizes the SEC to issue.**[219]

In other words, the specific proposals were manageable but the impact of the discretion granted to the SEC in its draft proposal was unknowable at the time.

His nine criticisms of the draft in many cases echoed points he had made elsewhere, including during the hearings on the Revenue Act of 1936 and during the SEC Investigation. He objected especially to restrictions on directors, on portfolio turnover, on borrowing, and on size, as well as some poorly thought out reporting requirements.

First, Paul believed that any provisions that made it more difficult to secure the services of capable directors would harm the interests of shareholders, and the draft had at least three such provisions. It prohibited directors of investment companies from serving as directors of companies in the investment companies' portfolios. This would have eliminated from consideration a huge pool of candidates; and it made no sense, to Paul, to exclude someone from consideration who, as an example, just happened also to be a director of General Electric, a company likely to be almost always represented in the portfolio. This was the only proposal that would have directly affected State Street. In the end, it was dropped, and extremely liberal rules, for instance one requiring that 40% of the directors be from outside the fund company, were adopted.

Also, officers and directors were required to report quarterly all personal transactions in securities that the fund had transacted in during the same quarter. This would not have eliminated anyone and could be seen as a legitimate protection against market manipulation; but Paul viewed it as burdensome.

On questioning, he brought up a third, related concern.

Cabot:	There is a provision in another part of the bill that the SEC can demand any document from any of these people and then can make public any of these documents. So, assuredly, they have it in mind.
Schenker:	*You* seem to have it in mind . . . . [emphasis added]
Cabot:	Well, possibly you gentlemen do not have it in mind today, but your successors might get it in mind. [Laughter]
	Many Directors will seriously object to the "snooping" provided for in the second provision and, in order to avoid subjecting themselves to this procedure, will prefer not to serve as Directors of an investment trust. The result will be that investment trusts will be forced to elect outside Directors—and the bill requires that these shall be in the majority [under the initial proposal]—from among those individuals who have no business affiliations, connections, or property of their own; and the boards will be filled with artists, architects, musicians, doctors, and the like.
Senator Taft:	And perhaps some lawyers? [Laughter]
Cabot:	I did not mention lawyers. I think that the shareholders will be hurt rather than helped by such a provision.

Paul apparently did not share in the laughter at Senator Taft's remark. He took this first objection very seriously.[220]

The second criticism, and the fifth, discussed below, dealt with Paul's concern that certain sections of the bill would force the breaking of contracts. In the example he gave, the SEC draft could upset the balance of power between preferred and common shareholders and make it easier for the preferred holders to liquidate the company, if they deemed it necessary to protect their investment. This, as Paul outlined the scenario, could have been unfair to the common shareholders.[221]

Third, repeating a point he had argued on several occasions, he opposed limitations on portfolio turnover because it was not a valid measure of conservatism; and he provided the following illustration.

> **Now Senator, picture the spring of 1933, when we went off the gold basis: We were conducting our affairs, running 60 percent in cash and Government securities and 40 percent in stocks; and we believed it became necessary and essential overnight to go practically fully invested. This law might make that illegal.**

Commissioner Healy disagreed that it would be illegal. But the language of the draft was ambiguous at best, which gave Paul the chance to retort that, "had the SEC seen fit to allow the industry to go over the wording of this bill prior to its introduction to Congress, we could have straightened out a great many of these difficulties."

To which, Senator Wagner replied, "However, Mr. Cabot, our committee is here for that purpose, you understand."[222]

Fourth, Paul once more opposed elimination of the funds' right to borrow on the grounds that investment companies were groups of individuals who deserved the rights they would have enjoyed as individuals acting alone. This strong point was central to his thinking but he weakened it by padding it with political bombast. Our country was built on borrowed money, he asserted; restrictions on borrowing by other industries would have impeded the opening of the West and the development of our natural resources. While the investment industry became too leveraged in the 1920s, so did others. That was no reason to go so far in the other direction at a time when, according to Paul,

> **The Federal Government wants to put to work the vast resources of unused capital and credit that lie idle today, with the thought in mind that with this capital at work people will be employed at useful production.**[223]

The fifth, sixth, and ninth criticisms dealt with the discretion given the SEC in administering the Act. The fifth, similar in spirit to the second, criticized Section 17 of the Act, which prohibited an investment company, in its charter or contracts, from authorizing the violation of any ruling from the SEC, even if the charter or contracts predated the ruling. Thus the SEC could force the rewriting of a charter or contract by issuing a ruling. The sixth criticized Section 13, which required a vote of shareholders to change a fundamental investment or management policy. Paul's objection was that the SEC had complete discretion to determine which policies were fundamental. Giving the SEC this power could slow the decision-making process during critical periods. The ninth criticism was a redundant blanket objection to all the discretionary powers granted to the SEC by the draft.[224]

The seventh criticized Section 8, which required funds to submit, among other things, a list of securities it had acquired or intended to acquire. Paul pointed out that they obviously did not know what they were going to acquire because "conditions will in all probability change in the future as they have in the past," and if they were forced to declare their intentions and execute on them, they would lose their ability to maneuver in the market. Brokers would know what they were required, or at least what they intended, to buy and sell and would "hold them up" on the price.[225]

The eighth criticism dealt with the SEC's attempt to regulate size. While Paul believed that there was most likely an optimal size, Federal legislation was not the way to get there.

> **If in the past there had been rigid limitations as to the size of other industries . . . the great growth of this country could never have taken place. For example, if years ago the automobile industry had been told that it could never expand beyond a definite size, it is probable that that great business could never have grown to its present importance. Other businesses are not regulated as to size, and I believe it is unsound to place arbitrary limitations on this industry, by law. I believe that, as in the case of other industries, competition will take care of the situation.**

David Schenker claimed that the idea of limiting fund size (to $150 million) originated, in part, with a comment that Paul had made to him to the effect that $50 million was as much as he would want to manage. While Paul denied saying this, it is consistent with other comments he had made during the 1930s and State Street's suspension of its sales campaign when assets had reached $35 million. In any event, it is plausible to argue that very large funds are inadvisable, but should not be illegal. No limitations on size were included in the final act.[226]

Of Paul's fourteen constructive suggestions the most significant, beyond those implied by the above criticisms, were the following. He wanted procedures to reduce "to a practical minimum" any dilution to existing shareholders that occurred as a result of sales to new ones. The sale of new shares, priced at the previous day's close, was a controversial tactic that could at times disadvantage existing holders. He proposed restrictions on the relationship between investment companies and investment banks and brokers, and between investment companies and their officers and directors. Perhaps most significantly, Paul wanted any investment manager or advisor with more than one client to have a "written agreement with respect to priority or *pro rata* treatment in the execution of orders, in order to avoid any possible conflict of interest."[227] But he believed that it was acceptable to put one client's trades ahead of another's if the arrangement was fully disclosed.

He ended his testimony with a final criticism and a final suggestion.

> Now, Mr. Chairman, I don't want to be too critical of the SEC . . .
> [but] I cannot but feel that this bill has been drawn hastily and
> under pressure. It appears obscure, redundant, and certainly
> over-complicated. I cannot but feel that had the SEC gone over
> the wording of this bill with the industry prior to its introduction
> to Congress some, if not much, of the difficulty would have been
> avoided.
>
> I hope that you and your committee, who have been so patient with
> us, will think that it is advisable to send this bill back to the SEC
> instructing them to redraft it in consultation with representatives of
> the industry chosen by you and that you will indicate prior thereto
> those broad principles and restrictions that you would want in the
> bill so that direct conflicts of opinion that would occur between the
> Commission and the industry would be minimized.[228]

The committee followed Paul Cabot's recommendation exactly. In essence, they ordered the SEC to draft a new bill in consultation with the industry. This was a major victory for a group of men whose major complaint was their lack of input into the original draft. A few days later Senator Wagner said,

> Again yesterday evening I read the statement of Mr. Cabot, which
> I thought was a very clear presentation of his views, and then I
> read carefully also his constructive suggestions. It would require
> many pages to incorporate them in legislation if you wanted to do it
> carefully. But I am sure his suggestions impressed every member of
> this Subcommittee, as they did me, because they were constructive
> suggestions and a recognition that something should be done.[229]

It is clear that in the mind of Senator Wagner, the Sub Committee (and Committee) Chairman, Paul Cabot's statement had been crucial to the Sub Committee's decision to entrust the drafting of the bill to a working group consisting of representatives of the industry and the SEC. Less than two weeks later the fund group was meeting with the SEC. Paul's recollection of these events captured the tone of the proceedings.

> [I said] we recommend to you that you instruct this SEC committee
> to sit down with our committee to see if jointly we can't draft a bill that
> will be agreeable to both sides. And that's what was done. [Senator

Robert] Taft later said—of course he hated the Democrats—you ought to have your head examined . . . . If you think that you can sit down with those Democratic bastards and get anywhere, well you're nuts. And I said, well I think I can; and we did.[230]

The industry group and the SEC first sat down together in late April 1940, drew up an agreement in principle covering the major issues, and in May circulated it to the industry. Over the course of the deliberations, all of the truly onerous proposals put forward by the SEC had been dropped. Paul's testimony had clearly had a significant impact on the Senators, but probably even more important was the coordination and the united front presented by all of the industry witnesses. Their presentations were consistent and realistic. They knew that regulation was coming and that they had to make concessions if they wanted to have an impact.

But probably the most important factor favoring the mutual fund companies was time. As the investigation dragged on into the late 1930s, the reforming zeal of Congress waned and, by 1940, was almost entirely extinguished by Washington's growing concern with the war. This was not the expectation in 1935. Had the SEC strictly observed the requirements of the Public Utility Holding Company Act and completed its investigation by the beginning of 1937, the resulting legislation might have been much tougher.

The industry lawyers and two lawyers from the SEC, Commissioner Healy and Chief Counsel Schenker, drafted the legislation. The following comment from an industry lawyer, Alfred Jaretzki, suggests the atmosphere of the proceedings.

After the hearings closed . . . with the approval of this Subcommittee we carried on discussions with Judge Healy and Mr. Schenker to see if we could iron out the differences which existed between our proposal and theirs; I want to say that personally, and as far as my group is concerned, we have never dealt with a fairer group of people than we did when we were dealing with Judge Healy and Mr. Schenker. On that basis, it was very easy to narrow down the points of difference. I think we persuaded them of some points and they persuaded us of others.[231]

While Jaretzki may have had good reason to be gracious and to minimize any conflict, the negotiations certainly appear to have been businesslike and cordial. After the industry had expressed satisfaction with the proposed legislation, it went back to the Subcommittee where Senator Wagner congratulated the negotiators.

I think I can speak on behalf of the entire Subcommittee in congratulating you gentlemen on reaching an accord. It shows what can happen when reasonable men sit around a table. It also seems to me that cooperation between government and industry, as is evidenced by the results here, is the way to secure reasonable, sound legislation.[232]

The industry did not have to make major concessions to win this support and praise from the liberal Democratic Senator from New York. And the final bill, which became law on August 23, was particularly favorable to the Boston-type, open-end funds. There were no limitations on the size of funds, few restrictions on directors and trustees, and little interference with the relationship between the sales and money management arms of a fund complex. And the open-end funds were able to promote sales through price maintenance to favored broker-dealers, thereby assuring good commissions to the brokers and strong networks of loyal dealers to the funds.

The Securities and Exchange Commission did retain some discretion in its administration of the Act; but its powers were generally limited to exempting funds from certain requirements. It could not add to their burden. For instance, they could excuse funds from filing certain reports, or even eliminate the reports entirely, but could not add to the filing requirements. This tended to increase the SEC's informal influence while preventing overly burdensome regulation. The SEC's one important prescriptive power was its right to standardize accounting policies so that all reports would be comparable, a requirement Paul had argued for.

The provisions of the Act generally fell into three categories: those that required disclosure; those that prohibited fraud or made fraud more difficult; and those that strengthened the control of shareholders. Paul strongly supported provisions in the first two categories and, while he opposed those of the third category in theory, saw no need to contest them actively.

A key disclosure issue was the frequent rapid and unannounced changes in funds' fundamental characteristics. An investor might purchase a fund of diversified, liquid companies and overnight, without his approval, have it traded for a group of illiquid stocks concentrated in one sector. Under the Act (Section 8), funds had to make a "recitation of policy" in their registration statements and change it only with the approval of the shareholders. Paul had worried that the SEC would have too much discretion in deciding what level of change would trigger a shareholder vote. The Act minimized, though did not eliminate, this concern by identifying changes in classification (diversified or non-diversified), borrowing policies, issuance of senior securities (for closed-end funds), underwriting, investment concentration, ventures into commodities or real estate, portfolio turnover, and other matters that the fund had declared to be fundamental, as matters requiring a shareholder vote.

Provisions discouraging fraud or strengthening stockholder control over their fund included the barring of known criminals from the business (Section 9), the requirement for an independent board of directors (at least 40% outside the management company) and independent investment advice (Section 10), the prevention of the sale of control or election of directors without a shareholder vote (Section 16), the requirement for SEC approval of exchange offers, in particular those that shift naïve shareholders from one fund to another solely to impose new charges (Section 25), and a prohibition on self-dealing transactions between management and the fund it managed (Section 17). This last also nullified clauses that could have been interpreted to excuse management from acts of "willful misfeasance, bad faith, gross negligence, or reckless disregard of [their] duties."

All of this was unobjectionable, compared to the proposals that were initially put forward by the SEC. As Paul had anticipated when he welcomed the SEC Investigation, the Act followed the practices of the Boston group closely. And Edward Leffler observed,

The Investment Company Act of 1940 was nothing new to me. It merely wrote into law the disciplines which I and my associates had long practiced.[233]

Paul and his allies had won a major victory; but his next service in Washington, with the War Production Board, would involve him in a more serious struggle.

CHAPTER V

MOSES AND JEREMIAH

I don't know what I should have done in life without the Club. When I leave Boston it is my shield. When I am in Boston it is one of my great diversions. The best people are always in it, the sort that you will understand and like. I once tried to understand a number of other people, but I am not so sure now that it was not a waste of time. Your own sort are the best friends and you will do well not to forget it.[234]

George Apley in a letter to his son

[Sidney Weinberg] was meticulous on the question of misrepresentation or complete honesty. I would say there never was a more honest, forthright fellow than him. That's probably one reason why I loved him so. Completely one hundred percent honest. And he'd never put up with any monkey business on any boards he was on.[235]

Paul Cabot

One evening in the late 1930s, while on a business trip to New York, Paul invited two close friends, Charlie Dickey of J.P. Morgan and Sidney Weinberg of Goldman Sachs, to cocktails and dinner at one of his clubs. The next morning, the club's acting president came up to Paul and cautioned, "You mustn't do that again, what you did last night."

Feigning innocence, Paul asked, "What did I do last night that I shouldn't do? Was I disorderly, making too much racket or something?"

He said, "Oh, no, no, no. You brought Sidney Weinberg in here and there's a rule that you can't bring a Jew into this club."

"I read all your by-laws and . . . there was no such statement in there, and if that is the way you feel about it, you can stick your club up your ass. I am through. I hereby resign." Paul walked out the door, never to return. [236]

115

Rose Kennedy, who knew what it felt like to be an outsider in Brahmin society, wrote resentfully of families such as the Cabots and Lodges who controlled the "routes to success." She called them "a self-perpetuating aristocracy," and while she admired many of their qualities, she considered them a "closed society."[237]

Rose was not wrong. To understand how unusual Paul's reaction was for a Boston Brahmin of his generation, one need merely turn to the popular fiction of the day. George Apley, protagonist of the 1938 bestseller, whom Marquand represents as having been decent and well-intentioned, felt that his life was "governed by the rigors of bluenosed bigots who have been in their graves for a century."[238] Similarly, even Santayana's hero, the gentle Oliver Alden, who appeared in print in 1935, when faced with disappointment began to resemble his bigoted Uncle Nathaniel and viewed himself as a "moral aristocrat" descended from people who "went . . . into a stark wilderness to lead a life apart, purer and soberer than the carnival life of Christendom."[239]

In these cases, fiction fairly represented reality. Only a few years earlier, President Lowell had worked to limit the number of Jews at Harvard and to keep African-Americans out of the dormitories.[240] Even Lowell's cousin and Paul's contemporary, Ralph Lowell, viewed as a champion of a more inclusive Boston society, had Jewish friends but failed to question traditional Jewish stereotypes, according to his biographer, who gives a few choice examples.[241]

Paul was the exception that proved Rose Kennedy's rule because he did not hold himself apart from others but embraced them. He made generalizations about people, generalizations that some would call prejudices; but they were based on his own experience of life, not the biases of his family, class, or city, and thus could be quite startling.

Sidney and Paul

Six months before Pearl Harbor, Paul moved to Washington where he, along with Sidney Weinberg, served on the War Production Board. Paul directed the Salvage Division where he had to deal with scrap dealers, and others who didn't know a Lowell from a Lawrence.[242]

> **When I was in Washington, and I had to deal with a great many scrap men, ninety-nine per cent of them were Jewish, and practically without exception, they couldn't have been finer people . . . . I felt that I must have on my staff a Jewish junk dealer . . . . A man named William Wolfe of Ohio [became] my Deputy. And we became close friends and still are [in 1980] . . . .**

He was uncanny in that when somebody came to my office to talk to me, he could tell right off whether the fellow was crooked . . . .

I hate to tell you that the very small percentage of Gentiles in the business were generally crooked as hell . . . . And sometimes the worst, sleaziest looking fellow would turn out to be the ablest and the most honest.[243]

Paul may have had a Brahmin's eye for who looked sleazy. His youthful letters from the army betrayed a discomfort around Jews, and he maintained his association with clubs that denied them membership; but he decided who was able and honest based on the facts. And these were the highest words of praise in his vocabulary.

To Paul, no one was more able and honest than Sidney Weinberg, who ran Goldman Sachs from the 1930s to the 1960s, roughly the same years that Paul was running State Street Research & Management. Sidney, seven years older than Paul, was born in 1891, one of eleven children, to the family of a Brooklyn liquor wholesaler. While Sidney was never poor, the size and the expectations of his family led him to quit school at an early age, fourteen, and start working at an even earlier one, nine. At a time in life when Paul was being pulled through the snow to school on his "Flexible Flyer," Sidney was selling evening papers in the snow at the Hamilton Avenue terminus of the Manhattan-Brooklyn ferry, or shucking oysters for a fish vendor, or carrying feathers for a milliner. With his Polish-Jewish heritage, Brooklyn upbringing, and eighth-grade education, no one could have been more different, at least superficially, from the wealthy Boston Brahmin who held two, almost three, Harvard degrees. Yet Paul never had a closer friend, or one more like him in character, intellect, and even sense of humor.[244]

Weinberg began working at Goldman Sachs as assistant to the janitor in 1907 for three dollars a week, but got a break in 1909. He had to deliver a flagpole to the Harlem home of Paul Sachs, a partner who also happened to be the grandson of Goldman and the son of the first Mr. Sachs, Samuel. Paul Sachs was something of a misfit at Goldman Sachs. His heart was never in banking and he did not stay long. As an undergraduate he had fallen under the influence of Professor Charles Eliot Norton, the most influential cultural and intellectual arbiter of his generation at Harvard. After a few years at the family firm, he returned to Harvard, where he eventually became Professor of Fine Arts and Associate Director of the Fogg Museum.

But shortly before he left for Cambridge for the second time, he "discovered" Sidney Weinberg and thereby probably did more for Goldman Sachs than he would have through forty years of his own hard work. Sachs answered the door himself when Sidney arrived by trolley car with the flagpole, and immediately struck up a conversation. Sidney no doubt saw this as an opportunity to impress

Sachs with his intelligence and charm. He did just that. Sachs liked him, urged Sidney to go to night school, and thereafter took an interest in his career. That career did not take off immediately; Sidney did not become a partner until 1927. But it began moving in the right direction. Said Sidney, "Paul Sachs was the first partner who ever really gave me a second glance. Until he took me in hand, I was an awful kid—tough and raw."[245]

Not by today's standards. Apparently, the worst thing that Sidney ever did in his youth was to place a want ad announcing that Samuel Sachs was about to assemble a chorus line for a Broadway show and wanted candidates to report to his office for personal interviews. The result, as one would anticipate, was a certain amount of confusion—but probably not as much as resulted from Paul's firing of his rifle into a college dance. Sidney's most violent act: he liked to put tacks on the chairs of company clerks. Perhaps Paul Sachs took an interest in Sidney because Sachs was not interested in investment banking, spent little time at the office, and therefore was not often, if ever, the victim of Sidney's pranks.[246]

In some respects, Sidney retained the persona of a kid through much of his life, at least when it suited his purpose to do so. Just as Paul Cabot sometimes assumed the demeanor of a curmudgeon, Sidney could put on the boyish charm to break the tension or add humor to a trying situation. When Franklin Roosevelt, who nicknamed Sidney "The Politician," wanted to make him ambassador to the Soviet Union, Sidney declined the offer. "I don't speak Russian. Who the hell could I talk to over there?" Henry Wallace showed up at a meeting of the Business Advisory Council of the Department of Commerce on the day that President Truman had relieved him of his position as Department Secretary. No one knew exactly what to say to him until, after a few awkward moments, Sidney strode up to him and remarked, "Well, Henry, I hear you got fired." At a General Foods board meeting, the directors had to sit through the formality of listening to a long string of numbers relating to the sale of a patent. After ten minutes of numbers, Sidney stood up and shouted, "BINGO," to the relief of everyone present.[247]

Unlike Paul, whose uncle was a director of General Electric, Sidney often seemed slightly in awe of the world over which he presided; and Sidney did preside. In 1930, when he was still in his thirties, a Goldman Sachs partner who had been director of eighteen corporations resigned and Sidney replaced him on nine of the boards. At one time, Sidney served on thirty-one boards, more than any other American up to that time. And he was fantastically loyal to every one of them. On the train to Chicago on his way to Sears and National Dairy board meetings, he regularly fought with the dining-car steward over the unavailability of Kraft Cheese, a National Dairy brand at that time. "Take it away. I won't eat it. Get Kraft." His family kitchen in Scarsdale looked like the household appliance pages of the Sears catalogue until he left that board and joined General Electric, a move which required a complete makeover of the kitchen. When he became a Cluett-Peabody director, he gave up Sulka shirts for Arrow. When a package of General Foods products contained some dog food, he almost bought a dog; and when he instead gave it to his son's poodle, he was horrified that the dog wouldn't eat it. Sidney used McKesson & Robbins hair tonic and smoked General Cigar cigars. Mrs. Weinberg bought all of her gloves and stockings from the Van Ralte Company, her light bulbs from GE, and, whenever possible, canned goods in Continental cans. She balked only at GE's luminescent light switches, which appeared to her like leering eyes whenever she turned the switches off.[248] But nothing demonstrated Sidney's loyalty—and his differences with Paul, who was more relaxed on these matters—more clearly than the infamous Maxwell House hoax.

Sidney and Paul were preparing to go sailing on Paul's forty-foot sloop. Since Sidney knew little about sailing and couldn't even swim, but had served as a Navy cook during World War I, he headed straight for the galley to check the provisions. There he was horrified to find a jar of Borden's instant coffee. Recalling their service together on the boards of Continental Can, B.F. Goodrich, and National Dairy, and threatening to jump ship if not appeased, Sidney claimed that he could not betray Maxwell House by drinking Borden's coffee. And he was sure that Borden's tasted awful anyway. At the next port, Paul purchased a small jar of Maxwell House instant coffee, which he periodically refilled from the much larger Borden's container. Sidney not only enjoyed it; he kept asking the others in the party if they had ever tasted anything so delicious.[249]

Sidney was almost totally ignorant of nautical jargon, or at least pretended to be, and Paul and their fellow sailor Charlie Dickey, who had been with them at the club in New York, liked to tell stories about Sidney's apparent confusion. One night, when all three were asleep on Dickey's boat at anchor in Somes Sound off of Maine's Mt. Desert Island, a storm suddenly struck. The two experienced sailors, who always kept an eye out for their non-swimming, non-sailing shipmate, threw Sidney a life jacket and immediately leaped up on deck to let out the anchor cable. Sidney, struggling below to get his life jacket on, heard one yell to the other, "Give me a little more scope," which meant a little more line. To which Sidney, who along with the others had been drinking that evening, replied, "Whatever that scope is, don't finish it all 'til I get there!"[250]

On another evening, Paul, Charlie, and Sidney were traveling up the Sheepscot River toward Wiscasset by motor when they ran aground. While they were still stuck in the mud, Paul and Charlie planned to row the anchor out into the middle of the channel so that when the tide freed the boat from the mud, they would swing around into the channel. Unfortunately, there was a thick fog that night and they could barely see the length of the boat. They knew that they had to row north to get to the middle of the channel but they had no way, in the rowboat, to know which way north was.

I put Sidney in [charge of] the main boat's compass—I showed him N on the compass, North, and I said "All you've got to do now is hold your flashlight, keep it all the time over N, and that will show Dickey and me what direction to row.

Well, we started out, and, of course, the first thing that happened, the thing's going all over the sky, the light. And we kept hollering back, "Put it on N."

Well, while we were rowing with this heavy anchor and the boat nearly afloat, of course it made the boat begin to twist a little bit. Sidney hollers back, he says, "I can't keep it on North. North's moving."

But we got off. That was the story about North moving.[251]

Sidney Weinberg's Twelve Commandments

In the sailing incidents and in others, Sidney seemed willing to play the naïf, even the fool. This willingness endeared him to his friends and associates, some of whom may have been uncomfortable in the presence of someone of Sidney's brilliance, were it not for his self-effacing manner. What stood out about Sidney, and about Paul, was their ability to take their responsibilities seriously without taking themselves seriously. Complementing this was their tremendous self-confidence, even at a young age.

When Sidney became a director of nine corporations in 1930, boards were just coming into their own as important forces in corporate America. Prior to World War I, the comparatively few national corporations that existed, primarily in the oil, steel, and railroad industries, were generally dominated by one or two powerful men—a Rockefeller, a Carnegie, a Harriman—who could choose and control their boards. In the 1920s, while corporations and the economy grew in size and complexity, the country prospered, crises were few, and boards remained passive. After 1929, boards began to assert themselves. The collapse of the economy exposed management mistakes that were hidden in the good times. Court rulings held directors responsible for mishaps. The Securities Act of 1933 and the Securities Exchange Act of 1934 regulated newly issued and previously issued securities, respectively, and specified requirements which corporations and their directors had to follow, or risk liability.

In 1930, Sidney could not have anticipated the securities acts, but he correctly sensed the tenor of the times. Young and inexperienced compared to his fellow directors, he nonetheless argued aggressively for their more active involvement in the affairs of their corporations and specified how this could take place. In 1933, with the first Securities Act and its explicit definition of a director's liability in mind, he wrote a memo to the heads of all the corporations he served. This "Memorandum re the responsibilities of Directors and an outline of the program suggested as the basis of cooperation between officers and Directors of a corporation," though "nothing more than a starting point for discussion" according to Sidney, is the earliest and clearest statement on these issues. He presented eleven proposals that seem as obvious today as the Ten Commandments but were desperately needed at a time when the country was in crisis and rules and relationships were changing. All eleven proposals had the goal of enabling the director "to exercise the reasonable care of a prudent man in the discharge of his duties."

They included: regular monthly meetings; an agenda to all directors well before the meeting and minutes shortly afterwards; corporate counsel at every meeting; procedures to give directors control over salaries; mechanisms to empower and limit executive committees of boards; the providing of monthly financial data and detailed auditors reports to all directors; and provisions for the approval of profit-sharing plans, bonuses, and the issuance of options and loans to officers and directors. What tied all these proposals together were the notions that directors were supposed to direct and that "outside" directors, like Sidney and Paul, had an especially important role to play.[252] Paul said this about Sidney's contributions.

He was an excellent Director. He did his homework before he went to the meetings and he had complete integrity and was well informed and in his inimitable way he had really great tact so that he could influence the management very greatly . . . . [253]

But while Sidney Weinberg's ideas on corporate governance had an enormous impact on the way corporations rebuilt themselves out of the wreckage of the stock market crash and Depression, Sidney's actions did not always measure up to his ideals. While always honest, on at least one occasion he was less conscientious than he might have been.

His worst corporate governance embarrassment ironically involved sailing. He and his family were vacationing on Nantucket when the CEO of McKesson & Robbins, F. Donald Coster, arrived in the vicinity on his yacht, *Carolita*, and invited the Weinbergs to lunch. Sidney, a fairly frugal man for someone of such wealth, rented an old rowboat to transport his family to the yacht, and as they approached, the captain of the *Carolita*, not expecting Mr. Weinberg to arrive in such a manner, waved them away. Only Coster's arrival on deck resolved the misunderstanding. They enjoyed a pleasant lunch and before departing, Sidney graciously wrote in the ship's log, "I'm for McKesson & Robbins and Coster, that's all." Unfortunately, Coster was in fact the notorious ex-convict and swindler Philip Musica and had been systematically looting McKesson & Robbins for years, right under the noses of Sidney and the other directors.[254] Years later Sidney wrote,

> [I]n the investigation that followed [the looting of McKesson & Robbins], when I was a witness, the attorney brought this memorandum [Re the responsibilities of Directors] forward and asked me why I had not operated as a Director of that company in accordance with the standards I had set up in the memorandum.

Sidney's answer clearly indicates how he viewed his eleven proposals.

> I pointed out to him that Moses had brought down the Ten Commandants from Mt. Sinai, that we all believe in them, but that unfortunately few of us live in accordance with all of them.

In other words, *nolo contendere*. He contributed $75,000 to the $600,000 out-of-court settlement. And Sidney decided that his "Memorandum" needed a twelfth proposal or commandment, "that the comptroller be present at all Directors' meetings, and that every board have a committee on audit composed entirely of outside Directors and, thereby, have direct contact with the independent auditors." As for Coster, ne Musica, he committed suicide, while the board was meeting to fire him, in December 1938. When the directors received word of his death, Sidney piped up, "Well come on gentlemen let's fire him for his sins anyway."[255]

Paul Cabot's Jeremiad

When a country loses its common sense and confidence, as America did in the late twenties and the thirties, it takes hundreds of clear-thinking leaders in government and the private sector to establish the rules, formal and informal, through which society rebuilds and functions. Sidney was one of those leaders. Paul was another.

As noted in Chapter I, Paul was sensitive to the potential abuses of the investment trusts because of his research on their British counterparts of the late nineteenth century. In 1928 he addressed the American Savings Bank Association and, without mentioning any institution by name, outlined some actual abuses that concerned him. The following quote is from the article based on that speech, the same one that was published by his uncle, Ellery Sedgwick, the editor of the *Atlantic Monthly*.

In my opinion there is to-day in this country a large and well-known investment trust whose shares are selling for far more than their intrinsic or liquidating value, which has continually managed its portfolio so that it can show the greatest possible profits and thereby obtain the greatest market value for its shares, regardless of their real worth. Generally speaking, in this trust during the past year the good securities that have appreciated in value have been sold and the poorer ones retained or increased, simply to show profits.

The Economist tells us that this is exactly the game they were playing in England almost forty years ago.[256]

American Founders Corporation, the dominant investment company organization of the 1920s, concluded correctly that Paul was talking about them and went to National Shawmut Bank, of which Paul was a director, and threatened to withdraw their account if Shawmut did not force Paul to stop talking about them. Paul reacted to this strongly.

They told me this; well I flamed up. I got so goddamn mad I said, why the sons of bitches, in the first place I didn't mention their name in this thing at all, and obviously it shows the shoe binds them since they are excited about it. I said I'll show them how I'm going to be shut up. I trotted up to the Atlantic Monthly, the editor of which happened to be my uncle, and gave him this speech and he published it . . . . It went all over the country and I got a hell of a lot of letters from it.[257]

Unlike Sidney, who had no important family connections and worked at Goldman Sachs for twenty years before becoming a partner, Paul's family gave him access and influence. Ellery Sedgwick, the husband of his father's sister, put Paul's piece into the March 1929 issue, a few pages in back of some newly-discovered poems by Emily Dickinson. Paul instantly became a spokesman for the industry in the eyes of many, including several politicians. Even John Kenneth Galbraith, something of a lifelong antagonist, noted that, due to his position, Cabot spoke with authority. But warnings from men in positions of authority were rare, and the response to them was negligible, according to Galbraith.[258]

Writing seven months before the crash and basing his article on remarks he had delivered several months before that, Paul began by tracing the history of the British trusts, using research he had done in London in the early 1920s, because

I strongly believe that unless we avoid these and other errors and false principles we shall inevitably go through a similar period of disaster

and disgrace. If such a period should come, the well-run trusts will suffer with the bad as they did in England forty years ago.

If Sidney was like Moses, presenting boards of directors with his eleven (and later twelve) commandments, Paul was closer to Jeremiah, warning that if America (Judah) failed to heed the example of the failed trusts of England (Israel), it would face "a similar period of disaster and disgrace."

Of course, the honest and ably managed companies would emerge from the difficulties eventually. This is what occurred in England, as seven of the thirty-one leading trusts "made headway" in the adverse market of the early 1890s, according to Paul's research. Even in the book of Jeremiah, the Lord was not angry forever. Paul went on to warn of specific dangers.

> **I shall now try to point out what in my opinion are some of the present dangers. Before doing so, however, I should like to emphasize the fact that the honesty and ability of the management are paramount and that good practices can be completely vitiated by dishonest and unsound investments.[259]**

In assessing the industry, Paul first distinguished between the broadly diversified trusts, with many small positions in a large number of issues, and the more concentrated and actively managed ones. The former permitted small investors to participate in the ownership of a widely diversified portfolio of securities, almost guaranteeing something close to average performance, as Massachusetts Investors Trust was doing at that time. One such trust was required to own at least four hundred securities. The Investment Managers Company, by contrast, followed the opposite strategy and was prohibited from holding more than thirty names. It provided safety of a superior sort, in Paul's judgment, for while it was not broadly diversified,

> **No one can get an issue into [its] portfolio . . . without proving to the Directors that it is not only good, but better than one of the existing issues for which it is to be substituted.**

> **In the other company almost any security will get by. The pet issue of each Director and officer can find its way in . . . . Another disadvantage to the highly diversified portfolio is either the inability of the management to follow closely so many issues or the expense of so doing. One of the worst of some of the present abuses is the ignorance and lack of attention of some investment managers.**

Managers of the former type of fund relied on diversification to cover for their inattention, one of the "cardinal abuses" of investment managers. This inattention was worse "where the managerial control rests in rather numerous hands," in other words where there was management by committee. Paul favored concentrated control in order to avoid the "delay and lack of positive action" that committee management entailed.

Paul next told of how he was asked by a broker to consider running an investment trust for them. He noticed that the portfolio included a very large block of shares that the broker had recently underwritten and asked the firm's representative if the directors would allow him to shift funds from that stock to that of another company in the same industry, if the latter company were, in his judgment, a superior investment. The representative said "No, not necessarily. This trust is part of our general machine, and if the selling of these shares adversely affected the first company, we would not make the sale." Paul pointed out the conflict of interest involved in using the public's money to help an underwriting client and place its interest above that of the investors in the trust.

This case illustrated two other abuses of investment trusts: "first, that of being run for ulterior motives and not primarily for the best interests of the shareholders; second, that of being used as a depositary for securities that might otherwise be unmarketable." He had observed both of these abuses in his research on the British trusts.[260]

Paul had expressed similar ideas in somewhat different form in testimony to a committee of the New York Stock Exchange in 1928. When asked what he thought were the present abuses in the investment-trust movement, he replied "(1) dishonesty; (2) inattention and inability; (3) greed." By "greed" he meant simply charging too much for the services rendered.

> **You may be asked to subscribe to a trust that is both honestly and ably run, and yet find it inadvisable to do so simply because there is nothing in it for you. All the profits go to the promoters and managers.**

This could happen in a number of ways. Insiders could own most or all of the equity stock, or warrants or options on the stock. And the trust could pay excessive managerial fees or have very high expenses. These devices were not necessarily objectionable if they were properly disclosed. Paul believed that publicity and competition could control these practices. But he objected if these provisions were unclear.

> **The most common method of accomplishing this result [i.e. obfuscation and confusion] on the part of promoters is an exceedingly**

complicated capital structure. There are many investment-trust prospectuses in which it takes literally hours to figure out just how profits are to be divided. To those not trained in finance the task becomes impossible, and the promoters have accomplished their purpose. Certainly a clear statement of how the money is supplied and the profits divided, together with a simple, straightforward capital structure, is highly desirable.

Another danger, usually the result of greed, takes the form of a very large funded or floating debt or an excessive issue of preferred stock.

The management and trustees, who in many cases had received common stock as compensation, received no return on it until they had paid all fixed charges, including interest and preferred dividends. This may have tempted them to take excessive risk through leverage and pyramiding or the purchase of excessively risky securities. "Let's either win big or win nothing," they might have said, since debt holders and preferred stockholders were paid first. In other words, a complicated capital structure with management holding junior securities encouraged reckless, all-or-nothing investment policies since terrible and mediocre performance produced similar results for the common equity holders.[261] Reckless, all-or-nothing investment policies, especially excessive leverage, led to disaster in 1929, and indeed contributed to the general panic.

For Paul, clarity, simplicity, and honesty were inextricably linked. He knew that a trust with an excessively complicated capital structure often had trustees who did not know what they were doing or had something to hide—in other words, trustees who were something less than able and honest. This is what lay behind Paul's preference for the Boston-type, open-end fund with its one class of shares leading to all shareholders being treated equally. It is also why this type of fund accounts for almost all mutual funds today.

Among the many parallels between the late 1920s and late 1990s was the formation of exceedingly complicated investment funds whose structures offended the common sense of the clearest thinkers of their day. When Long-Term Capital Management (LTCM) sought the aid and the capital of Warren Buffet during its crisis, Buffet's objection to the fund, according to Roger Lowenstein, biographer of Buffet and chronicler of the LTCM saga, was the overly complicated structure.[262] If Paul took hours to figure out how profits were divided by some of the trusts of his day, he would have required months to understand LTCM's capital structure or Enron's deals with special-purpose partnerships owned and controlled by its own corporate officers. He would not have been tempted by either of these "opportunities" so popular with "sophisticated" investors at the end of the century.

Both 1929 and 2000 marked peaks in what Galbraith refers to as the "bezzle, an inventory of undiscovered embezzlement," which is a measure of corruption that is as cyclical as any financial index. In prosperous times, when people are making money, they relax and look less critically at exactly how it is being made. Unscrupulous operators take advantage of this by perpetrating various types of fraud. "The bezzle increases rapidly," according to Galbraith. When the prosperous times end, everything goes into reverse. Investors are more skeptical, even suspicious. Morality improves and the "bezzle" shrinks. The stock market boom and the ensuing crash caused a traumatic exaggeration of these normal relationships.[263]

During a bull market, defects of character and judgment can be hidden. Money is available and investors, accountants, and journalists are less diligent. When the tide goes out, the mendacity and foolishness are exposed for all to see. Paul understood this; but before the crash, he did not see the need for tougher regulation. Few did. While Paul saw the abuses as clearly as anyone, he believed that publicity and education were superior as remedies to laws and regulations.

> **[A]ll these laws can do is to hamper able management and fail to protect the public against inability and dishonesty. No law can replace the necessity for investors to think intelligently and to investigate a situation before investing their own money.[264]**

On this issue, Paul stood with the Investment Bankers Association and others who, like him, feared burdensome regulation,[265] but there is every reason to believe that these sentiments were based on principle, since they were consistent with every element of his personality. Unfortunately, while Paul had a sense that tough times were ahead, he did not know that a market crash of unprecedented magnitude was seven months away and, until the 1930s, he underestimated the demand, and the need, for reform legislation.

Paul concluded his article with a discussion of the likely performance of investment trusts during a period of declining security prices, a timely topic in March 1929. He felt, not surprisingly, that it was during periods of decline that well-run investment trusts would prove their value.

> **The investment-trust manager should be a financial expert similar in his profession to the doctor of medicine. When we most need a doctor is when we are sick. Equally it should be . . . true that when the investing public most needs expert assistance is during a period of falling security prices . . . . I should not go so far as to say that the well-run trusts will not lose money during a period of deflation; but certainly they should, and I believe will, lose less money than the average investor. With conservative capitalization, sound**

policies, and able management, the investment trusts will make more money than the average investor in good times and lose less in poor times.[266]

Paul, like Sidney, was fooled by a swindler, Ivar Kreuger of Swedish Match, who, like Donald Coster, eventually committed suicide. Kreuger had built a business empire around flagrantly fictitious accounting, predatory pricing, and the acquisition of national match franchises by lending needy European governments money at attractive rates. After World War I, all European governments were needy. He bribed Europe into granting him monopolies with money he had swindled from American investors, including State Street, and especially Lee Higginson. And although his profits were fictitious, he always paid high dividends to his existing investors by selling securities to a new group of victims.

In early October 1929, Kreuger uncharacteristically disclosed the secret of his success to the *Saturday Evening Post*.

Whatever success I have had may perhaps be attributed to three things: One is silence, the second is more silence, while the third is still more silence.[267]

He always kept his investors guessing. But after the 1929 crash, gullible investors were hard to come by, and Kreuger made a bad situation worse by refusing to retrench his operations. He felt that any sign of weakness would raise suspicion. Without fresh funds, his empire as well as his mental health began to fall apart. By the early 1930s he was reduced to forging counterfeit Italian government bonds and putting them on his balance sheet.

Paul was suspicious. But in this case he succumbed to the "delay and lack of positive action" that he criticized in others.

In the beginning I was not suspicious. He came with the highest recommendations from Lee Higginson, and the suspicion grew over the years, particularly on the basis of the way he answered a lot of the questions we asked.

He'd always have an answer, and he was pretty plausible . . . [We] said to him, now, Mr. Kreuger, you give the earnings of your company in toto, but you are earning different amounts of money in each country which you are in. We want your earnings country by country.

He said, I would be very glad to give you those earnings, but they will be meaningless. Of course, I bit and said, why? And he said, for

example, our principal wood we use in matches is aspen, and they grow a lot of aspen in Czechoslovakia, and if the price is low for aspen in Germany, let us say, high in Czechoslovakia, we will buy our aspen in the place where we can buy it cheapest and import it to the other country, and thereby make no money, say, that year in Germany and a lot of it in Czechoslovakia or vice versa, so it will mean nothing to you. And that was the kind of answer he had to everything.

[Later] I was highly suspicious. As a matter of fact, when at one point he said he had discovered a gold mine in Sweden . . . I said, well, this is too much for anybody and we started to sell all of our holdings in the match empire, and one morning my uncle called me up early in the morning to let me know that Krueger had committed suicide. I said, "oh, oh."[268]

Steven Heard and Bill Morton, the two junior State Street partners, were skiing in North Conway, New Hampshire, when they heard the news. They each said to the other, "No audited statements," a comment on the quality of Krueger's financial reporting. Heard and Morton immediately drove down to Boston, opened the office on a Sunday, and telephoned a sell order to London for the Monday opening. They managed to get their stock off, at a concession price, but before it collapsed totally.[269]

Max Winkler concluded his book on Ivar Kreuger with the Latin proverb, "Mundus vult decipi; ergo decipiatur." (The world wants to be deceived. Let it therefore be deceived.)[270] Paul expressed the same sentiments, but in his own words.

The most important quality is management that's able and honest. A hell of an easy way to get taken to the cleaners is by some goddamn crook like Ivar Kreuger.[271]

The War Production Board

While Paul, as well as Sidney, focused almost exclusively on business during the difficult decade of the thirties, as war approached they temporarily abandoned their careers and turned their attention to the larger needs of the country. In 1939, the government began recruiting businessmen and engineers to help direct the mobilization of American industry. Many of them, the so-called dollar-a-year men, were business leaders who earned enough in the private sector so that the government could gain their services only through appeals to their patriotism.

Perhaps to emphasize their public spiritedness and appeal to their pride, the government paid them virtually nothing. According to an Office of Production Management (OPM) memo, the dollar-a-year program sought "nominees of outstanding experience and ability . . . in full sympathy with the defense program . . . [for] positions of a responsible administrative, technical, or consulting nature." Said nominees had to have been receiving a salary higher than the OPM could legally pay and be individuals of "high integrity and good moral character."[272]

Arguably the most important of these dollar-a-year men, other than the chairmen of the OPM and its successor agency, the War Production Board (WPB), was Sidney Weinberg, who served in the senior staff position at the WPB. The later agency superseded the OPM (and other agencies) after the attack on Pearl Harbor, and due to the war emergency had more power than those established during peacetime. For instance, shortly after it was created, President Roosevelt delegated to its chairman his authority, under the Second War Powers Act, to allocate all materials needed for war production. The WPB's membership included Chairman Donald Nelson; the Secretaries of War, Navy, Commerce, and Agriculture; Vice President Henry Wallace; and Roosevelt advisors such as Harry Hopkins and Harold Ickes.[273]

According to a high-ranking government official and friend, "Sidney [was] a sucker for anything patriotic." On two occasions, during World War II and during the Korean War, he took leave from Goldman Sachs to help mobilize industry for war. For years he displayed a government check for sixteen cents on his office wall, his pay for one particular two-month stint.[274] WPB Chairman Donald Nelson explained that Sidney had been a director of his company, Sears, Roebuck & Co., as long as he could remember. The Sachses of Goldman Sachs were related to the Rosenwalds of Sears, Roebuck. In addition, Sidney had belonged to as many boards and was acquainted with as many business leaders as anyone in America. For this reason, he decided, the investment banker was the best man to set up the dollar-a-year program.[275]

While one of Sidney's closest friends, Paul was only one of hundreds he brought to Washington, beginning in May 1941. Paul explained his service as follows.

> **My good friend, Sidney Weinberg, had gone down to Washington to serve in what [became] the War Production Board . . . . And he got a man named McConnell . . . to offer me a job down there . . . I was too old to get into the service. I was in the service in the First World War. And I thought it was my duty to the country to go down there.**[276]

Three things are particularly revealing. Paul was frustrated that he "was too old to get into the service." Like Sidney, he thought it was his duty to serve, even though he had done so in World War I. Also, like Sidney, he was working in

Washington nearly six months before the attack on Pearl Harbor. Paul's letter of nomination was sent to the head of the OPM on June 23, 1941, and he began work around that date.[277]

Sidney had an unusual surprise for Paul when he arrived in Washington, according to Charlie Flather, who tells the following story.

> **When Paul moved to Washington, Sidney took an ad in the paper. It appears that a very well known Madam's establishment had been recently raided by the police and closed. Sidney's ad announced that the Madam was open for business again and listed Paul's address and telephone number as the new location. Naturally, there was a constant stream of phone calls and visitors until the word got around that the ad was not true.**[278]

Paul's daughter Chris remembers receiving some very strange and somewhat unsettling phone calls while she was struggling with her geometry homework.

Paul worked briefly for McConnell, but for most of his three years in Washington ran the Salvage Division of the Bureau of Industrial Conservation, which became the Conservation Division of the WPB.[279] In late 1942, the Salvage Division broke away from the Conservation Division and reported directly to the WPB's Director General for Operations. Paul's boss at the Bureau was initially Lessing J. Rosenwald of Sears, Roebuck, who reported to Nelson, who reported to the President. But Rosenwald, a man too sensitive for the rough and tumble of Washington, resigned as a result of some embarrassing and probably unfair newspaper columns.[280] It is indicative of Rosenwald's character, however, that while he was the son of one of the founders of Sears, Roebuck and Nelson's peacetime boss, he was willing to work as his subordinate in Washington to help the war effort. After Rosenwald resigned, Paul reported to Donald Davis, who had been president of General Mills.

Before the establishment of the WPB in January 1942, Nelson's functions were carried out by William S. Knudsen, head of the OPM, where Paul Cabot worked for several months as well. Nelson had worked at the OPM and the Supply Priorities and Allocations Board, another predecessor agency. Knudsen, a former head of General Motors, became an Army Lieutenant General in charge of production for the War Department when the OPM was disbanded.[281]

Nelson devoted a chapter of his memoirs to the dollar-a-year men, in part to praise their contribution and in part to discuss the conflicts and controversies that swirled around them. These included the prominence of businessmen over union leaders that some thought gave the WPB an anti-labor bias, the problem of gearing up for the war but avoiding post-war overcapacity, the temptation of favoring one's own former company in the expectation that one would return to it after the war, especially since so many men continued to be paid by their companies, and the problems some senior executives had reporting to government bureaucrats that they considered their inferiors in status and ability.[282]

The Salvage Division consisted of an Industrial Salvage Branch, composed of senior industry executives who had the knowledge and authority to scrap plant equipment; a General Salvage Branch, which worked through the state salvage committees to recover scrap from homes, farms, and small businesses; a Scrap Processors Branch, or Automobile Graveyard Section; and a Special Projects Salvage Branch to handle waste material whose use was obstructed by a legal, political, or financial situation.[283]

Nelson described the importance of Paul's Salvage Division as follows. While industrial scrap, the largest share, automatically returns to the raw-materials market, the demands of the war required them to shorten the "flow-back time lag and make sure that all the scrap produced by industry went back to take the place of raw materials." Nelson estimated that the incremental quantity of material made available through the efforts of the Salvage Division was about six million tons per year. If we assume that five million of this was steel, it would have amounted to about five percent of American steel production during the war years.

Nelson pointed out that for the year ending February 1, 1943, the number of automobiles in junkyards declined from 1,500,000 to 400,000. During this period, 3.75 million tons of steel were removed from these yards. As another example, between March 1942 and the end of the war, over fifteen thousand special projects, negotiated by the Salvage Division according to Nelson, produced almost 3.25 million tons of scrap. These included abandoned railroads, unused streetcar tracks, bridges, mines, buildings, oil wells, sunken vessels, and lumber equipment.

Then there was the drive to recover scrap metal and waste paper from individual homes and farms. Here Nelson credited the press, radio, and the movie industry, which sprung into action once the Salvage Division had explained the need.[284] There was also a great public relations benefit in giving average citizens another opportunity to participate in the war effort.

Every state had one paid federal junkman from the General Salvage Branch who would organize committees of volunteers to run salvage drives. Then professional junk dealers would separate the material, prepare it for use in factories, and transport it there. An October 1942 Review of the General Salvage Program concluded that,

> **The policy of dealing with this national problem requiring the active support of millions of people by calling upon State leadership and control within the State by its own citizens was the chief factor which sustained the General Salvage program over so many months and produced extraordinary results.[285]**

For almost three years Paul crisscrossed the country supervising these activities. Paul Morgan, his young associate, remembers him as very much the provincial Bostonian on these trips in spite of his schooling in Arizona, military service in Kentucky, and employment in London. Paul remembered a luncheon in his honor at the Brown Derby in Los Angeles as being the place that had something to do with a hat, and the English actor seated next to him, Basil Rathbone, as "Wishbone."

Morgan also recalls that Paul was uncomfortable dealing with the print and broadcast media, especially being interviewed.

> **One time he was scheduled for an appearance on a Jack Benny radio show and was so nervous that he asked me to come to his house for breakfast to have a cup of coffee with him while he went over his brief script. My coffee was in the normal Harvard mug which is twice the size of any normal cup, but his was ten times the size. I have never seen before or since such a large cup. It was really a bowl. And did he drink from it? Heavens no! He poured the coffee from the "cup" into its saucer, swirled the coffee around for a while and then slurped the coffee from the saucer. I must say the baked beans were excellent.[286]**

It was at around this time that Bing Crosby recorded one of his least-remembered songs, advertised as "the theme song of the NATIONAL SALVAGE CAMPAIGN under the auspices of the CONSERVATION DIVISION of the WAR PRODUCTION BOARD." The words, very representative of the time, went as follows.

> **Junk aint junk no more____ 'cause junk can win the war____**
> **What's junk to you has a job to do,____ 'Cause junk aint junk no more.____**
> **Pots and pans and garbage cans, ____ the kettle that doesn't pour,____**
> **Collect today for the U.S.A.,____ 'Cause junk can win the war.____**
> **From the attic to the cellar start looking if you please;____**
> **All your trash will go to smash the tricky Japanese.____**
> **Old automobiles, old iron wheels, the shawl that Granny wore;____**
> **Take a tip from Uncle, Junk'll Win the War.[287]**

Nelson, writing after the war was won, made it sound free of conflict and stress. But during the emergency, the demands for materials were urgent. A memo Paul received from Leon Henderson of the Office of Price Administration captures the feeling of that time. Henderson wrote,

> **The present shortage of wood pulp is daily becoming more acute because of the unprecedented demands being made upon industry.**

Waste paper collections have now reached the highest point in history, but are still inadequate. The relieving of this situation is your job. [We] can only point the way and serve as a clearing house for information and suggestions.[288]

The papers from the WPB show a level of bureaucratic squabbling that was confusing at best and counter-productive at worst, and Paul Cabot was often in the middle of it. The various branches of the salvage division often got in each others' way, and their respective responsibilities had to be continually restated, often by Paul. The salvage division as a whole had conflicts with the Requisitioning Branch of the Division of Industry Operations. These were resolved through a joint memo issued by Paul and his counterpart at the Requisitioning Branch. The Chief of the General Salvage Branch, who reported to Paul, at one point sent to his regional offices a packet of four manuals and six agreements and directives that spelled out that branch's relationships with the Office of Price Administration, the Office of Civilian Defense, the Requisitioning Branch, the Rubber Branch, the Iron and Steel Branch, and the other branches of the salvage division. He then noted that there were a lot of other agreements that he did not bother to send.[289]

While Paul's situation was not as trying as that of the men and women on active duty, his job did involve sacrifice. For one thing Paul, who slept outdoors on a sleeping porch in Needham, Massachusetts, twelve months a year, could never adjust to the heat of Washington.

I went to sleep one night with my head in the ice chest, because I thought I couldn't get a breath of air. My neck was so damn stiff the next morning, with the ice chest door banging on it all night.

Many of the wives and children left Washington during the summer and half-a-dozen men would share a house, which always happened to be Paul's house. Every evening they would enjoy cocktails and dinner together. But Paul recalled that there was no late-night drinking or poker because they were all tired from working so hard. Occasionally they had a distinguished guest to dinner, like Secretary of the Navy William F. Knox. These events sounded a bit like dinners at the Porcellian Club at Harvard. When asked to repeat some of Secretary Knox's stories, Paul claimed that they were unrepeatable, and that went for his own stories as well. There was one difference between the Club dinners and these gatherings in the heat of Washington, however. When asked if they dressed for dinner, Paul answered that no, they undressed for dinner, on account of the heat.

While Paul complained about the heat and the hard work in Washington, he seemed to recall those days with fondness. His family was with him for most of the time and he had the opportunity to work with many of the leaders of American business—the heads of Goldman Sachs, General Motors, and Sears, Roebuck of course, but also Charles E. Wilson, head of General Electric, and Spencer Shore, a business school classmate who ran Eagle Picher. Following a dinner party at the Cabots' house, Shore put four new tires on Paul's car. To the surprise of most Americans, but surely not to Shore, tire rationing began shortly thereafter.

On one occasion, when Paul had gotten tickets to fly home for a weekend, Sidney as a joke told him that there was going to be a meeting to reorganize their agency and that his attendance was required. But a mutual friend, Frank Crocker, told Paul that Sidney had made up this story. This gave Paul the opportunity to turn the tables on Sidney, and he told him that he had cancelled his airline tickets on account of the meeting. This sent Sidney into a panic. He "called up the President of every airline—I think he probably knew them all personally—and tried to get me reinstated," remembered Paul. But he failed to do so.

So Sidney then called Frank and told him that he was going to call Paul and pretend that he was William Knudsen, Paul's boss at the time, Midwestern Swedish accent and all. He would tell Paul that the meeting was off and perhaps Paul could then get his own tickets back. Frank relayed this information to Paul, but unfortunately Knudsen himself actually did call just when Paul was expecting to hear from Sidney, so Paul told an assistant to brush Knudsen off. When Knudsen called back, the assistant was more insistent and Paul agreed to speak with him. Still thinking it was Sidney with a fake Swedish accent, Paul yelled, "You piss up a rope." But it was the real Knudsen, who replied, "Nobody in the General Motors Company has ever said anything like that to me."

> **So I scooted around as fast as I could and just told him what had happened, and told him the truth, and he laughed like blazes and thought that was a hell of a good joke and kidded me about it ever afterwards.** [290]

But Paul got even. According to Paul Morgan,

> **Paul and Sidney were on an Army Air Corps plane en route to a meeting, with Donald Nelson and several other big shots . . . some six in all. They hit some very rough weather whereupon the pilot told them to don their parachutes. However, they discovered that there were only five chutes. This prompted Paul and the others to look at Sidney and tell him that since he was the smallest he'd have to hang on to someone else in case of a bail out. Paul told me the story with tears of laughter running down his cheeks thinking about the expression on Sidney's face.** [291]

Two Friends

Treasurer Paul Cabot, Sidney Weinberg, and Overseer Sen. John F. Kennedy at the Harvard Commencement in 1959 at which Mr. Weinberg received an honorary degree, arranged for him by his friend Paul Cabot.

While Paul and Sidney had similar worldviews and compatible personalities, it was hardly inevitable that they would become close friends. When Sidney went sailing with Paul and Charlie Dickey, it was a Harvard man, a Yale man, and a P.S. 13 man. And while Paul and Charlie, as institutional investors, were clients of Sidney, when it came to sailing Sidney was always the guest. If Sidney had been an important customer, it would have been natural to invite him along and show him a good time. But Sidney Weinberg of Goldman Sachs, the banker, broker, and salesman, was there because Paul and Charlie loved having him around.

Interestingly, Sidney's competitors from Morgan Stanley and First Boston had backgrounds similar to Paul's. The Wall Street trading houses founded by Eastern European immigrants and their sons, like Goldman Sachs and Salomon Brothers, had many talented men with little formal education in important positions. But Goldman Sachs had broadened its franchise to encompass investment banking and advisory services, which is why Sidney served simultaneously on thirty-one corporate boards. This made Goldman more the peer of Morgan Stanley, with its Ivy League graduates, than of Salomon. But in the 1970s and 1980s, when Paul recalled his early years in the business, it was as if Sidney were the only investment banker on Wall Street. And a picture of Sidney, Paul, and Senator John F. Kennedy at the Harvard graduation where Sidney received an honorary degree hung for many years on Paul's office wall.

Service to Sidney and Paul did not only mean patriotic service. While they were ambitious men anxious to make their way in the world, there was an element of service in every aspect of their business careers. Sidney once said, referring to his work on philanthropic boards, "My fundamental philosophy is that a man can't be only a businessman and get any satisfaction out of life." And in his business career as well, Sidney was always thinking of the social and ethical implications of his actions. Of his paid corporate directorships he once said, "I regard being a Director of a large corporation as a semi-public service. A man in my tax bracket gets nothing out of it except terrific responsibility, and he'd be silly to assume that responsibility unless he looked upon it as a public service."[292]

Referring to Sidney's work as a director, Charlie Wilson once wrote, "Sidney has an uncanny understanding of the needs of industry." Never was this truer than in 1931 when he arrived in Akron for a B.F. Goodrich board meeting just as a run was starting on the city's banks. Seeing this as a potential disaster for the company and its employees, he stayed on in Akron after the meeting to try to ease the situation. For ten days he studied the banks' books and, having satisfied himself that they were basically sound, he called New York and convinced some financiers there to put up enough money to see the banks through the crisis. The Akron banks stayed open.[293]

Paul's moral sensitivity showed most clearly when he was considering the interests of investors of limited means and sophistication. And, in his role as treasurer of Harvard, he thought carefully and independently about the ethical way to raise, manage, and spend endowment funds. When the three partners established State Street Investment Corporation, they sought the advice of experienced financiers. The consensus among these older men was that the partners' idea, essentially the modern mutual fund, was a bad one and that 1924, actually near the beginning of the bull market, was the wrong time to start. To err on the side of caution, they overrode their own judgment, invested only their own money, and did not sell to the public until 1927.

> **This was a new idea—it was wise to try it out for a number of years with only our own money, on the basis that if the idea was no good and it wasn't going to work, we wouldn't hurt anybody except ourselves.**

Throughout his career, Paul favored delivering good performance to existing clients over spending resources trying to win new ones, as we saw in Chapter II. When asked why he spoke against the American Founders Group he answered simply, "They were doing what I thought was absolutely wrong. Indeed, probably immoral, crooked."[294]

Paul brought an independent moral standard to the management of Harvard's funds. He felt that it was immoral to ask for money when you don't need it,[295] which certainly would be a strange notion to fundraisers today, and no doubt was then. He favored conservative spending policies because donors had a right to expect their gifts to last.

There were limits to materialism and greed in both of these men. Today, business interests frequently argue that a low tax rate is needed to encourage socially productive entrepreneurial activity. One gets the impression with Paul and Sidney that a high tax bracket almost freed them from the worry over how much they were earning. Both men lived simply in large and comfortable but unpretentious houses. Both used public transportation regularly. Paul's suits, coats, and hats were well-worn even by Boston Brahmin standards. When an overnight guest at Sidney's home in Scarsdale left his suit and shoes outside his bedroom door one evening, Sidney pressed the suit and polished the shoes himself rather than explain that he did not have a valet.[296]

Sidney handled the differences in their backgrounds with confidence and humor. Paul once invited Sidney to a dinner at Harvard that Sidney could not attend. Whatever the reason, he responded that he already had an academic event planned for that evening, a dinner for a P.S. 13 classmate whom nobody had seen for twenty-five years. When Paul asked where the man had been, Sidney replied "In Sing Sing. He shot our teacher for giving him a lousy mark." Sidney was not above having Ivy League pretensions, however. P.S. 13 has a school song that any neutral observer would conclude is an adaptation of Cornell University's "Far Above Cayuga's Waters." It begins:

**Near where East River rolls its waters
Toward Atlantic stream
Worked the hardy sons and daughters
Of Public School Thirteen.**

Sidney never accepted this. He maintained that it was Cornell that had stolen the song from his *alma mater*; and he never stopped chiding John L. Collyer, chairman of the board at B.F. Goodrich as well as at Cornell, for this larcenous act. [297]

Paul never felt distant from Sidney because he was a Jew. Similarities in character, intellect, and personality drew them together. Likewise, Paul was fond of William Wolfe for a half century after they had worked together at the Salvage Division of the War Production Board. And Paul liked and was well-respected by several Jewish faculty members whom he had worked with at Harvard.[298]

By basing generalizations on personal experience, Paul was saved from the prejudices of some of his peers. But this also limited his ability to empathize with those with whom he could not easily identify because of his lack of first-hand contact. While Paul was Treasurer,

> **Some editor of the *Crimson* called me up at night. He asked me if Harvard owned Middle South Utilities or Mississippi Power and Light. I told him we did. He said that they wanted me to sell them, that they were unfair to Negroes. I told him that he was a goddamn little squirt. I had a partner on the board and happened to know that they'd been better than almost anybody else down there. "Go jump in the lake . . . to hell with you," I said.[299]**

Paul's statement may well have been true. But its tone is decidedly less sensitive than his very sympathetic remarks about Jewish junk dealers. Like others of his class and generation in Boston, he had little interaction with African-Americans. They were not present on Wall Street, much less in the Boston investment fraternity, or in senior positions in Washington, or at Harvard during Paul's working career. They were rarely even servants in Brookline or Back Bay.

Paul was neither liberal nor politically correct in the modern sense. He simply made up his mind about people and groups based on the people he knew well. Paul's feelings toward Jews came from specific individuals, most of all from Sidney. This came through most clearly in Paul's interview with Jessica Holland of the Columbia University Oral History Research Office. Holland, whose interests were broad, was anxious to explore the friendship between Sidney and Henry Ford II, whose grandfather was notorious for his anti-Semitism. Henry and Sidney had been friends for years through their common membership on the Business Roundtable, which Sidney had helped found. But they became especially close when Sidney represented the Ford family during negotiations with the Ford Foundation over the Foundation's decision to sell Ford stock. This decision was complicated because Foundation stock was non-voting; voting rights had to be attached if it was to be tradable on the New York Stock Exchange; and there were tax implications for the family if they transferred some of their voting rights to the Foundation for cash. The negotiations lasted two years (1953-1955) and included not only the family and the Foundation, but also the stock exchange and the I.R.S. They were so complex that Charlie Wilson, then chairman of the Foundation's Finance Committee, and Henry Ford fought over who would get to hire Sidney to represent them in the negotiations.[300]

Holland naturally asked Paul about Henry's reaction to Sidney's death in 1969, but Paul could not answer for Henry without answering for himself. With the emotion in his voice clearly audible on the cassette tape, Paul replied,

Same as mine. We both adored Sidney. Had the greatest respect for him and were going to miss him something terrible. I heard him say at a meeting that was conducted in the Ford Building of the Detroit Harvard Business School Club, introducing Sidney, he introduced him as "my closest friend." And I'm sure that was true, right up to the time Sidney died.[301]

Paul's character reflected his background, along with his strong will; but Sidney shared many traits with Paul in spite of his different upbringing. One could argue that cultures that give individuals a strong sense of self, a sense of honesty and of right and wrong, have more similarities than differences. When Oliver Alden's fictional ancestors, and Paul's real ones, "went . . . into a stark wilderness to lead a life apart, purer and soberer than the carnival life of Christendom," they drew their strength from the example of another tribe attempting to build a society in the wilderness, the ancient Israelites. The archetypal Puritan sermon, common in New England as late as during Paul's childhood, was the Jeremiad. He clearly retained something from all of the sermons that his mother brought him to on Sundays. The Old Testament impulse to smite the wicked and reform society was part of the cultural background of both Paul and Sidney.

Paul felt strongly that abusive practices had to cease or the good would suffer with the bad, as was the case in England in the nineteenth century (and Israel in the eighth century B.C.E.). Doing Moses one better, Sidney proposed what amounted to eleven (later twelve) commandments that enabled directors to actively direct and to keep corporate America on the right path. Paul was no Puritan in the common sense of the word; and neither he nor Sidney was particularly religious. Both, by their conduct, strongly opposed the Puritan-inspired reform of their day, prohibition. But they shared a sense of who they were and a kind of honesty, without which all of their ability and ambition would have counted for little.

Chapter VI

Harvard's Treasurer

[T]he office of Harvard's Treasurer is different from that of most colleges and universities. There simply is no investment committee—the committee consists of Mr. Cabot. He likes it that way. "You can move faster and you know where the responsibility lies," he says . . .

HARVARD Today Magazine.

Paul Cabot has the unique ability to weigh many conflicting pieces of evidence, trends, and arguments, and then come up with a valid decision when many men would still be wavering. And then he also has the wide circle of friends and acquaintances who have access to experts in many fields. When the signals that he is receiving do not make sense to him, he picks up the telephone, or makes a quick trip out of town, to talk with someone who knows the facts of the matter.[302]

George Bennett quoted in HARVARD Today Magazine

For many years, when Paul Cabot was Treasurer of Harvard University, Charlie Flather had the job of briefing him before his bi-weekly meetings with the Harvard Corporation. Paul had traditionally given this task to the most junior analyst, but when it was Charlie's turn to relinquish these duties, he requested to stay on. He felt that it was a matchless opportunity to learn from a brilliant investor. Charlie recalls,

[Paul] was always direct. I always knew where I stood . . . . I particularly recall how much fun it was and what a great sense of humor he had. On one occasion, when Harvard purchased a hotel near Harvard Square with the intent to turn it into married student

> housing, the transaction was fairly complicated. We went through the
> various items . . ., and finally came to an item labeled "miscellaneous,"
> which was slightly over $40,000. As I knew he would, Paul asked me
> what the miscellaneous was. My response was that it was a package
> purchase and that we had to buy everything including the reception
> desk's registration forms, the pencils, and the paper clips and other
> office supplies. Paul asked in an incredulous tone, "$40,000 for paper
> clips?" and I responded that most of it was the bottles in inventory
> for the hotel's liquor lounge. He looked up at me and said, "Get a
> truck, and have them send it over."[303]

Paul Cabot's method in investing the Harvard endowment was identical to
his method in investing other funds under his control, except that he was totally
on his own, rather than a first among near equals. As Harvard Treasurer, he
had no partners; and he was only held accountable after the fact to a Board of
Harvard Fellows who held him in high esteem. Paul attended all-day meetings of
the Corporation every other Monday,[304] but little time was devoted to financial
affairs, less still to the endowment. Paul remembered,

> The discussions of financial matters were practically zero. I had
> charge of that . . . . Every time, I'd begin the meeting and tell them
> what I'd done and what I was going to do.[305]

We can divide Paul's investment method into three parts: the search for
"pieces of evidence, trends, and arguments;" the resolution of anomalies within
the evidence; and the taking of action based on the above. This is common to
all sound investors; what was noteworthy was the quality of the execution. And
the key to the execution was Paul's passion to get to the heart of a matter, to
get things right. This is what lay behind Paul's and his partners' eagerness to
interview corporate executives in person, and especially to visit them at their
offices and factories. Significantly, as recently as the 1980s, analysts' reports at
State Street Research & Management were called "interviews," because the
heart of the report was the commentary of management, of their customers, or
of other industry experts. The analysis and recommendation were clearly labeled
so that the analyst's opinion was not confused with the evidence. This was the
case even when management's comments were thought to be disingenuous.
The event which triggered an action was the discovery of "conflicting pieces
of evidence," opposing arguments or "signals that . . . do not make sense,"
anomalies that suggested the mis-valuation of a security by at least some market
participants.

Paul Cabot Returns to Harvard as Treasurer

Paul began his long association with the Harvard Treasurer's office in 1928 when Treasurer Charles Francis Adams asked him and his partners to advise the University on common stocks.[306] Harvard paid State Street (SSRM) for this service through the management fee on shares of SSIC that Harvard had purchased. Also, Adams agreed to serve as a director of the mutual fund. When Adams left Harvard to become Secretary of the Navy in February 1929, Henry L. Shattuck succeeded him both as Treasurer and as a State Street director, though for a period Adams and Shattuck served together. Their pay was only twenty dollars per meeting, about one hundred dollars per year; but they could keep a close eye on their money.[307]

Paul's work with Adams led to a rumor that he would succeed Adams in the office, though Paul was only thirty years old when Adams resigned. After a Corporation meeting on February 25, the Boston Post lead headline shouted, "CABOT TO TAKE ADAMS' PLACE." The Boston Transcript asked "Paul Cabot for Harvard Treasurer?"[308] The rumor of Paul's assuming the Treasurer's post was either false, or the Corporation changed its mind when the word got out. Shattuck, a man knowledgeable enough about the stock market not to need Paul's advice, took over; and State Street's involvement with the Harvard endowment was minor over the next two decades.

These decades were tough ones for Harvard finances and the Harvard endowment, though it had nothing to do with Paul Cabot's absence from the scene. The Depression hurt both alumni giving and endowment investment performance. Inflation became a problem before fundraising and endowment income recovered, in part because President Conant (1933-1953) had little interest in development. And enrollment and tuition income dropped, at least for a while, during World War II.[309]

Treasurer William Claflin, who succeeded Shattuck, de-emphasized the role of the endowment in the budget and foresaw an era when the university would finance its activities more from current revenue and less from "receipts from accumulated wealth." Perhaps reflecting the experience of the Depression, he was more interested in the safety of the endowment than the return; and naturally during the war he felt an obligation to buy government bonds. In 1944 he defended his 31% allocation of the endowment to equities against those who thought it was too *high*.[310]

But Claflin's tenure as treasurer ended as the result of a *non-financial* dispute with President Conant. In December 1947 the Corporation approved Conant's candidate, William Marbury, to replace a retiring fellow, but by an unusually narrow

5-2 vote and with Claflin the more ardent of the two opponents. Marbury hailed from Baltimore, not the more usual Boston or New York, and he was a graduate of the law school, not Harvard College, the usual prerequisite to Corporation membership. Depending on one's vision for Harvard, this non-traditional background could be regarded as positive or negative. The Overseers, who had to confirm Marbury, asked Shattuck, at that time a non-officer member of the Corporation, whether a vote against Conant's candidate might lead to his resignation. Shattuck could not answer but Conant made it clear that "If this election is not confirmed, it will be apparent to the Treasurer and the President that a majority of the Overseers think that the Treasurer and not the President ought to run the University." Claflin and Provost Buck had taken an active role in managing day-to-day affairs at Harvard during and immediately after the war, while Conant was back and forth between Cambridge and Washington, advising the administration on scientific issues, including nuclear weapons policy. Some, perhaps Conant among them, suspected that Claflin enjoyed his power too much. The Overseers did eventually confirm Conant's choice; and Claflin resigned a few months later.[311]

The two leading candidates to succeed him were two friends from the Class of '21, Thomas S. Lamont and Paul Cabot. While knowing each other in college, they became friends only toward the end of their time there when Lamont's father, Thomas W. Lamont, chief executive at J.P. Morgan, built a summer home, Sky Farm, near the Cabots' home at Pulpit Harbor in North Haven, Maine. The younger Lamont and Paul also later became directors of J.P. Morgan.

According to Paul, Thomas S.

> **was about one of the closest friends I ever had . . . . I was very fond of him and his wife . . . . He was devoted to Harvard.**

> **We got to know each other pretty well in college, and then his family moved to North Haven, where I saw a lot of him every summer. Cruising together and boating together and playing golf together and tennis.**

> **And his wife was a friend of all of ours, whom we all knew very well. Her name was Eleanor Miner . . . —he met her at North Haven. She and her father and mother and her brother all lived up there in a little house called Kent Cottage.**

> **Then, of course, I saw a lot of Tommy after I became a Director of what was at the time J.P. Morgan . . . up to the time of his death.**

His father was one of the senior partners, Thomas W. Lamont . . . .
Tommy (S.) . . . went there I think right after college . . . and when I
became a Director, he was a partner.

The Lamont family differed from most of Paul's friends, and from most
wealthy families, in one notable respect, its politics. Paul described the elder
Lamont as

Very interesting, vigorous, thoroughly gentlemanly, kind, thoughtful,
and intelligent. He was very much taken by the late Lord Maynard
Keynes . . . He was a fairly liberal-thinking man, but an extremely
kind man. He was always terribly nice to me.

I would say he was liberal in thinking that Maynard Keynes—maybe
his philosophy was pretty good. I imagine he'd change his spots now,
if he were alive . . . .

His wife was very liberal too. Pretty far to the left. A good deal farther
than Mr. Lamont was, but obviously his wife must have influenced
him . . . . Whenever you dined there with them, they talked about the
current affairs of the nation and what was going on in the world and
what they thought about it.[312]

Paul's description of Thomas W. Lamont is more interesting for what it
leaves out than for what it includes. Lamont was a liberal internationalist, but he
almost invariably supported Republicans at election time. The one exception was
when he supported Cox and FDR in 1920 because of Harding's opposition to the
League of Nations. He was open-minded toward Keynes's economic policies, but
disagreed with him on international questions such as policy toward the defeated
Germany after World War I.[313] And while he may have been "very much taken by
the late Lord Maynard Keynes," Paul does not mention that, for a while, Lamont
was also very much taken by the late Benito Mussolini, or at least pretended to be
while pursuing banking business from the fascist regime. Lamont was public in his
support for *Il Duce*, even mentioning him favorably in a Harvard class report. He
rationalized this by suggesting that many of Mussolini's problems were a matter
of public relations. Paul had not mentioned this, perhaps influenced by Thomas
W. Lamont's personal kindness and his friendship for son Tommy, or perhaps
influenced by Lamont's later disillusionment with Mussolini and his 1937 trip to
attempt to persuade the Italian dictator not to join forces with Hitler. Paul also
did not mention that the Lamonts had made the greatest imaginable sacrifice for

their country, losing a beloved son and grandson, Thomas W. Lamont II, when his submarine was lost in the Pacific in April 1945.[314]

Lamont was admired by the left as well as by business associates. According to the poet John Masefield, the Lamonts' "political views, national and international, were ever generous and liberal." According to Peter Vermilye, who worked at J.P. Morgan before coming to State Street (SSRM) to head up the pension fund management business, Lamont "was the heart of J.P. Morgan for decades," as well as "a force in politics, literature, and philanthropy."[315] Paul, and nearly everyone who knew the Lamonts, saw Lamont, Sr. very much as he wished to be seen—liberal, cultured, and successful.

Tommy's brother, Corliss Lamont, was less diplomatic. Paul recalled,

> **He . . . has a very extreme leftist in Corliss Lamont. Oh, he's way to the left. He's practically a Communist Socialist . . . . He's pleasant enough personally . . . . We never discuss [economics] because we would fight if we did.**[316]

Paul did not exaggerate Corliss Lamont's views. During World War II, the Columbia philosophy instructor, known as the "Silk-Shirt Communist," was chairman of American Friends of the Soviet Union. Even his mother thought that Corliss seemed "fairly daft on the subject of Russia." Interestingly, according to Ron Chernow, Corliss considered his radical views to be an extension of his parents' liberalism, not a rejection of it.[317] Corliss used part of his inheritance to fund the collection of the papers of Santayana and other philosophers.

Tommy (Thomas S. Lamont) was regarded by Paul and others as reliable and balanced, an establishment figure with the intellect and independence to be a constructive critic of the system that had so favored him. In 1949, as a member of a visiting committee, most of whose members were concerned about the leftward drift of the economics department, Tommy worried about

> **getting new men in the Department who might be so far to the right as to be unaware of a changing world . . . . What we need are teachers to expound all theories, not propagandists for any.**

In 1959, he complained to Nathan Pusey that the Business School did little to alert its students to

> **some of the faults of our corporate institutions and of the so-called free enterprise system, which need attention if the system is to be preserved. The Harvard Business School would be more worth its salt if it could produce just a few more cynics and skeptics.**[318]

These were not Paul's views, but they were the views of one of his closest associates at Harvard.

Paul was appointed Treasurer on October 18, 1948, and Harvard contracted State Street Research & Management for "research and analysis."[319] Tommy joined the Corporation a few years afterwards, and they served together for thirteen years. While we do not know the Corporation's reason for choosing Paul, neither man was likely to sacrifice his career to work for the University full-time, and Paul's Boston office was a more suitable second headquarters for Treasury than Lamont's Manhattan locale. Paul had more investment experience, and perhaps most important, a fully-staffed investment team ready to support him.

Harvard may have been undecided about the advisability of having a part-time Treasurer. When Corporation Fellow Grenville Clark interviewed Paul for the job, he initially told him that he would have to leave State Street to accept the position. Paul told President Conant that

> **To have me serve as Treasurer and not have the backing of my organization ... would be like asking a carpenter to come and build you a house and leave all of his tools at home.**

Conant either agreed with Paul or shifted his position quickly enough to get him to accept the job.[320]

In addition, Harvard agreed that under certain circumstances, State Street's transactions could take precedence over Harvard's, just as they had over the Shawmut's. Believing that these arrangements were thoroughly proper if fully disclosed, Paul had written Conant that,

> **It is realized that the handling of the University account will be quite different from the problems of our present handling of the funds of the State Street Investment Corporation. A large proportion of the University funds will be in bonds, preferred stock, and other similar obligations which are rarely held by State Street Investment Corporation. The University funds will be more permanently invested, and not subject to more rapid "switching" of State Street Investment Corporation. *None the less there will be occasions when both accounts will wish to buy or sell the same security at the same time. It is understood that when these occasions develop State Street Investment Corporation is to have precedence.*[321]**

This letter was made a part of the records of the Harvard Corporation. There is no record of Conant's response, but the administration was clearly on notice and apparently did not outwardly object, though different individuals may have felt otherwise. John Thorndike, an assistant to both Cabot and George Bennett in their roles as Treasurer, and a Harvard graduate, felt uncomfortable with the arrangement nearly fifty years later. But George Bennett, Paul's principal assistant and his successor, did a study demonstrating that this practice had not hurt performance because State Street was usually early on its buys and sells and Harvard usually got as good or better prices.[322] While the conclusion of this study is probably correct, because Harvard did do well relative to State Street, the study has not survived and cannot be audited. Even if it were proven that Harvard was not hurt by this, however, an arrangement in which Harvard took a back seat to State Street would not be permitted today, especially since so much of Paul's personal money was at State Street.

In managing the endowment, Paul took advantage of his team at State Street, but made all of the investment decisions on his own, sometimes extremely rapidly. As *HARVARD Today* explained, "If he feels that the facts show a decision can be made, he will make it at once, rather than delay."[323] But the article did not mention that Paul sometimes did delay until State Street had completed its trades; nor does there appear to be any published reference to the fact that State Street's transactions took priority over Harvard's.

Since Paul ran the State Street (SSIC) portfolio ($290 million in 1948) and the Harvard portfolio ($212 million that same year), the equity portion of the Harvard portfolio did look a lot like State Street Investment Corporation. As Paul explained when asked how he could do two jobs at once,

> **Investing other people's money, you can't ever say how much time do I give to A and how much time do I give to B. I could tell you how much time I give to studying General Electric or General Motors or Ford Motors. The application of that knowledge takes about two seconds.**[324]

In other words, the money management business profits from tremendous economies of scale. As long as you are not so big as to run into liquidity constraints, driving the price up every time you buy and driving it down every time you sell, managing $500 million (SSIC plus Harvard) is not that much harder than managing $300 million. But while Harvard's performance does not appear to have been hurt by illiquidity overall, it may have made a difference on some trades.

Due to the nature of the relationship between the endowment and the fund, State Street was able to run the Harvard portfolio for an extremely small fee, cost plus a profit that never exceeded $100,000 per year, or a total of about $300,000 per year. George Putnam Jr., Treasurer in the early 1970s, actually offered State Street a raise, which George Bennett, then head of State

Street and a former Treasurer (1965-1972) refused.[325] But State Street reaped benefits beyond the revenues generated. Brokerage commissions were very high during the years that Cabot and Bennett ran the endowment (1948-1972). The Harvard portfolio accounted for a large percentage of State Street's funds under management, and thus a large percentage of the commission business that it could allocate to brokers. These commissions were bartered for Wall Street help with research and trading that benefited the entire firm. In other words, State Street Research & Management got a lot more attention from Wall Street on account of its managing the Harvard assets, especially when it became clear that Paul was increasing the weighting of common stocks in the portfolio. So, while the Harvard account was not highly profitable, there were ancillary benefits and few costs to State Street.

One of Paul's first actions as Harvard Treasurer was to begin raising the common stock allocation, from 42.2% when he took over in 1948, to 57.4% by 1955. He did this by investing new money in equities and through the appreciation of stocks, not by selling bonds. Looking back more than a half-century later, this move seems prescient. But for the first eight months after Paul assumed office in October 1948, it did not seem that way at all. The S&P 500 stood at $16.19 on Paul's first day as Treasurer, but eight months later, mid-June 1949, it had fallen over 16% to $13.55. Paul had not shifted much money into equities by that point, so the loss to Harvard was small; but he was always outspoken in advocating his opinions and he must have been embarrassed by a correction that began the month after he took office as Treasurer. The post-war bull market that seems almost foreordained today did not seem so then. The financial trauma of the 1930s was a recent memory and many felt that the economy and the market would return to its pre-war state once the country demobilized. Even Paul was uncertain enough to worry a great deal. Nearly forty years later he remembered the 1948-1949 period as an extremely difficult time. And he was very much on his own.[326] What *TIME Magazine* wrote in 1962 would have been equally accurate in 1948. The analysts at State Street fed Paul "a ceaseless stream of information" on which he based his investment decisions. "Judgments and decisions, though, [were] his alone, subject only to *ex post facto* review by the University Fellows."[327]

According to a *HARVARD Today* article clearly written to appeal to donors, the U.S. Department of Health, Education, and Welfare wanted to investigate details of the investment process, including how recommendations were presented and who made the decisions. But Harvard's process only existed in Paul's head. When they were told that all of the decisions were made by one man, and that his recommendations were generally in the shape of buy or sell orders, they were "dumbfounded," according to the magazine, but could not dispute Harvard's successful record.[328] In other words, Harvard, and Paul, put performance over process; and for them, at that time, it worked. As the money management business became more systematized in the last quarter of the twentieth century, performance without a clearly defined process became suspect. But the period before 1975 was, arguably, one of less efficient markets; individual genius was a bigger factor in the market, and especially, in the public perception of the market.

Paul's virtually single-handed management of the endowment of a major university was unprecedented at the time and probably has been done only once since, by George Bennett, his successor. Cabot has received many honors for his work, most famously a doctorate from Yale that, upon his retirement from Harvard in 1965, recognized "your dramatic achievement for your own university [which] has brought long-overdue and appreciative attention to that host of unsung fiscal officers at Yale and elsewhere whose acumen provides the ways and means for the ends of education."[329] Harvard granted Paul a doctorate a year later.

Paul contributed to the endowment both through security selection (picking the best stocks and bonds) and asset allocation (increasing the proportion of equities). The calculation of that contribution, however, is a difficult exercise that depends upon the measurement of many thousands of transfers into and out of the endowment, all calibrated to movements in the financial markets. Also, there was no predetermined benchmark against which performance was to be measured.

A Putnam Management Company Report from the summer of 1955 noted a more than doubling in the endowment "since Mr. Paul C. Cabot became Harvard's Treasurer." The report dates his tenure from June 30, 1948, a few months before he actually assumed office. Of the $236 million increase, from $206 million to $442 million in this period, $65 million came from new money and $171 million from capital appreciation. However, the $65 million in new money about equaled the total amount of investment income drawn from the endowment for operating and capital purposes during these seven years. Thus the endowment appreciated by about $236 million, including income, from its base of $206 million, an increase of 115% in seven years or 11 to 12% per year. But since we do not know the timing of all of the transfers into and out of the endowment, that 11 to 12% per year is too precise. A fairer guess would be between 10% and 13 %.

This is a decent estimate for Paul's first seven years as Harvard Treasurer. A more difficult question is how good was this? A rough estimate of a benchmark for Harvard during this period, matching the dollars in each asset class by year with the average performance for each asset class, suggests that the endowment could have appreciated by between 8 and 9% per year through indexing (June 30, 1948 to June 30, 1955). So it appears that State Street's security selection contributed at least 1%, and possibly quite a bit more, to overall performance per year above what Harvard's particular mix of assets would be expected to yield.

It is likely that the actual number is close to 1%, because even this would suggest that Harvard did better in the equity portion of the endowment than State Street Investment Corporation did during this period. This was possible because Harvard paid a lower fee; the mutual fund included some cash, which had a lower return; and Harvard did not have to consider the tax implications of its capital gains. The senior State Street partners had most of their wealth in their fund and managed their tax bills carefully.

Security selection was only one part of Paul's contribution. He also made an impact by shifting money from assets that averaged little more than 3% appreciation per year during this period, to equities that rose at a 13.7% rate. If we posit a 10% differential in return between Harvard's equity assets and other assets, the value added by moving from the 42% equity position of 1948 to 47.5%, the Harvard average for the 1948-1955 period, was about $12 million, or almost $2 million per year on average. Thus, between 1948 and 1955, State Street's management, in total, probably added at least $5 million per year to the value of the endowment, at minimal cash cost to the university. Some would argue that the added risk to the endowment from the heavier equity exposure represented an additional cost. But considering the long investment time horizon that a wealthy institution like Harvard can afford, the risk was reasonable and worth taking.

By mid-1955, asset allocation had more or less stabilized, near 57.5% common stocks, 37.5% bonds, 4.5% preferred stocks, and 0.5% real estate. The common stock percentage had risen 15 percentage points between 1948 and 1955, while bonds were down by 10 percentage points and preferred stocks were down by 5. It fluctuated over the ensuing decade, but there was no strong trend.

Seymour E. Harris, author of *The Economics of Harvard*, and a teacher there for forty-three years, attempted to measure the performance of Harvard's equity investments, consisting of the endowment and a few smaller funds, for the years 1950 to 1965, the last fifteen years of Paul Cabot's seventeen year tenure. He opened his discussion by declaring that "Harvard's record seemed to have been rather spectacular in the years 1950 to 1965," but then, perhaps unintentionally, demonstrated that measuring that record is impossible. The increase in the common stock portfolio for the period was 473%, or 12.3% per year, while stocks overall appreciated by 380%, or 9.3% per year in price, in other words excluding dividends. Paul, however, did not distribute all of the dividends to the university; he held back on some and reinvested them. Also, as Harris noted, this result could have reflected the transfer of funds into and out of the accounts or into and out of equities. On the other hand, because stocks outperformed bonds by

7% per year during this period, it appears that Harvard, at least after 1955, was continually rebalancing its portfolio back to bonds to maintain a safe balance. If the 1950 allocation had been untouched, equities performing only in line with the market would have risen to about 85% of funds invested, whereas they actually rose to only 56%.

This writer's cautious conclusion is that while it is difficult to distinguish between performance from stock selection, performance from asset allocation, and the interplay of gifts and distributions, Paul appears to have served his university well. Overall, Harvard's investment funds rose from $245 million to $952 million between 1950 and 1965, or 9.5% per year, slightly more than the stock market and 3% more that a mix of common stocks, bonds, preferred stocks, and real estate that tracked Harvard's average allocation. [330]

The *HARVARD* Today article listed the following tenets as parts of Paul's "down to earth" attitude toward Harvard finances: "never spend from principal; never borrow from the government or anyone else; invest not just in businesses but in people, in good management."[331]

The first rule, prohibiting the spending of principal, is an almost inherited stricture passed from father to son among Boston trustees, and dates from the days when corporations distributed almost all of their profits as dividends. Some would argue that growth companies, by their nature, invest most or all of their profits back into their business and that institutions that require income are justified in periodically taking some capital gains to supplement their income. This is correct in theory but sometimes leads institutions to overspend when times are good; and it can be discouraging to donors to see their gifts dissipated rapidly, even if they are dissipated in a good cause.

Paul's opposition to borrowing definitely went against the conventional wisdom of the day, but again probably mirrored the preferences of the Harvard alumni and other wealthy donors. The government subsidized loans to educational institutions for certain projects like dormitories, and some economists argued that borrowing by universities was justified because inflation, then thought to be a permanent feature of our economy, had the effect of transferring the burden of the debt to the larger society, a socially desirable outcome to their mind. Actually it only transferred the debt if inflation exceeded expectations, since expectations are incorporated into interest rates. It exceeded expectations for decades, but not forever. Paul felt that it made no sense for Harvard to lend money to the government, through its ownership of bonds, and then turn around and borrow the money back. He felt that Harvard would pay for the subsidy by having to abide by the restrictions imposed by the government, which he termed "bureaucratic tomfoolery." And as for borrowing at low, subsidized rates and lending at higher rates, he likened this to "running a margin account."[332]

Paul's faith in management presents an interesting contrast to other equally talented investors like Warren Buffet, who believes that when a good management takes over a bad business, that it is the reputation of the business that prevails. Perhaps each was right for his time but neither is right for all time. In the most active period of his career, between 1923 and 1965, Paul experienced depression and war but, after 1929, relatively little structural change. While great industries like steel declined, the decline was gradual and strong managements could control their destinies. During Buffet's career, which took off just as Paul's was winding down, the rise of the economies of Europe, Japan, and Southeast Asia, the growth of world trade, the rise of information technology and the service economy, the fall of the East bloc, the bull market in equities, and the growing influence of the free-market model around the world put in motion forces so powerful that managements, in some cases, could not manage. In other words, Paul's faith in management worked for him, but had he retained his influential roles into the 1970s, when competition from Japan began to seriously damage the steel and auto industries, for example, he would have had to change his thinking or suffer a decline in his performance and reputation.

Indeed, Paul's performance, if not his reputation, did suffer during his later years, when he failed to fully appreciate structural changes in the economy and the stock market. As we shall see in Chapter VIII, even in the 1950s he sometimes stuck too long with older industries, and he was later than some to fully appreciate the stars of the 1950s market, like aerospace, drug, and office equipment stocks. During much of Paul's tenure, Harvard's largest industry positions were utilities, oil, and insurance—good performers but not great performers. The utility industry, including telephone, was considered a growth industry, as continuing electrification, the growing use of appliances, and the growth of the telephone network contributed to strong unit volume growth. It also benefited from the attractive economics of an industry with declining costs, due to improving technology and economies of scale, and the protection and stability of the regulatory system. Oil represented a large portion of the endowment fund in part because it was a large industry. But it also offered more opportunities than in later decades, due to the expansion of the automobile industry, capable management, and strong and conservative financial management. Insurance was a way to capitalize on the improving financial markets and the growing role of risk-management. Paul, whose family was wealthy and diversified, and thus did not need insurance, liked to say of his personal relationship with the industry, "always a partner, never a customer."

Paul had to fight hard on behalf of his principle against spending principal. Virtually all the Harvard presidents and deans that he served with wished to loosen the spending rules at least somewhat. Whereas before he took office, endowment income was distributed to the faculties when received, Paul held it back until the following year. And by always underestimating the amount of income likely to accrue, keeping what he called the "university rate" artificially low, he created a reserve fund that by 1956-57, and for a while after, had come to equal an entire year's endowment income.[333] In other words, Harvard could budget with monies already on hand. The Boston trustee traditionally did not spend principal to support current expenses. But Paul took this one step further and generally threw at least part of the endowment income back into the investment pool.

Paul did more to control expenses than just withhold money from deans. On one occasion he was sitting next to Boston's Cardinal Cushing at a dinner. He told the Cardinal that Boston and Cambridge were always after him to have Harvard pay full taxes on its property but that he told them he wouldn't even talk about it until they persuaded the Catholic Church to pay taxes on their properties. According to Paul, Cardinal Cushing replied, "Mr. Cabot I can guarantee you we are never going to pay a nickel's taxes on any of our properties; and by the way, if either city gives you any kind of trouble please call my office, and I'll settle it for you in minutes."[334]

Nathan M. Pusey

Paul, as a full voting member of the Harvard Corporation, attended all meetings; and while financial affairs generally occupied only the first few minutes, he stayed all day and made himself felt on virtually every issue, apparently not his agreed-upon role at the beginning of his tenure. Tommy Lamont wrote a memo to President Pusey and Fellow Francis H. (Hooks) Burr in which he complained,

> **I recall that when Paul became Treasurer of Harvard University he swore that he would not take any interest in affairs of the University other than investment matters. After a year in office he was the first man to have ideas on every Harvard problem running from real estate matters to future plans for the Divinity School and how bad our teaching of French was.[335]**

But Paul's most important non-financial role at Harvard by far was the part he played in recruiting Nathan M. Pusey as Harvard's President in 1953. Paul remembered a telephone call he received at home late one night in Needham.

I had gone to bed exhausted, and my wife woke me up and said, Appleton, Wisconsin calling on the telephone. And I said, oh, to hell with it. Tell him to call in the morning. I want to go to sleep. Well, she kept hounding me until I got up. And it wasn't Pusey on the telephone at all. It was Tommy Lamont. I had heard a rumor that Pusey was a Prohibitionist. I didn't like the idea at all. And Lamont is such a thorough fellow. He'd gone all the way out to Appleton, Wisconsin to see the Puseys . . . . And he called up in the middle of the night to tell me that he'd just had two Old-Fashioneds with Nate Pusey. I said, I'm glad I got up.[336]

Nathan Pusey, who led Harvard through the 1950s and 1960s, had many qualifications for the Presidency; but Paul Cabot and Tommy Lamont might well have ended his candidacy that night had he indeed been a "Prohibitionist." The six members of the Harvard Corporation, one short because the Presidency was vacant, and including Paul as Treasurer and Tommy, had to screen about fifty candidates for the position and come up with a manageable number. Since they were the ones assigned the task of screening Pusey, they might have ended his candidacy had they found him too provincial.

Paul recalled,

[Pusey] was not on the list from the beginning. None of us knew him. Didn't know anything about him.

Sherry Logan . . . at that time . . . was working for the First National Bank of New York, and he was a Harvard man, a friend of all of ours. And he called up my friend, Tommy Lamont, one day and said, a lot of these small colleges, the Presidents and so forth, come in here begging money from the Baker Foundation . . . . I see a lot of these fellows and . . . there's a fellow named Pusey, who is the head of . . . Lawrence College in Appleton, Wisconsin . . . . He is outstanding, and he is a Harvard graduate.

I was in New York when this happened, and Tommy Lamont said, bring the guy around to J.P. Morgan for luncheon and we'll all have lunch in there together and discuss this fellow—see Pusey and see what we thought of him. As a result of that luncheon, I and Lamont had no doubt that this was the man we wanted. So after that we recommended him highly to the other members of the Harvard Corporation, and they all eventually saw him and agreed . . . .

After we had elected him in the Corporation, we had to get him approved by the Board of Overseers, and I had to do that [as Treasurer] because there was no President [of Harvard at the time.] The President and Treasurer are ex officio members of the Board of Overseers, so it was my job alone to sell Pusey to the Board of Overseers. They couldn't nominate, but they could veto.

I can remember the columnist [Joe Alsop] . . . jumped all over me and said, never heard of the man . . . . I said, well, you don't know everybody in the world quite yet. And we had a kind of funny time about it, but the Board of Overseers finally went along . . . . He was just insulted that he never heard of the man. He thought he knew everybody of importance everywhere.[337]

Paul was especially anxious to get a good man into the office at Massachusetts Hall, and soon. He was one-fourth of the committee, along with Provost Buck and two Fellows of the Corporation, which ran Harvard after President Conant resigned in January 1953 to become United States High Commissioner for Germany. And he was too busy with other responsibilities to run a university.

Paul was not alone in supporting the man no one had ever heard of; the final vote of the Corporation was unanimous and the Overseers favored him overwhelmingly. But it was, nonetheless, in character for Paul to champion the candidacy of an obscure Midwesterner, the first non-Easterner to head the university, and by Harvard standards, a nontraditional candidate. Based on their meetings, Paul had decided that he was indeed able and honest.

So had Tommy Lamont, who wrote to Pusey that

[I]t may have appeared to you that the Corporation acted with almost indecent haste but we have seen you and liked you and we have checked you out rather exhaustively . . . we felt we couldn't do any better for Harvard by further investigations . . . .

[A]nd the added help of the drama implicit in choosing a Harvard man, born in the Midwest, the head of a small Wisconsin college, a man especially interested in college education and in the liberal arts tradition, and a Classicist. But we didn't choose you for these particular qualifications . . . We chose you because you were the best man.[338]

Why did Paul and the other fellows decide unanimously, most of them after only one meeting, to pluck the President of a small Midwestern college out of obscurity to lead America's preeminent university? What the Corporation saw in Pusey was a man shaped both by his secular humanistic education and his religious faith, a man who knew what he stood for and whose comfort with himself made him a capable administrator and leader, as well as university spokesman and fundraiser.

Soon after taking office, Pusey proved that he deserved the trust and high regard of the Corporation and Overseers. In the first days of his administration in 1953, he had a run-in with Senator Joseph McCarthy. Pusey had clashed with McCarthy, a native of Appleton, at Lawrence, and his experience there had served him well. But leading a national university presented a new set of risks and opportunities. At Harvard, not only was Pusey under a microscope, but he faced potential adversaries, including the Harvard faculty, who knew that whatever he did and they did could immediately assume national significance.

In the fall of 1953, McCarthy challenged Harvard over the Communist Party affiliation and Fifth Amendment plea of a faculty member. Pusey's response had the appearance of balance without compromising academic freedom or any other interest of the university. He asserted the college's opposition to Communism, because Harvard "is dedicated to free inquiry by free men;" and he honestly and accurately minimized the importance of Communism at Harvard. But when Overseer and Massachusetts Governor Christian Herter called on Harvard to dismiss any faculty member who exercised his constitutional right to plead the Fifth Amendment, Pusey opposed him vigorously, even though Pusey personally deplored the use of the Amendment in such cases. This won him an endorsement from the faculty. "Stubborn in the right, strong in his convictions as an administrator and as a man . . . he has made himself President of Harvard in name and deed."[339]

A few months earlier, Charles Cabot, the brother Paul was closest to, had defended Harvard's refusal to dismiss three professors, even while criticizing the professors for pleading the Fifth Amendment when questioned about their past Communist Party affiliations. Said Charles, a Massachusetts judge, in his valedictory speech as President of the Harvard Alumni Association,

> **The failure of Harvard to discharge these few is for the high purpose of preserving inviolate the principle that the scholar must feel absolutely free to speak his thoughts, no matter how heretical or unpopular those thoughts may be . . .**

> **The professor is protected far more than most in freedom of thought and speech, no matter how distasteful that thought and speech may be to the university that employs him.**

> The professor has a particular duty to speak up and tell his thoughts
> at all times, and particularly when summoned by governmental
> authority. Freedom to speak does not mean freedom not to speak,
> except that no person may be forced to be a witness against himself
> in a criminal case .... The professor, like the university, is not above
> the law.[340]

It may appear at first that Judge Cabot was articulating a new, narrower interpretation of the Fifth Amendment protection against self-incrimination; but given the occasion, he was more likely only voicing his disapproval of the professors' silence, expressing a moral obligation, not restricting their legal rights. Paul almost certainly shared his brother's sentiments. In the case of Wendell Furry, a member of the Physics faculty who had concealed his Communist Party membership (and that of others applying for sensitive positions) while working at the MIT Radiation Lab, and who pleaded the Fifth Amendment, Paul took a moderate position, supporting Conant's move to strip Furry of tenure and give him a term appointment, while others wanted to dismiss him for "grave misconduct."[341]

Pusey faced a very different challenge toward the end of his presidency, and took positions that hastened its end, but arguably served Harvard well in the long run. While "stubborn in the right" and "strong in his convictions," he lacked the flexibility to defuse the political protests at Harvard in 1969, in particular the occupation of University Hall, which, in a controversial encounter initiated by his administration, was forcefully broken up by the police. Given the mindset of the leaders of the occupation, perhaps no one possessed sufficient flexibility to defuse the crisis; but that was not clear at the time and the initial reaction to Pusey's action was unfavorable in some circles. By remaining consistent and rational in his actions, loyal to his principles, and articulate in their defense, however, he hastened the day, not far off, when Harvard again could put its traditional priorities, the advancement and dissemination of knowledge, above politics.[342]

By the time Pusey announced his retirement in 1971, the hostility toward him had waned and his performance during the crisis was seen in perspective. Professor Daniel Patrick Moynihan spoke for much of Harvard when he wrote that, "You were strong when many were weak. And you were true when truth was hard to perceive and harder still to avow."[343] Not everyone was supportive. Pusey had his critics on the left; and skeptics, like Joe Alsop, felt that they had been right in opposing his election in 1953.

> And I am not sorry that I did, to this day. We [Alsop and J. Robert
> Oppenheimer] were both sure that he would be a morally impeccable
> President; but we were equally sure that he would be unable to

enforce the new standards of intellectual rigor, which we thought to be essential. What has happened since, seems to me to have verified our forecast.[344]

Paul, like most other members of the governing boards, felt close to President Pusey.

Nate Pusey, who is one of my closest friends, is a very warm., thoughtful, nice fellow to be with. Conant was always meticulously polite, but I always thought of him as a cold scientist with not much warmth and not much fun to him.[345]

On the occupation and the other disturbances at Harvard in the late 1960s, he was characteristically direct.

The small hard core group [of radicals] not only lacks discipline but to a greater or lesser degree they are immoral sexually and otherwise, they are extremely rude and ill-mannered, they are intolerant and bigoted, and they are physically and mentally dirty.[346]

While Paul was blunter than the other Corporation Fellows and Overseers, and a bit overwrought, his views on Pusey and on the demonstrators were fairly representative. But Paul's description of the radicals was an overgeneralization. One student, when asked about plans to desecrate the Dean's desk, replied, "Good God, no. [It] was used by Mr. Eliot."[347]

Pusey returned their support, especially in Paul's case. While the President's frequent thank you notes, on the occasions of his many special services and special gifts to the University, were understandably effusive, notes that he never expected Paul to see were equally so. When Pusey thanked Charles Mortimer of General Foods for his pledge to the Paul C. Cabot Professorship Fund at the Medical School, he wrote that

[I]t honors one of the best friends the University has ever had, a man who has been my close associate, friend and advisor through the past eleven years. Nothing could please me more than to know that Paul Cabot is being honored in this way and that you are participating in this happy enterprise.

The note made an impression on Mortimer. He sent it on to Paul after scrawling on it in pencil, "**To Paul C**. I'd be damned proud to have Nate Pusey say something like this about me—But **you** deserve it."[348]

At Paul's memorial service in 1994, the then President *Emeritus*, eighty-eight years old but looking fifteen years younger, spoke of his friend with great feeling, with the clarity and force of a man in the prime of life, and totally without notes. He spoke of Paul's service to Harvard, of how he had relied on him as Treasurer, and of their friendship.

Since Paul retired as Treasurer in 1965, Pusey was the last president that Paul served with. Perhaps this was fortunate. Paul did not feel the instinctive liking for Pusey's successor, Derek Bok, that he had felt for Pusey; and Bok would not have followed Paul's lead on financial matters as unquestioningly as had Pusey. But even out of office, Paul tried to influence Harvard's management of the endowment when he feared that Bok might favor the more liberal spending policies advocated by former Dean Mc George Bundy, at that time president of the Ford Foundation.

Mac Bundy and Derek Bok

Paul's ideas again assumed national prominence in 1972, seven years after he had left the Treasurer's post. Mc George Bundy had taken over as president of the Ford Foundation several years before. Bundy was acknowledged by all to have been extraordinarily brilliant, but even those closest to him noted his tendency to jump into a subject he knew little about, quickly make himself an "expert," and then feel that through sheer brilliance and logic he had mastered it beyond the capabilities of lifelong practitioners—not a trait likely to endear him to Paul Cabot.

Yet Paul liked and respected Mac Bundy, and knew his family well. President Lowell was Bundy's grandmother's brother; and George Putnam Sr. was Bundy's mother's brother. In short, Cabot and Bundy came from the same social world. Had Mac not followed his father to Yale, some felt he would at some point have followed in his great uncle's steps as president of Harvard, a Harvard undergraduate degree seemingly the only credential he lacked. As Treasurer, Paul worked well with Bundy, the Dean of the Faculty of Arts and Sciences. He recalled,

> **Mac Bundy had a Scotchman working for him on his finances and so forth, who was a corker. And the Scotchman and I and Mac got along beautifully. We never had any trouble whatsoever.**

Paul compared Bundy favorably to the dean of his other *alma mater*, the business school, who had many more people working on finances but was much more difficult to work with.[349]

On the subject of endowment management, however, Paul Cabot and Mac Bundy were at opposite ends of the spectrum. At the Ford Foundation, Bundy's policies effectively, though perhaps unintentionally, encouraged colleges and universities to invest their endowments aggressively and spend a percentage of the total return, rather than just the income. An influential Ford Foundation report, *Managing Educational Endowments*, argued in 1969 that the pressure for income distorts asset allocation decisions by encouraging institutions to invest heavily in higher-yielding assets, even if they do not offer the best long-term total return. At the time, colleges and others were investing in bonds to boost income when stocks, the report suggested but did not quite say, were more attractive. Better to ignore the distinction between income and capital gains and go for the best risk-adjusted returns available. This was sound advice.

But the report went on to argue,

> **[R]etained earnings today are often more profitable to the stockholder over the longer term than those he receives as dividends. Many well-run companies in our present economy achieve rates of return on their invested capital that the average stockholder finds difficult or impossible to match in his own security selection.**

In other words, retained earnings are not only as good as interest and dividends, or as the Foundation stated in its report, "we see no reason in theory why credit for [the retained earnings] should not be taken in current operations through modest periodic supplemental transfers in excess of dividends and interest." Retained earnings are actually superior, according to the report, because the well-run companies, presumably those that pay little or no dividends, can invest the capital more profitably than can the average investor.

To the moderately sophisticated chief financial officer of a small college, all of this must have sounded like an endorsement of growth stocks. Equities historically had had better returns than bonds. One should therefore buy stocks and supplement one's budget by spending part of the capital gains. Furthermore, the best companies, or those that looked like the best companies in 1969, paid little or no dividends because they had superior investment opportunities and superior managers, or those thought superior at the time, allocating their capital.

Unfortunately, by the time the second edition of the report appeared in 1972, the Foundation had to backtrack on at least the inferred message of the report. Robert Barker, the chairman of the committee that authored it, complained that

> **subsequent public comment has made it clear that some of our readers believed that we were recommending common stocks and some went so far as to find an endorsement of growth stocks.**[350]

Of course they did. The report did not make asset allocation recommendations, but it did state that retained earnings were often more profitable than dividends; and it implicitly criticized the holders of bonds, which had the higher current income but the inferior long-term total return.

The Foundation, due to its prominent role in support of higher education, had the prestige and power to influence college investment policies. Unfortunately, it was exerting this power and influence near the top of the bull market. The institutions that followed the Ford Foundation's lead ended up spending a high percentage of their endowment at the peak, endangering their financial security, and in some cases were forced to cut spending significantly when the market fell by almost half in 1973 and 1974. According to his cousin, George Putnam, Jr., Mac Bundy felt terrible about this. And Paul Cabot told the following story about Bundy's reaction.

> I was down at the Mill Reef Club in Antigua, and by chance Mac Bundy was there. And he was a good deal younger than me, and he very politely came up to speak to me . . . in reference to the Ford Foundation statement [on endowment spending policies], which was fairly fresh at the time.

> I said, Mac, I've got one piece of advice for you. I said, you take the whole Ford Foundation portfolio, put it in your ass pocket, go to Monte Carlo and put it on the red, and if you win you're going to be a hero.

> He laughed, kind of sickly, and that was it.

> But at that time, when I said this, why, the boomerang had hit all these people that were spending their capital. And it did bust a lot of little charities.[351]

And hurt some that were not so little.

> Yale set up a group and then had a formula, under which not only did they spend taken gains, which in my opinion is completely improper, but if a stock went up, let us say from ten to twenty and they didn't sell it, they would spend the untaken gains in addition to the taken gains. I thought that that was completely stupid, illegal, immoral, bad, and so it has turned out.[352]

This was indeed risky policy in the 1960s and the Ford Foundation unintentionally led some charities astray. In establishing their spending formulas, there was no margin of error for untoward events. And the charities did not recognize the overvaluation of the market in the 1960s, much less anticipate the inflation that would plague it in the 1970s. But was it "completely stupid, illegal, immoral?" Not necessarily. If stocks go up in part because of the reinvestment of retained earnings, the distinction between income and capital appreciation, realized and not, loses significance. To some extent, Bundy and his Ford Foundation colleagues had logic on their side; and the highly successful investment management style adopted in recent decades by Harvard, Yale, and others owes a lot to their approach. But Paul's instinctive conservatism, while not informed by the latest financial theory, would have served these charities better in the 1970s.

The important decision, however, is the determination of the level of spending, not as Paul argued, the separation of capital from income. In the 1960s, the payout formulas used by many schools and charities were too generous. Restricting spending of the endowment to income would curb spending, but this was a clumsy way to do it. Conservative payouts tied to total return could preserve endowments for the future, and do so in a more rational manner than an income-only policy would dictate.

Paul reacted emotionally against the spending of capital gains because the traditional prudent Boston trustees, including his father, were strongly against it. But most of Henry Cabot's career fell during the period, before 1920, when corporations paid out virtually all of their earnings as dividends. And other traditional investments—bonds, mortgages, even real estate—had no equivalent to retained earnings. So spending capital necessarily was cutting into future earning power. But as the proportion of earnings that were paid out as dividends declined after 1920, the absolute prohibition against spending principal lost relevance. It had value to the extent that it discouraged overspending when times were good. But the thoughtful consideration of an endowment's resources and an institution's needs served that institution better. Bundy's ideas were not wrong; rather their timing was unfortunate and the spending formulas of many institutions were too liberal. The reader will recall from Chapter III that Paul and his partners shifted $10 million of State Street Investment Corporation's capital to surplus to maintain the payout to shareholders when they were hard-pressed in February 1932. To some extent, Paul's change in attitude in these matters represents the difference between being thirty-five years old and being seventy-five.

In the midst of this, Paul wrote President Bok on this issue and circulated his letter widely among Harvard alumni.

**When Derek Bok came in as President of Harvard, I was a little
nervous that he might be inclined to do the same thing [as Yale] and
I wrote him an open letter which was given considerable publicity
all over the country, particularly among Harvard men . . . showing
that Yale's policy [of spending capital] was fast driving them into
insolvency, and that Harvard's policy, if we stuck to it, would take us
through good times and bad times.**[353]

Paul was actually more than "a little nervous." He began by saying he had

**heard that you and other members of the Harvard Corporation are
considering the use of capital for current expenses [specifically part
of capital gains] in addition to your present policy of using *all* of
income on the endowment funds of the University.**

Paul underlined *"all"* because as Treasurer he had not even spent the
endowment income, only a percentage of it. He called the spending of capital
gains a "dangerous, unfair, unwise and possibly disastrous policy."

He then claimed that ever since Harvard was founded in 1636, we have had,
"other than for short periods," nearly continual inflation—not actually true but a
reflection of a great preoccupation of the 1970s. Paul guessed that the Corporation
would agree that inflation was likely to continue, in spite of "rather futile attempts
which, at best, may only slightly slow the present rather rapid *rate* of inflation."
He was probably correct that the Corporation agreed with him; but of course, if
they did, they were wrong.

Paul next argued, "If one spends capital, obviously, there will be less in the
future to earn money on." Less than there would have been surely, but not actually
less. If a company reinvests $100 million of retained earnings, and the stock
appreciates by $100 million, and Harvard sells $50 million of the stock, there is
still $50 million more to earn money on; not the $100 million there might have
been, but more nonetheless. This calculation is more complicated in an inflationary
environment, but nonetheless valid.

Paul then suggested that this policy, which he calls

**robbing the future to take care of the present . . . is tempting to any
present incumbent. He'll probably be dead or out of the picture long
before the inevitable fallacy of such a policy comes home to roost.**

This statement is unfair. There is no evidence that Bok ever thought this way. In
fact Paul, with his ultraconservative spending policies, appeared willing to rob
the present to take care of the future. He went on to say to Bok,

> **Your two predecessors as President of Harvard, with whom I served, always backed me one hundred percent in refusal to spend capital. Indeed, the income we "availed" ourselves of was, in fact, less by a few million every year than the income earned.**

Paul then pointed out the superior size and growth of the Harvard endowment, compared to Yale, which he correctly attributed to larger gifts, his own investment policy, and the endowment spending policy, which he had strongly influenced. But if growth of endowment were the only goal, they should not have spent any of it. Yale did spend more of its endowment than Harvard did for a number of years, and this no doubt was unwise; but that is no reason to honor a line between capital and income, when that line is determined by the dividend payout and accounting policies of corporations and the asset allocation of the endowment. By demonstrating Yale's overspending and its endowment's declining contribution to its budget, he made the case for conservative spending policies. But Paul wanted not only to maintain the endowment relative to inflation, and endowment income relative to the size of the budget, but also to tie policy to an accounting distinction that was relevant in Paul's father's day but not in 1972.

After noting the negative impact that spending principal would have on donors, an important point made more so by Paul's letter, he went on to suggest steps to cut expenses, including fewer students, no growth in scholarships, fewer faculty, more teaching by faculty, no new buildings, and fewer activities.[354] All of these were defensible proposals, but whether or not they were worth taking in the interest of endowment growth was a policy question that went well beyond issues of finance. The trade-off between the interests of the present and the future is more than an investment matter; and the distinction between principal and income is not helpful in analyzing it. Nonetheless, Paul's letter won the argument, at least for a while, probably because of his credibility with wealthy alumni donors.

His stature with the alumni stemmed from his well-deserved reputation as an astute investor and businessman. But it also reflected his active university service, particularly in fundraising, and especially his role in the Program for Harvard College from 1957 to 1960. Paul traveled the country speaking at alumni events at places like the Harvard Club of New York; and he solicited gifts from wealthy donors.[355]

The Program was a coordinated, university-wide campaign to raise $82.5 million for buildings, faculty salaries, and scholarships—more than twice the size of any previous campaign at any university and the first major campaign since Paul was an undergraduate. It owed a large measure of its success to an innovative marketing campaign that made good use of the media, including radio and television.[356] And an interesting sample of that marketing campaign was a story on Paul in the *New Yorker*.

On the day that Paul spoke at the Harvard Club on behalf of the campaign, the *New Yorker's* "*Talk of the Town*" columnist interviewed him for a feature. The column described Paul as this "ruddy stentorian Cabot of fifty-eight. When we met him he was wearing a Porcellian pig on his watch chain, a conservative gray flannel suit, and a rakish plaid tie . . ." Paul stated in the interview that the decision to go forward with the campaign was made at Pulpit Harbor in North Haven.

> **Tommy Lamont of J.P. Morgan, and Alec White of White, Weld, and I all have houses there and President Pusey was vacationing up the coast at Northeast Harbor, and David Rockefeller brought him down on his boat. Some of the others flew up. We voted to go ahead, and persuaded Alec to act as general chairman, and we were in business. We didn't know how much dough we were going after, except that it would be a hell of a lot. The President and his staff later presented a report on what they needed, and we told them to cut it to the bare bones, and they did. Eighty-two and a half million does not sound like bare bones, but it is.**

Paul explained that the next step was to solicit the present and former members of the Corporation and the Board of Overseers.

> **We figured it would help to underwrite our success if the guys running the show put their dough on the line. Now our special gifts boys are completing their research on how much money our wealthier alumni have. In a deal like this, you've got to go for the rich cats first.**

When asked how he felt about prospects for the fund drive, he answered, "I wish I felt as confident about my tennis game."[357] When a friend, Arden Yinkey Jr., read the article, he wrote Paul,

> **I have spent enough time in the publication field to know that in many similar interviews the reporter has had to fabricate a character for public consumption . . . . However there's no doubt that this story accurately reflects the subject. No reporter would have enough imagination to create the *real* Cabot.[358]**

The campaign reached its goal but had to be extended one year.

Jack Kennedy and Ken Galbraith

The campaign, which set the standard for other major universities, and the Kennedy administration, which drew many faculty members and countless graduates to Washington, marked the apex of Harvard's influence and self-confidence in the twentieth century.[359] Something of Harvard's smugness is suggested by Mc George Bundy, then National Security Advisor, who described a cocktail party he gave for Pusey and Kennedy in 1961 as "a little gathering of the President, the President, and the professors they are sharing." But no event symbolized Harvard's ascendancy in the early 1960s better than the Board of Overseers meeting that President Kennedy, who continued his service on the Board when he became President, held at the White House in 1963. Kennedy wrote Pusey, "There is much to see of Harvard here in Washington—not only Dumbarton Oaks and the Hellenic Institute, but Harvard men actively serving their country at every level."[360]

Of the Overseer's meeting itself, Paul recalled that

> **President Kennedy turned the meeting over to Pusey . . . . Of course, there was a little confusion about a couple of Mr. Presidents around, and Pusey ran it . . . just exactly as if it were being run in Cambridge . . . .**

> **One of the retiring members . . . got up to make his farewell speech and suddenly . . . he fell flat on his face. We all suspected that maybe he was drunk, but as a matter of fact, the poor fellow had a heart attack.**

> **Kennedy handled it beautifully. He immediately said, "We've got a lot of eminent doctors on the Board of Overseers. We've got doctors in the White House. And I'm told the wisest thing to do is just to leave him lay and let the doctors go to it, and so let's all move out of the room into the adjoining room."**

> **Half of the gang went out to listen to one of the members . . . playing the piano. The other half, including me, went in to sit with the President in an adjoining room.[361]**

At this point, Paul sat down on a couch between Kennedy and Pusey, slapped President Kennedy on the knee, and asked, "Well Jack, how do you like your new job?" When Paul confessed, "I didn't vote for you but I'm willing to give you a chance," the President answered, "Mr. Cabot, you'll have a chance to undo your mistake." Paul did support Lyndon Johnson in 1964.[362]

> **This was at the time that Khrushchev was raising hell in Russia. Suddenly from the next room, somebody feeling no pain, hollered back, "Don't worry about Khrushchev, but for God's sake, look out for Ken." Ken being Kenneth Galbraith. Prior to this time, I and others had tried to prevent Galbraith being given tenure at Harvard.**[363]

In 1949, Paul led the opposition to tenure for Galbraith on the Corporation, while his brother Charles did the same at the Board of Overseers. Paul had known Ken during the war when he was number two at the Office of Price Administration; Charles had worked with him after the war, on the Strategic Bombing Survey. Charles' experience in particular had turned him strongly against Galbraith, and Charles had influenced Paul.

Galbraith had been given the task of editing a report on the bombing originally drafted by Charles and had used the opportunity to modify the conclusions to better fit his own thinking. By his own admission, he had overstated his case to give himself extra bargaining room. In discussions held to resolve the differences, Galbraith argued with what he called more arrogance than tact,[364] apparently showing more self-awareness than he is sometimes given credit for.

Other incidents occurred that, in Paul's retelling of Charles' version of events, cast Galbraith in a poor light. But these others were primarily matters of personal style and philosophy. As Ken admitted, Charles had seen him acting in an "uncouth" manner; and he did not share Charles' natural deference toward the military. Galbraith no doubt raised tough and important questions about the effectiveness of the bombing of German cities and he believed that he, more than others working on the survey, had the independence to see the facts as they were, not as the generals wanted the panel to see them.[365]

But while he was less in awe of the military than were his colleagues, and this served him well, he may have overestimated his powers of observation and his ability to see beyond his own prejudices. As recently as 1984, on a trip to the Soviet Union, he had observed great progress in the economy. He based this not just on statistics, but on his observations of people on the street and in their restaurants, theatres, and shops. The key to their success, in his view, was their efficient use of manpower.[366] The Soviet economy was then falling apart and it collapsed five years later.

One could conclude that both Galbraith and Charles Cabot made important contributions to the Strategic Bombing Survey, which was conducted by a panel of imperfect men whose differing points of view kept all the members more or less honest, and the final report balanced. But this did not guarantee that the members would end up liking each other. Paul felt the animosities present among the panel members intensely, even though he experienced them secondhand.

At Harvard, Galbraith developed a reputation as a social critic rather than as a scholar on the cutting edge of his field. Clearly he had world-class ability, but ability devoted to criticism and public debate more than to the advancement of his discipline. If scholars serve society by developing insights and then systematically building on those insights, Galbraith specialized in the first part of the job. His most original concepts like "the conventional wisdom," "countervailing power," and producer manipulation of consumer response had an enormous impact on public debate in their day, and "conventional wisdom" has entered the everyday vocabulary of journalism and the social sciences; but his analysis did not go far enough to have lasting influence on the leaders of economic thought. In addition, Paul, Charles, and many of their background objected to Galbraith's ideology, which they saw as contributing to the Keynesian, even socialist, orientation of the Harvard economics department.

> **That evening [with the Overseers at the White House] I said to Kennedy . . . "How in the world can you stand that so-and-so Galbraith? Why did you make him ambassador to India?"**

> **Kennedy said to me, "That is the furthest away place I could think of to send him and get him out of my hair."[367]**

Paul told this story many times and loved doing so, even though he knew that the post was an important and sensitive one. In 1963, the Corporation, including Paul, had to approve an extension of Galbraith's leave of absence, and his tenure, so that Kennedy did not have to change ambassadors in the middle of a crisis between India and China. According to Paul, "It didn't make us like him any more."[368]

In the end however, John Kenneth Galbraith enjoyed the last laugh, both literally and figuratively, if for no other reason than for his ability to put the myriad conflicts of his career in perspective and to avoid feeling embittered toward his former adversaries. At a conference at Arden House, the former Harriman family residence, attended by Galbraith and Charles Cabot, a shortage of bathrooms compelled the attendees to walk down a corridor filled with them and systematically try each handle until they found a door that would open. Galbraith recalled turning the knob to one of the doors, then feeling it turn from within. Out from the bathroom emerged Charles. Ken had prepared for their possible meeting, in case the matter of Charles' opposition to his bid for tenure came up. After an exchange of pleasantries, Charles moved on, but he then hesitated, giving Ken the impression that he had something on his mind. He again moved on, again hesitated; and Ken became convinced that Charles wanted to talk about their differences. Charles spoke. "Kenneth, there is something I must tell you." Galbraith smiled encouragingly. Charles continued, "It won't flush."[369]

Chapter VII

North Haven and Needham

> But what I most hold to, most cherish in my memories of Dad, is his merriment, and his love of merriment. He loved to laugh, and to make others laugh, even if to laugh at him . . .
>
> He was a complex man in some respects; a man of contrasts. Along with his love of good fun, there was an element of mayhem in him. His sometimes hot temper was hitched to a short fuse.[370]
>
> **Frederick Cabot, at Paul's memorial service**

Productive people tend to love their work. Certainly Paul did. This chapter suggests that they also need to get away from it. They need vacations and homes and, if they can afford them, vacation houses. Paul was refreshed and restored by his vacations, by his homes, and especially by his house at Pulpit Harbor.

Paul's grandfather, who bought the land on Heath Hill in Brookline in 1871 for his home and eventually for those of Henry and Anne and of Bob and Ruth (Paul's parents, aunt, and uncle), made an even more significant purchase in 1880, land that has provided a summer retreat for six generations of Cabots, in North Haven, Maine.

North Haven

Phoebe Washburn Barnes recorded the following exchange (abbreviated here) between Paul and his brother Charles for her book, *The Pulpit Harbor Cabots.*

PAUL—My grandfather, Walter Channing Cabot, first came down on a steam yacht named the Fidget . . . .

CHARLES—I don't think so. Go ahead.

PAUL—He brought his daughters, amongst others, with him on the yacht; and when, in about 1880, he steamed into Pulpit Harbor, the ladies determined they wanted a place to go ashore where they could spend the night. So my grandfather built the Big House that is now the part of my property that I have more or less turned over to my children. Since his time, the house has been added to, and added to . . . .

CHARLES—You left out the most important thing, I think. When Grandfather cruised in here with his various daughters, he went to see old John Crockett down there where Bun Smith lives now; and he said, "I'd like to buy some land out there. I like it." "What do you want to do that for?" says John Crockett, "It's nothing but rocks and spruce trees." And the story goes he sold it to him for one dollar an acre. Six hundred . . . roughly . . . I think.[371]

All five of Walter Channing Cabot's children inherited the houses and property, but over time Paul's parents bought out Paul's father's siblings, and when they died, it all went to Paul and his siblings. Charles designed a more advantageous form of ownership, three trusts known legally as The Crockett Farm Trust, The Pulpit Harbor Trust, and The Dead Horse Trust. This prompted Phoebe Barnes to inquire about the etymology of the latter name.

CHARLES [chuckling]—That's quite a story and didn't happen until 1950.

PAUL—Harry [Paul's and Charles's oldest brother] had bought the farm and gone into partnership with Malcolm Crockett . . . . He and Harry farmed it for a while. Then Harry inherited [a farm] in Walpole, New Hampshire and Malcolm got drowned . . . Charles and I decided to buy in; and Harry sold us each a third of the farm . . . .

CHARLES—Well, the autumn before Malcolm got drowned he shot this white horse he'd had for years; because the horse was old and couldn't work anymore. It was too cold to bury him; so when [Malcolm] drowned that next May.

At this point, Charles and Paul argued about what month Malcolm drowned.

PAUL—Well anyway, Malcolm had just shot the horse before he drowned; and it lay there all winter. That spring my son, Neddy, called me up and said that Malcolm never got to bury the horse; and the horse had blown up and was very ripe. He didn't think with the prevailing winds the Chestons were going to like any part of it. So . . . the four of us. Poodles [second brother, Powell] was here . . . . Harry was supposed to be the expert. He was the farmer. We had a tractor with an old scoop and he dug a big hole, which turned out to be not big enough, along side the horse. He couldn't get it very big because he hit a ledge; but he got it what he thought would do. Then the problem was how to get the horse into the hole. Harry said, "No problem. We'll just tie a half hitch around his legs, and put the tractor on the other side of the hole and drag him in." And oh, that horse smelt something awful. Poodles ran to the side of the hole and blew his lunch. I came awful close.

CHARLES—We tied the rope around one hoof and the whole hoof came off.

PAUL—The whole LEG came off!

CHARLES—We finally got him buried; but his belly kept goin' up and down. We'd go over him with a tractor.

PAUL—And the tractor fell into the horse! Harry kept saying, :We gotta do this right. We gotta tamp 'er down. It don't look good if we don't." So we went over it and over it; and the back wheels of the tractor fell into the horse! And then we couldn't get the tractor out.

CHARLES—So that's how the Third Point became Dead Horse Point; and why the trust is known as Dead Horse Trust.[372]

The Cabot compound at Pulpit Harbor in North Haven was comfortable enough but far from ostentatious. Shortly after the Second World War, Cleveland Amory had described it as a compound of "Spartan-simple houses," totally devoid of luxury and more than a mile from the nearest telephone, which was located in the old Crockett farmhouse. There was no dock, only a few small boats that could be brought to shore by means of running lines. He contrasted this with the house across the bay, belonging to Thomas W. Lamont, whose guests, according to Amory, "have been known to carry away with them an impression of Boston high society as a sort of esoteric cult of St. Francis of Assisi—an impression which is by no means unpleasing to the cautious Cabots."[373]

Charlie Flather, who visited the family there while Paul was alive, feels that Cleveland Amory exaggerated the Spartan simplicity of the houses, which he describes as "comfortable, livable, practical, and relaxing." But Charlie, himself no devotee of fashion, notes, "They clearly had not felt the touch of the decorator."[374]

Use of the telephone was indeed problematic, a state of affairs that reflected not only the culture of North Haven, but the pace and intensity of the investment management business in Paul's day. While no twenty-first century professional investor strays too far from his cell phone or her Blackberry, Paul was willing to take a break from the action, let his portfolio rest, and give himself time to think. Perhaps a lifetime of summers in Maine had taught him how to slow down. Charles remembered that when he and Paul were boys, they would bike over to the village of North Haven whenever they could, and

> would spend nights at Sum's [Sumner Roberts' house] up Seal Cove; or with Dickie Hallowell. I can remember getting a postcard from Ma from Pulpit Harbor just two miles away . . . because there were no telephones . . . saying, "Don't you think it's time you boys came home for a while?" And we'd bike home for a night or two.

Not only was the telephone a mile away in the Crockett's kitchen, but, according to Paul's sister Susan, making a call was a far from pleasurable experience.

> The kitchen . . . had a high aroma. There were usually dirty dishes in the sink and dirty clothes around, and this poor, worn-out-looking woman there.[375]

Even the Lamonts had to contend with the telephone system. According to Charles, when Thomas W. Lamont died, he left $50,000 in a trust to the town. The trustees were Thomas S. Lamont, a lawyer, and the chairman of the North Haven selectmen. The lawyer called the selectman to tell him about the gift. When he finished, he asked him to keep the conversation private. The selectman answered, "Too late, too late." When the lawyer asked him what he meant the selectman responded, "Well while we've been talking I've heard five receivers go up."

Phoebe Barnes remembered the time Anne Morrow Lindbergh sent her family a telegram telling them that she and Charles would be flying up the next day. The central telephone operator became so excited over the news that she forgot to deliver the telegram. As a result, the entire town knew that the Lindberghs were coming—except for the Morrows, that is.

Things got better when electricity and telephone service came to Pulpit Harbor in the 1950s. But improvements came slowly. The system of running lines was a good example. According to Charles, who wrote a school essay on the family compound in 1915,

> **The rowboats were kept on "a row-off,"[also known as a haul-off] which was a complicated set of ropes reached by the steps that went down to the water.**[376]

In other words, this complicated but primitive system of outhauls existed virtually unchanged from the time Charles wrote his essay, and probably long before, until Cleveland Amory visited after World War II, and in fact well into the 1950s. Frederick Cabot likens it to an old-fashioned rope tow at a ski resort.

Boats and sailing were major interests of the Cabots. Without their boat, *Fidget*, they would have never discovered North Haven. As Phoebe Barnes charmingly puts it, they were "so bewitched by what they saw" that they decided to settle there. And major family passages were related to the purchase and sale of favorite boats. According to Barnes, the sale of the *Fish Hawk* in 1919 marked the end of Paul and Charles' boyhoods.

Some of their favorite boats were the ones the boys built themselves. Charles recalls,

> **Paul and I had a raft which we built. I remember well paddling across the harbor to Izzy Beverage's store where you could buy a big pink peppermint for a penny . . . . The raft was quite a contraption. Why we were allowed to paddle it across the harbor, and why we didn't sink, I don't know to this day. Once across, we'd let down a gangplank and go ashore . . . . It was great fun!**

One wonders if they had been reading *Huckleberry Finn* at the time.

And they raced dinghies—*Snipe, Wharf Rat, and Tobac*—the last being Cabot spelled backwards. Paul claimed that he and Charles "got so good at tipping over that we could climb on the side without even getting wet and sit there dry as a bone waiting to be rescued."

Charles remembered one race in which "Old Man Agassiz" had Susan as his crew and Charles sailed into the side of his boat.

> I was on the port tack, tipped way over so I couldn't see under the sail. All of a sudden, WHAMMO . . . . His language was so unbearable and so loud that his wife . . . told him he should apologize to my sister.

Charles added, in 1978 when Paul was eighty,

> Paul won't say it but he's won his share of races . . . and is still winning them. He's got a Fox Eye, the Samana, he's raced for years . . . . Even this season he won half the July and half the August series; and, also, the Fourth of July race.[377]

The most famous boat to visit Pulpit Harbor was FDR's Presidential yacht *Sewanna*. On July 11, about three weeks after the passage of the Revenue Act of 1936 and immediately after a meeting with Massachusetts Governor James Michael Curley, he took a three-week working vacation to Hyde Park and Campobello, spending a night near Paul's summer home at Pulpit Harbor. On this so-called vacation, he also dedicated the Triborough Bridge in New York City, attended a reception held by the Roosevelt Home Club of Hyde Park, and the wedding of the minister to Denmark, and he called on the Governor General of Canada.[378] While the President was attending to these duties, three of his sons, James, Franklin, and John, headed up to Pulpit Harbor aboard *Sewanna* to rendezvous with their father.[379]

Paul was the first to spot the Roosevelt boys that Saturday.

> I was up at my summer place in Pulpit Harbor, Maine and one day I noticed this nice schooner that came into our little cove. It kept coming in and dropping its anchor and picking it out and going out and so forth and I didn't know what was going on or who it was but we had an extra mooring handy so I rowed out to these fellows, and said wouldn't you like to have a mooring. They said yes, thank you very much. Well it turned out to be the three Roosevelt boys . . . and a friend . . . . They said they were waiting for the old man, the President, and they were all going to cruise up to Campobello where the old man had a summer house.
>
> They came and played tennis with us and then I said, wouldn't they like to come and have dinner with us and they said sure, so I got some of the local people around from the village, girls, and so forth, and

I said, now I don't want anybody to talk politics. I said, these people are my guests, and I said we'd really get acrimonious if we talked politics so forget it.

Well of course I was the very first one to break the thing, and I looked at Jimmy Roosevelt who then was living and working in Massachusetts, and I said, why do you want to back such a goddamn crook as James Michael Curley who's been to the klink? And I said he's terrible; it's disgraceful of him to back that bum. And oh he said, we [thought] it [was] the only way we [could win over] Al Smith.

Well I called Curley everything I could think of in the book and one of the Roosevelt boys, I guess it was Franklin, . . . said, well Mr. Cabot I couldn't agree with you more. He said, that's the most awful man, that Curley, and my brother Jim ought to know better . . . . but you've neglected to say the worst thing you can about Curley. I said, I've called him everything I can think of, what have I missed? He said, he's such a goddamn spendthrift.

Well this was at the time that Franklin D. was pouring money out. I didn't know what to say. I just looked at my feet and figured maybe the old man's a little tight in his allowance to them.

The President came in the next day, and the boys invited me out onto his boat.[380]

North Haven is a small place that had never before received a Presidential visit. It is likely that every resident of the island knew that the President was arriving that weekend, as was reported in the *New York Times*. Certainly Paul did. And the elder Lamont, a Roosevelt advisor, was a neighbor. It would be in character for Paul to deliberately intercept the Roosevelt boys, claim it was a chance encounter, and never really expect anyone to believe him.

Some years later, Paul's eldest daughter Virginia, who was nicknamed Christmas after her birthday and later called Chris, made a sign at the entrance to the Cabot compound at Pulpit Harbor that read, "WELCOME TO CABOTVILLE. NO LOWELLS HERE." It was inspired by John Collins Bossidy's ditty about the Lowells speaking only to Cabots and the Cabots speaking only to God; and some members of the family were anxious to distance themselves from the more formal Lowells. Actually, several Lowells had spent time at the Cabots' summer home, and had left evidence of their visit. In the

1970s, there were still some old silhouettes of family members and guests in the dining room, including Mr. and Mrs. Abbott Lawrence Lowell and his sister, Amy Lowell.[381]

When *Life* Magazine wanted to do a feature story and a series of photographs of the family in 1957, Paul and his siblings refused. "So they did the Lowells," remarked Paul. *Life* told the Lowells that it would do nothing to "detract from the dignity" of their family. But the Lowells may have looked more like "One of America's Great Families," the title of the piece, in any case. Ralph Lowell, the family patriarch, in particular had a great deal of natural dignity, [382] while the Cabots, in spite of their wealth, presented an unostentatious, even scrappier, appearance.

But Paul had a sense of dignity as well, or at least a sense of propriety. Domie Lowell told the story of how he and Paul bumped into each other at the airport in Chicago on their way home to Boston and sat together on the plane. The plane made one stop along the way in Buffalo. Once airborne, the flight attendant came along to record the passengers' names and destinations.

> **My name is Lowell and I'm going to Boston.**
>
> **Paul was engrossed in some figures, sheets on his knee, pencil working back and forth. When the stewardess came to him with,**
>
> **"Your name sir?" There was Paul sprinkling a few more figures.**
>
> **"Cabot."**
>
> **"Are you getting off in Buffalo sir?"**
>
> **"Hell no! My name is Cabot, I said. Where the hell do you think I'm getting off?"**[383]

Cabot is indeed a Boston name. But it is North Haven where the Cabots relax, regroup, and even get reacquainted, as the following story from Susan shows.

> **The story concerns the year that my son, Charlie, was a freshman at Harvard and Paul had been its Treasurer for some time. One day Charlie appeared and said,**
>
> **"Mother, you know I thought I saw Uncle Paul the other day as I was walking across the yard. I wasn't sure; but I looked**

at him very hard. If he'd flinched or shown any sign, I'd have spoken to him; but he didn't. He walked right on so I didn't say anything."

A few days later I saw Paul and he said,

"Susan, you know I think I saw your son, Charlie, walking across Harvard yard the other day."

I said, "Yes, Paul. He's a freshman and could be there."

"Well, I wasn't sure it was he. I looked at him very hard, but he showed no sign of anything; so I walked by."

I said to myself, damn it all! We've got to do something about that. If Paul doesn't recognize his own nephew, we'll have to go back to North Haven so he will! That was in 1952 and we went back in 1954.[384]

Lil and Chris in the 1930s. Chris felt pressure to set an example for the younger children.

Paul and Virginia Cabot with Lil and Chris, seated on the floor, Paul Jr. standing, and the twins, Ned and Fred, on their laps.

Anna (Anne) McMasters Codman Cabot with her twin grandsons, Ned (left) and Fred Cabot. Paul's children remember that their grandmother supervised their religious training—"with a vengeance," according to one of them.

**Paul (far right) and his surviving siblings in the 1960s.
Charles, Powell, Susan, and Henry.**

Needham

Paul's home in Needham was another refuge. Daughter Chris remembers it as pastoral, though its neighborhood is suburban today. In 1929, a newspaper story described, perhaps exaggerated, his weekend activities.

> **On Sunday afternoons in the winter Mr. Cabot may be found in a spirited amateur hockey game with his neighbors and their children on the pond on the Lee estate in Westwood.**

> **Mr. Cabot's rose garden is his hobby. His home, looking over the Charles River valley towards the Dedham Country and Polo Club, is situated near a ledge and in order to build his garden he had to do a lot of blasting. This gave him a big hole to play with, which he filled with loam for his roses.**

> **He rides horseback with enthusiasm. He gets exercise also playing squash.**

> **Robert M. Tappan, of the National Shawmut Bank, yachting enthusiast, says he is a fine racing man and cruiser and one whom anyone would like to have in his crew.**[385]

Paul's wife Ginny took all of this well—Paul's outrageous personality, his busy career, and his hyperactivity—as he acknowledged in this self-deprecating comment in the Harvard Class of 1921 50th Reunion Book.

> **I have had a happy life with a wonderful and long-suffering wife, and we both look forward to a few more years of the same.**[386]

The irony was intentional and the self-deprecation sincere. As Paul knew, his qualities of a direct, no-nonsense manner of speaking and nearly inexhaustible self-confidence, useful attributes in the business world, may not have worked as well at home, at least not on every day of their seventy-year marriage. The best one could say is that these qualities, which could have been unbearable in a man who took himself too seriously, were lightened by Paul's sense of humor and his willingness to laugh at himself.

Perhaps he did not take himself seriously enough at times. An interviewer asked Paul whether he confided his troubles to Sidney Weinberg, whether they discussed matters that were bothering them. On at least one occasion, they did.

> **When Sidney's first wife Helen died, we—Dickey and I took Sidney on this long cruising trip in the Caribbean—I think it was just the thing that he needed to snap him out of it.**[387]

Paul acknowledged that they did share their troubles, but protested,

> **I don't know that things ever did bother us too much. We had an awful lot of fun together.**[388]

In many ways, Paul was a lucky man and a happy one; and to some extent things did not upset him because his life was relatively free of problems. Yet the Cabot home was not an altogether peaceful home, nor was it an easy one in which to grow up, first because of Paul and Virginia's high expectations for their children, second because of what Frederick saw as the "element of mayhem" in his father. Chris felt pressure to set an example for the four younger children. And because, like her father, she has an independent spirit, they often clashed. Chris is outspoken, like Paul, but very much has her own ideas—in some respects quite at odds with his. Paul called Chris a "revolutionary" because she worked for Henry Wallace's Presidential campaign and, as a Mills College undergraduate, volunteered to wait on tables for delegates in San Francisco for the founding of the United Nations.

Chris has the sense that she was always disappointing her father. First, she was not a boy; and she felt that her parents had wanted a boy as the oldest. Second, she refused to attend Radcliffe, which she had heard too much about while growing up. Third, she married a New Yorker, not a Bostonian. In truth, it is hard to believe that Paul was disappointed in his oldest child. The Cabots eventually had three boys and two girls. Chris attended good schools, including graduate school at Boston University. In making a career teaching dyslexic children, she fulfilled her grandfather's guidance of "trying to make something worthwhile of our lives and have a regard for the well-being of" others. Finally, in marrying John Wood, a founder of the Boston investment firm Standish, Ayer & Wood, she chose someone whose career closely paralleled that of her father. Still, however Paul felt, Chris believes that she has disappointed him; something in Paul's personality must have created this anxiety.

It is clear that Paul either goaded his daughters or was unusually insensitive to their feelings. Frederick told this story at Paul's memorial service.

> **None are more susceptible to being mortified by their parents than teenage daughters, as were Chris and Lil when he escorted them and their mother to a fancy dinner at the Kimball House in Northeast Harbor. After an all-day sail under a hot sun, he was arrayed in a ragged shirt with a frayed collar, and in baggy khaki pants [his usual yachting costume] and he'd slathered his red nose with zinc ointment. He was terribly thirsty, and he demanded a lot of water from an apparently neglectful but more likely overburdened waitress. His patience was never great. That evening it was soon used up, so he hoisted his fingerbowl and drained it. This action so shocked the impeccably turned-out guests at an adjoining table that they all rose and left, casting reproachful backward glances and murmuring disapproval.**[389]

Frederick tells another story about Chris, Lil, and their father, about the day "when he quite literally 'lost it.'"

> **When Chris was about eleven and Lil was nine, on a hot summer day after hard exercise, Dad had taken a bath at noon and was sitting on the terrace of the Needham house before lunch.**

> **Chris and Lil were poking holes through the screen, which enclosed the terrace. Paul was wearing only a bathrobe and slippers.**

183

"Stop that!" he commanded. Chris and Lil didn't stop.

"Stop that or I'll give you a spanking!" They didn't stop. They kept on poking holes in the screen.

At this point, according to Frederick, "his sometimes hot temper, . . . hitched to a short fuse," got the better of him.

He bellowed, rose, and pursued Chris and Lil around the house.

Paul could outrun them, but the "kids," as he called them whenever he told the story, could cut closer to the corners of the house. With Paul's weight and momentum, he would swing wide and lose on the corners whatever he gained on the straightaways. Frederick continues narrating the scene.

In the course of the pursuit, first the slippers came off. Then the belt of his bathrobe let go, along about the second time around the house, and one can imagine the impression he made: red face, full frontal nudity, bathrobe streaming out behind. The kitchen staff (Irish cook, Hannah Shea, and a maid) were watching the whole event and laughing. "Go it gals!" they'd yell whenever the hunter and the hunted passed by. The pursuer never caught the pursued. After the third circuit, Dad gave up.[390]

This was the "element of mayhem" that Frederick saw following his father everywhere. Even on Sunday,

Morning might begin with a bang, or even two bangs, and a double-blast from Dad's shotgun into nearby trees from his bedroom window, aimed to quell noisy bluejays or crows, or perhaps thieving squirrels.

Then he'd preside at breakfast, a stomach-churning, traditional affair of baked beans and codfish cakes, which he'd season with a semi-liquid slurry of salt, lots of pepper, and Tabasco Sauce and vinegar.

Sunday dinner, a full-course extravaganza beginning with soup and concluding with ice cream and chocolate sauce, always featured a roast: beef or pork or chicken or turkey or lamb. If Dad could have his way, this roast was a bird or beast raised on the property. He'd salute the contents of the inborne platter by name: "Old Whitey" if pork or ham; "Old Blackface" if lamb; and "Midnight" if beef or veal. This practice rather dampened the appetites of guests unfamiliar with it. After dinner, Dad smoked a cigar, and when in a particularly good mood he'd chant,

> "Old Mother Har!
> What 'cha doin dar?
> Sittin' in a corner
> Smokin' a seegar?"

The element of mayhem in Paul would not have been quite so obvious if he did not so often have a gun in hand. Had he lived a few years later, he could have been a walking advertisement for gun control. Frederick tells us that

> He loved bird shooting—duck shooting at the Long Point Club on Lake Erie, where he'd spend a few days in October and November for many years. On an early visit there as a guest of one of the members he was fussing with the safety of his shotgun while out in the marsh in a skiff with a guide. His gun went off and blew a hole in the bottom of the boat. He and the guide had to peel off their shirts and stuff them in the hole to keep from sinking. Embarrassed by this turn of events, Dad apologized.
>
> "That's all right, Mr. Cabot," the guide replied. "Don't give it a thought. The members do it all the time."

On another occasion, at the Eagle Point Club in Florida, Paul was asked how his shooting expedition had been. "Great! And I even shot Charlie Coolidge!" who had been peppered from a distance by a spent #9 shot.

And while Paul liked to tell stories about Sidney Weinberg's mishaps at sea, he suffered quite a few of his own. Frederick remembers,

> Once when cruising with his men friends, an annual ritual for many years, his Coleman camp stove . . . flared up in a semi-explosion . . . . So he abandoned it and served an evening meal of martinis and shredded wheat. "No one complained," he reported . . . .
>
> Yet he could add an element of dignity to a pratfall. Standing once at the bow of the Kestrel to hoist the jib as she felt her way out of crowded Camden harbor in a stiff southwesterly, he was knocked overboard as a wind-gust slapped the boom across. He went

> straight down, feet first, like a plumb-line, disappearing for a long,
> anxious moment. When he popped up, it was in reverse order of his
> disappearance: first his battered straw hat still on his head; then his
> corncob pipe clenched in his teeth.

**As I've noted, a key winning aspect of Dad's merriment was his
willingness to play something of a fool in his own stories.**

Yet the atmosphere that Paul created, the mayhem that followed him everywhere, was not equally congenial to all. Paul had a distinctly masculine way about him, something that his children, at least his daughters, may have resented at times. As a tennis player, Paul was known as a "yeller," and "women and children were warned away from his offending language," according to Frederick, a frequent doubles partner.[391] Virginia was quieter than Paul, as of course everyone was, and a certain amount of natural deference may have been reinforced by the fact that Paul contributed to the support of his in-laws; and she may have feared that too much conflict would endanger her parents' welfare. But her children nevertheless remember her as a moderating influence on their father's behavior.

Paul was very fond of his wife's family, and while he was no aesthete, he enjoyed his father-in-law's music and took an interest in his career. Frederick Converse had composed a humorous orchestral piece, *Flivver Ten Million*, based on the much ballyhooed sale of the ten millionth Ford. According to Converse,

**He who wishes to express American life or experience must include
the saving grace of humor. I wondered what Mark Twain would have
done with such a theme if he had been a musician.**

His piece included a muted Ford automobile horn to represent the cry of the newborn infant, the ten millionth of its family to serve the American consumer. Not surprisingly, one of the first performances took place in Detroit, with the Converses, the Cabots, and the Fords all present. But because of either its flippant tone or its violent ending (it concluded with a car crash, possibly suggested by Serge Koussevitzky) the elder Henry Ford and Mrs. Ford did not like it at all. While Paul remembered it as "beautiful," he believed that the Fords were insulted by it.[392]

Paul's domineering personality may have robbed his family of some of the feminine influence that his strong-willed mother had given to him and his siblings. Chris definitely felt that something was lacking in her upbringing, except for one year when she lived with her grandmother. At home in Needham, there was very little cultural activity, even with a composer in the family. For Chris, "it was a real eye-opener," when as a teenager living in Washington during World War II, she had a Jewish boyfriend who took her to plays, movies, and concerts. During the year that she lived with her grandmother, whom Paul's children regarded as the leading intellectual in the family, Anne Cabot had a major influence on her education. Paul believed in college for all of his children because he wanted them all to be able to support themselves. But her grandmother, according to Chris, "pushed [her] intellectually" and opened her mind to learning, just in time for college.

There is a feeling in Paul's family that he was hard on the three older children—Chris, Lil, and Paul—but had learned to relax by the time the twins, Fred and Ned, came along when Paul was nearly forty. But the best statement from Paul of his mature thoughts on child-raising are comments he made about his brother-in-law, Junius Morgan, a man who should have been a naval architect but allowed himself to be pressured into the family business.

> **He was, in my opinion, an extremely nice man. I was very fond of him. But it was a wicked shame that he was made to be a banker. He was very interested in marine architecture and that is what he wanted to be, and I think he would have been an excellent one, but his father refused to let him and told him he had to join J. P. Morgan.**

Junius had no understanding of banking, according to Paul, and he spent his time entertaining clients and talking about everything but banking. One time, after the election of a new President, Paul and Junius went out for a drink. Paul made reference to the election; and Junius surprised him by asking whom they had chosen.

> **You mean to say they never told you who they were going to nominate?**
>
> **No, Paul, they never tell me anything.**
>
> **I told my two closest friends on the Board, Tommy Lamont and Charlie Dickey, that it was an outrage for them not to at least inform Junius Morgan what was going on.**
>
> **He should have been allowed, in my opinion, to be what he wanted to be, a marine architect.**[393]

Jeff Wyman was married to Paul's sister Anne, but for only sixteen years because she died at age forty in 1943. But he vacationed at Pulpit Harbor into the 1980s. According to Susan, Jeff liked the old ways. The first thing he did when he arrived was to turn off the electricity and get out the old kerosene lamps. He hated the telephone. His days consisted mostly of long walks and painting. Susan continued,

> **Oh, there are Pulpit Harbor stories without end we could tell you. And memories, mostly happy ones; but some less free from heartache and contention. It is the happy ones we want to pass on, however, because they go back to Grandpa and Grandma Cabot and to my father and mother. It is the good memories that explain why their children and grandchildren come back and build on Cabot land, and account for the Pulpit Harbor heritage, still being passed on to new generations of Cabots.**[394]

CHAPTER VIII

LETTING GO

In order to avoid being raped they consummate a legitimate marriage, but in either case they lose their virginity. [395]

Paul Cabot, on the plight of a company trying to avoid a takeover by a predatory conglomerate, Testimony to the House Committee on Ways and Means, March 12, 1969

December 8, 1941, was not a "Day of Infamy," but a poor one on Wall Street nonetheless. The stock market had closed on Saturday with the S&P Index at 9.38, down 11 percent for the year. On Monday it fell another 4.4 percent and on Tuesday an additional 3.2 percent, 7.5 percent in the two days following the Japanese attack. Paul was already working in Washington. He had not predicted Pearl Harbor any more than he had predicted the 1929 Crash, but he was in the right place at the right time. He had anticipated war in the forties, just as he had anticipated financial turmoil in the twenties. In neither case did he have a clear picture of what would happen; but in both cases he sensed danger.

In Boston his partners dealt with the unfolding events without him. The year before, when the Nazis had invaded the Low Countries, the market tumbled and State Street, under Paul's leadership, had bought into the market's weakness. Tactically, it turned out to be the right thing to do, though they raised their cash position a few months later. We do not know whether his partners called Paul to discuss the market after the Japanese attack, but their experience following the Nazi invasion almost certainly influenced State Street's actions following Pearl Harbor. They bought into the market weakness, reducing their cash position from 25 percent to 13 percent; and this time it was more than a tactical triumph. The market almost doubled over the course of the war from its December 1941 level. [396]

The State Street annual report for 1943 contained a notable announcement. In September of that year, Paul had returned to the active management of the fund.[397] During 1944 it moved in new directions both as a business and as an investment vehicle. At mid-year it acquired the Spencer Trask Fund through an exchange of shares, the first of nearly 30 similar acquisitions over the course of 35 years that netted State Street (specifically SSIC) hundreds of millions of dollars in assets.[398] Paul and his partners disliked the distractions of selling. But growth through acquisition appealed to them. With the help of brokers like Sidney Weinberg's Goldman Sachs, they marketed to smaller funds and family holding companies. George Bennett recalled,

> **That was less distasteful to the three original partners than getting back into the so-called selling racket because we were dealing with individual groups and entities on a one-on-one basis and this didn't require a lot of selling.**[399]

On the investment front, they became more active as well. The 1942 Registration Statement had noted that while SSIC does not seek to control companies, "it does from time to time express its views to the managements of companies in which it invests."[400]

But in 1944 it took this one step further. The annual report for that year announced that

> **During the past year your management has taken an increased interest and participation in a variety of problems affecting the companies whose securities we hold in our portfolio.**

Taking a page from J.P. Morgan's book and trying to influence the internal policies of companies where they had an investment stake, State Street took a particular interest in public utilities dissolving or reorganizing under the provisions of the Public Utility Holding Company Act of 1935. It also became involved in several railroad reorganizations during this period. It reported that during 1944 it had intervened in two proceedings before the SEC and also that "our efforts have been a factor in improving our position as investors."[401] George Bennett, who had worked on the utility industry from its rebirth at the time of the 1935 Holding Company Act, initially at First Boston Corporation and after 1943 at State Street Research, masterminded the utilities investment strategy.

George F. Bennett

George, who succeeded Paul as CEO of both the mutual fund and the management company in 1958, is, in later life, viewed as an establishment figure because of his Harvard pedigree and his successful business career. But his origins, in some respects, are as far from the privileged world of the Cabots and Saltonstalls as were Sidney Weinberg's. Unlike the State Street founders, who probably never set foot in a public school, George graduated from Hingham High School, where he excelled both at his studies, graduating *summa cum laude*, and in athletics. George enjoyed the benefits of a Harvard education and the valuable contacts he gained there, but he is very much a self-made man as far as money is concerned. And his contacts came about initially as a result of his athletic achievements, as a football and track star at Harvard and as a decathlete on the 1932 Olympic Team. A shoulder injury kept him out of the Games.

**George F. Bennett, Paul's choice to succeed him at
State Street and at Harvard**

George's athletic talents gave him the kind of privileges that Paul had inherited from his family. Like Paul, George had a confrontation at a party in his dormitory room, though his weapon of choice was a fire hose, not an ROTC rifle. But while Paul apologized to the dorm's disciplinarian, George wielded the dorm fire hose to keep the campus police at bay. Yet like Paul, George got off easy. His contribution to the track team was judged invaluable and he escaped expulsion.

A former partner, speaking of him in middle age and later, refers to George's low-key aggressiveness, his ability to usually remain calm and even-tempered, but to have his way through the strength of his will. While Paul's ambition was fiery, George's is more smoldering. He is usually warm and approachable, where Paul could be hot or cold but not always approachable at either temperature. Yet George can be very combative. This showed in his business career, but probably even more when he was Treasurer of Harvard (1965-1972), where his political and religious beliefs ran against the grain of many. George was a John Connolly Republican who had no trouble shifting to Reagan when the latter eclipsed the former. But in some ways he reminds this writer more of Connolly, a man thoroughly comfortable with the exercise of power in both government and business. Perhaps because of his relatively humble origins and his later success, he is very confident of his beliefs. In 1974, he told *Fortune* Magazine, "I do not consider myself an intellectual, but I think I'm a lot smarter than one."[402] Some who worked with him as Treasurer feel that the Harvard community underestimated him because of his conservative views. Paul, who admired FDR, liked JFK, and opposed Goldwater, looked like a "limousine liberal" next to George.

George is also more ambitious than the three founding partners were, and he never shared their aversion to marketing the fund and growing it. He recalled, in about 1990, that

> **Paul Cabot, in particular, felt you could do a better job of management with a modest size Fund, rather than a fund that was too large . . . . He also found the "selling racket," as he used to call it, repulsive. In other words, he didn't want to be beholden to brokers . . . . It was about then that I came on with the firm. They had just terminated selling when I was employed. Of course, I was always pushing to opening it up or enlarging it.**[403]

However, Paul and George had a defining trait in common: their devotion to their friends. George may be the only person who managed to maintain a close relationship with both Henry Ford and Lee Iacocca after the former fired the latter. Iacocca, who had been hurt by the way he felt he had been treated by the board at Ford, wrote that between jobs at Ford and Chrysler he had maintained his contact with George and "soon learned that he had been my one real friend on the Ford board." In addition to serving at Ford, George was on the board at Hewlett-Packard, and Bill Hewlett served on the board at Chrysler. It was George's recommendation to Hewlett, according to Iacocca, that got him his job at Chrysler.[404]

But George's circle of friends and admirers extended beyond his peers. Bob Beck, a young analyst in the 1960s, remembers his first impressions of George as "the steadiest person at State Street, an aggressive salesman for the funds, and a defender of the analysts." George believed that the research and judgments of analysts should carry as much or more weight than the accumulated wisdom, and prejudices, of the older, more experienced portfolio managers. Bob liked him for this, as did many, many others.

In spite of his conservatism, George always has a youthful energy about him. In his seventies he raced test cars at the Ford track. In his eighties, he could tire out his sons, scuba diving off of Bermuda. In 2005, at age 94, he was still making his birthday swim across Quissett Harbor in Falmouth, Massachusetts, a distance of more than one half-mile. Because George never wearies, or at least never shows it, he has always approached investment ideas, even from the newest analysts, with enthusiasm. George is by nature more cautious than Paul, but where Paul became more conservative and pessimistic with age, George never seems to change.

Perhaps George's spirit comes from his faith, or vice versa. As a young husband and father, when alcohol was taking a toll on his personal life, it was Jesus, he believes, who saved him. He became a devout Christian who takes the Bible very seriously and almost literally. He is personally closer to Billy Graham and Chuck Colson than to most of his business and political friends. While Paul in old age, like an Old Testament prophet, feared the wrath of the financial markets, or maybe even the wrath of God, George always sounds like he believes the good luck he has enjoyed in life will go on literally forever. But at Harvard, George was about as popular as Chuck Colson, before Colson found the Lord, and for some of the same reasons. Where Paul often showed genuine anger, George is a more controlled man who appears to enjoy a good fight, like Colson once did, and especially enjoys winning.

And win he did. Leaving aside the 1920s, a very unusual period, the record of the firm under George is comparable to the record under Paul, at least until the partnership was sold in 1983. The table below shows the performance of State Street Investment Corporation, compared to the S&P 500, annualized by decade.

Table 7
Annualized Investment Performance

	State Street Inv. Corp.	S&P Index	SSIC Relative Performance
1924-1929*	50.7%	21.3%	29.4%
1930-1939	3.3%	-0.1%	3.3%
1940-1949	10.7%	9.2%	1.5%
1950-1959	14.4%	19.4%	-4.9%
1960-1969	9.9%	7.8%	2.1%
1970-1979	6.8%	5.9%	1.0%

*From July 31, 1924

Again leaving aside the 1920s, and also the 1950s, we see that performance relative to the broad market, represented by the S&P 500, declined from about 3% ahead of the market in the 1930s to 1% in the 1970s, *per year after payment of fees*. Even 1% net on average for a decade is quite good. The decline, in my judgment, reflects the growing efficiency of the market.

The decade of the twenties is not hard to explain. That kind of performance is achievable today only in emerging markets, like those of Brazil and Russia, which is exactly what the U.S. market was in the 1920s. The anomalous performance of the 1950s is harder to understand, but can be blamed on both Paul and George. Paul was CEO for the first eight years of the decade; George led the firm for the last two, when performance was only slightly better. Paul's investment strength was his passion for facts, logic, and intellectual honesty; but he was a focused man who thought intensely about a relatively narrow range of topics. When something new and different disrupted his world, he was not the first to recognize it, especially during the second half of his life. In other words, the intense focus that characterized his pursuit of information and his analysis of it, the sharpness of his vision, took something away from his peripheral vision, his ability to spot things on the horizon. This is not surprising in someone who, in his youth, took to business and financial topics but was bored by literature, music, and even some of the sciences.

In many ways the 1950s was a stable decade for America, but for the stock market it was a new era, the first "double-digit" positive decade since the 1920s, with stocks up over 19% per year. And the bull market in the 1950s was led by newer industries, such as aerospace, drugs, and office equipment, just as it had been led, in the 1920s, by the then-new industries such as radio, automobiles, chemicals, and electric utilities. These older industries, the ones that were new in the twenties, did well in the fifties, but not as well as the overall market, and not nearly as well as the glamour industries of that era. Paul, George, and their partners generally did a good job of picking stocks. They owned the best utilities and the best oil companies. But in the fifties, the action was elsewhere. Even if they had picked the best stocks in each industry, it could not have made up for the fact that their portfolios had too many utilities (which underperformed) and too many oils (which only matched the market), but not enough aerospace, drug, and office equipment stocks. Add to this their practice of maintaining very large cash reserves, and their half percentage point fee, and you have a performance problem. At that time, there was more emphasis on absolute than relative performance; and by this measure the 1950s was a great decade for almost everyone. But many competitors did better than State Street.

George was the utilities specialist before he became CEO, and he had an important impact on performance, since utilities were the firm's largest industry "bet." But he was more than an analyst. He was, at various times, director of seven utilities, including some when he was quite young. Like most analysts, he liked the industry he studied; and more than most, he liked the people. He was loyal to his friends, sometimes to a fault, and he stuck with some utilities and other stocks too long.

According to Charlie Flather, who succeeded George as utilities analyst, Niagara Mohawk presented just such a case. It had lost a large amount of its low-cost, hydro capacity in a rockslide and it never again performed at its former level. Yet Charlie had to use what he termed "salami tactics" to get it out of the portfolio because George did not like to have shares sold of companies he served as a director.[405] But George's understandable unwillingness to pay capital gains taxes on these shares was also a consideration. George is a buy-and-hold investor who believes in buying what he considers to be the best companies and best managements and sticking with them through thick and thin, rather than trading in and out. If one's initial choices are good and if the world does not change too much, this tack can work well because it avoids liquidity problems, transaction costs, and capital gains taxes. But in the 1950s the world changed a great deal.

Paul, as CEO and President of the fund until 1958, retained final authority over all investment decisions. George was the analyst making recommendations to Paul, who made the decisions, so until 1958 Paul was still the person most responsible for the performance of the fund, in good times and bad. Yet sometimes the press was too easy on Paul. During the last third of his life, his personality and achievements made him a favorite among journalists, who tended to overlook his mistakes; and George sometimes suffered unfairly by comparison. A 1974 *Fortune* article credited Paul with steering "State Street through the Depression, World War II, and the Fifties with great success,"[406] giving the impression that the performance slump commenced when George took over in the late fifties. In truth, the performance slump began in 1950 and ended in 1960, shortly after George became CEO. Ignoring these facts, *Fortune* claimed that George is "cut from skimpier cloth" than Paul. But he is really just cut from less colorful cloth.

Paul was a leader of the generation of industry pioneers. Born toward the end of the nineteenth century, they were often, like Paul, privileged sons of Boston trustees. They attended private schools before Harvard, and they were clubmen, usually Porcellian. They were principled and public-spirited individuals who saw themselves more as professionals than as businessmen. And most were more interested in their reputations, including their reputations for investment performance, than in maximizing profits.

George was a leader of the next generation. Their origins were more diverse and their backgrounds more humble than those of the founders. Most were white Protestant Americans who had gone to elite colleges, if not Harvard; but one grew up in Shanghai and earned two degrees from Boston University. They were businessmen first, and very ambitious, probably none more so than George Bennett. George was the first in Boston to take a Brahmin investment management firm and turn it into a real moneymaker. Since Paul created State Street, the professional firm, and George turned it into a great business, each had a claim on the wealth produced by the business and each had a say in its future, as we shall see.

Paul Cabot's Role as a Corporate Director

When Paul retired as CEO in 1958, he completely divorced himself from the running of State Street (SSRM and SSIC). He trusted George's judgment and never interfered.[407] So after 1958, and especially after retiring as Treasurer of Harvard in 1965, Paul devoted an increasing share of his energy to his corporate directorships. The *Fortune* magazine issue of July 15, 1966, profiled America's leading directors, including Paul, and discussed their influence. It noted the contributions that directors could and did make—represent a company to the broader business community, objectively judge a company's performance—and especially singled out "the financial genius of Sidney Weinberg," who served on over 35 boards. *Fortune* identified the six companies on whose boards Paul served at that time—Ford (where he was later replaced by George), Continental Can, Eastern Gas & Fuel, Morgan Guaranty, National Dairy, and B.F. Goodrich.[408] On four of these boards, he served with Sidney Weinberg, and probably upon Sidney's recommendation.

At Ford, Paul stood clear of the details of the automobile business and concentrated on directorial responsibilities like monitoring executive performance and compensation and insuring the integrity of financial reporting and communications with investors. But his reactions to people and events are revealing.

Henry [Ford II] never liked his grandfather, but Henry adored his father, Edsel. So when he put his father's name on the car, he had

quite a lot of sentiment in so doing. But I'll never forget, when we heard at the Directors' meeting . . . of how badly it had done and how it wasn't working, either that night or the next morning Henry said, "Production stops today," in spite of all of this sentiment. It was a hard thing for him to do . . ., but it was the correct business thing for him to do.[409]

Of course Henry got the news before the other directors; and he no doubt had consulted with operating management. But Ford Motor, even in the fifties, had some of the feel of a nineteenth-century trust dominated by a single personality.

To Paul, this was not altogether a bad thing.

I think [Henry Ford II] is completely fair and completely decent, and I think he was one of the ablest . . . chief executives that I had any experience with . . . . He was very good at picking people, shoring up the organization of the company, of understanding the details of it, handling the people under him and with him, and of his general knowledge and grasp of world affairs.

Paul mentioned Robert McNamara, Arjay Miller, Ed Lundy, and of course Lee Iacocca as among the talented people that Henry Ford identified and sponsored.[410]

Paul's relationship with General Lucius Clay at Continental Can was more problematic. He had supported Clay's election as chief executive in 1950, in part because Sidney had recruited him, and in part because Paul had formed a favorable opinion of him during the war, when Clay was Deputy Director of War Mobilization. Unlike the navy admirals Paul had to deal with, he felt that, "Lucius understood our problem immediately and gave us first-rate cooperation."

As Paul got to know him better, however, he developed some doubts.

Lucius was the most arrogant, stubborn, opinionated man I ever met. I remember sitting with him and Sidney Weinberg at Sea Island, Georgia, just after Ike was elected in 1952, discussing possible Cabinet appointees. Lucius had a definite opinion about everyone. Good or bad. Yes or no. Finally, I said, "Jesus Christ, Lucius, there's a word 'maybe' in the English language. Don't you ever use it?"

After the war, Clay served as United States High Commissioner for Germany, from 1947 to 1949, which included the period of the Berlin airlift. When President

Kennedy faced another Berlin crisis in 1961, following the building of the Berlin Wall, he persuaded Clay, a hero to the Berliners, to accept a position as his special representative in Germany. Clay asked the nominating committee, on which Paul served, whether he would get his job as CEO back upon his return. Paul said that he could not answer that until he had spoken to Tom Fogarty, the man whom they were about to elect as the new CEO.

> **Clay turned to me and he says, I command you not to speak to Fogarty. I said, you can go plumb to hell. I'm going to talk to whomever I want. And did.**

> **When he was going to Germany, he wanted to know what . . . we were going to pay him . . . . It was illegal for corporations to pay people in the Armed Service anything . . . [and I] said no. I'm going to vote that we are not going to pay you a damn thing. And went out of the room, both of us mad . . . .**

> **Ten minutes later we go into the Directors' Meeting. Clay tells them . . . about going to Germany, and says, of course, I'm expecting no pay whatsoever. He . . . had learned in the interim that what I told him was true, that we legally could not pay him anything.[411]**

Of his later trip to Germany and his relationship with Continental Can, General Clay told an interviewer,

> **I absolutely turned the company over to Mr. Fogarty and went on my way. I was still chairman, but I was on leave, and I took no role whatever in the company. Mr. Fogarty used to send me reports in Berlin. I read them, but I never made any comments. As far as I was concerned, he was running the company . . . . I gave up the chief executive's job when I went to Berlin, and I had no intention of taking it back.[412]**

Clay returned after seven months in Berlin; and after doing a few special projects for President Kennedy, became a senior partner at Lehman Brothers.

Paul became involved with Eastern Gas & Fuel in the late twenties through his uncle Ellery Sedgwick of the *Atlantic Monthly* magazine. Sedgwick, a shareholder of Allied Chemical & Dye, asked Paul to look into the details of a proxy fight between Allied and The Koppers Company. Paul first visited Allied, which Sedgwick was inclined to support in the dispute. He found the management there arrogant and not forthcoming. He then visited H.B. Rust of The Koppers Company.

Rust had owned a boiler business which he had sold to Babcock and Wilcox, and became President of Koppers in 1914, when he led a buyout of the company, which was founded by Dr. Heinrich Koppers in 1907. Between 1914 and 1929, he had expanded the business from coke to other coal chemicals, gas and gas by-products, metal fabrication, equipment manufacture, and the production of automobile and aircraft piston rings, along the way developing many new industrial processes and winning awards for the company's scientific and engineering excellence.

In contrast to the management at Allied Chemical, Paul found Rust to be polite, open, and communicative.

> **The only thing that threw me for a loss was that he had St. Vitus Dance, and every time he would say yes, his head would shake no . . . . But I was greatly impressed with him. I told him that I'd come up fully prepared to give it [the proxy] to Allied Chemical, but I gave it directly to Mr. H.B. Rust, and he never forgot it.**

A few years later, Rust asked Paul to help him set up a new company, which involved Koppers acquiring Boston Consolidated Gas. This was unpopular in Boston, where many of the business leaders—at for instance the company's engineering firm, Stone & Webster, and its law firm, Gaston, Snow—understandably wanted the company to remain under local control. But Paul thought highly of Rust and he felt that a deal would be in the best interests of the shareholders of Boston Consolidated Gas, so he lent Rust his support and made some enemies in Boston. Rust prevailed and Paul became a director of what became Boston Consolidated Gas's parent company, Eastern Gas & Fuel. Unbeknownst to Paul, while Eastern was being organized, the lawyers needed a name to put in as president in order to file the papers of incorporation. They used Paul's name without telling him. Years later in an Eastern Gas & Fuel annual report, a list of all the company's presidents appeared. Much to Paul's surprise, his name headed the list.[413] In 1935, however, The Public Utilities Holding Company Act forced Koppers to divest Eastern Gas and Fuel. Paul stayed with Eastern, and thus separated from Koppers. Rust died shortly thereafter.

Paul had many connections with Morgan Guaranty, or J.P. Morgan as it has also sometimes been called, and made many new connections while on its board. First there were the two Thomas Lamonts. Through the Lamonts he met Junius Morgan, who introduced him to Robert Fleming and probably to his wife Virginia Converse Cabot. He also knew a later president at Morgan, George Whitney, through the Porcellian Club. Interestingly, Whitney consulted Paul when he was looking for a new president for Montgomery Ward. Paul recommended Justin Dart, who later merged his company with Kraft.[414]

During the period that Paul served on the National Dairy board, they owned the Kraft brand name, and Paul got reacquainted with J.L. Kraft, who had founded Kraft in 1903 and was still a director of National Dairy. At their first meeting together, Kraft recalled the financing mistake he had made almost 40 years before and asked, "Paul, what does Jim Trimble think of me now?" Paul answered, "I don't think he's changed his mind." To Paul, J. L. Kraft would always be a great merchandiser but "a babe in the woods" when it came to finance.[415]

While Paul served on the board of B.F. Goodrich, the company had to fight off a takeover attempt from Northwest Industries. Almost certainly for that reason, he testified before the House Ways and Means Committee on the subject of conglomerates, and the unfair tactics they employed when attempting to take over another company. His testimony, delivered in March 1969, is the clearest statement we have of Paul's reaction to the abusive practices of that era. And since many of these practices were adopted more broadly in the 1990s, Paul was addressing issues very similar to those we face today at the beginning of the twenty-first century.

Ironically, a practice Paul and others introduced in the 1920s can be seen as making the conglomerate boom and bust possible. Paul studied the earnings prospects of companies and related projected earnings to price, valuing every stock with a price-earnings (P/E) ratio. In the twenties, this was an advance because the traditional method of valuation, dividend yield, did not take account of retained earnings. But earnings can be manipulated through accounting in ways that dividends cannot be. In particular, companies that make acquisitions have enormous discretion in how they report their earnings. The conglomerates of the 1960s, and others since, manipulated their earnings in order to push up their stock price. Since most acquisitions were made through an exchange of stock, a higher stock price made acquisitions more affordable. In other words, acquisitions gave companies opportunities to boost reported earnings, which pushed up their stock price, which facilitated more acquisitions, which kept the "Ponzi scheme" going. The key was that investors focused on earnings, but did not seem to care about the quality of earnings—that is, how earnings and earnings growth were achieved. The conglomerates faltered only when their managements lost control of their many and diverse businesses; they produced earnings below what the market expected; and their stock prices collapsed. When the stocks of the conglomerates became undervalued relative to the stocks of their intended targets, the conglomerate takeover boom ended.

George Soros tells a story about the conglomerate boom of the 1960s that illustrates this perfectly. A key misconception of that time was that earnings growth was equally valuable whether it was achieved internally or through acquisition. After the boom's collapse, Soros was having lunch with the president of Ogden Corporation, the man to whom he had sold his brother's engineering business. The Ogden president complained that his earnings were collapsing because "I have no audience to play to." In other words, with a depressed stock price he could no longer manipulate his earnings by using his stock to acquire companies.

Soros notes that the conglomerate boom affected only limited sectors of the stock market and economy; so when it threatened the establishment, the establishment was willing to expose the abuses. In contrast, during the 1990s, the establishment was complicit in the abuses, which therefore lay largely hidden until the boom collapsed.[416] In the case of B.F. Goodrich, friends and fellow board members no doubt prevailed upon Paul to speak out in defense of certain principles; but his testimony makes clear that it was the principles that moved him to action, not his loyalty to any establishment group.

In his testimony before the House Ways and Means Committee, Paul implicitly acknowledged the impact that government policies had on the economy and the financial markets and argued for policies that minimized the human and economic dislocations that resulted from the then-current frenzy of takeover activity. This represented a departure from the position he had advocated in 1928-29, one that assumed that government's role in the economy should be restricted to requiring openness and disclosure so that market participants could act in an informed manner.

Paul first declared that,

> It's my opinion that most of [the conglomerates] do and already have done our economy great harm, and that in the long run their shareholders will suffer.

He then went on to describe how they acquire operating companies.

> Company A, a small conglomerate, first quietly buys in the open market all the stock it can up to 10% of the company to be acquired.

Buying more than ten percent would have required a filing with the SEC.

> Company A then is very likely to go to other large pools of money and on a confidential basis say to these pools, "We are about to make a tender offer for Company B at an apparent price far greater than the present market price. Why don't you buy a big block of the stock and then when we make the tender offer you will vote with us and can make a large, quick profit on that offer." After a delay to permit the purchase of shares by those who will support the tender offer, Company A makes a public statement of the "takeover" offer followed by registration with the Securities and Exchange Commission.

Paul explained that the offer generally took the form of subordinated debentures convertible into the stock of the acquiring company, or convertible preferred stock, or warrants to purchase an already overvalued stock for an even higher price. He called the securities "funny money" because their intrinsic value was often far below the price at which they initially traded, and he claimed that the entire process was inflationary because it inflated securities prices. Overvalued securities can indeed contribute to inflation, though over a sustained period they can contribute to deflation as well if they lower the cost of capital and thereby encourage the building of excess capacity.

The process was disruptive even if the conglomerate did not win the battle for the target company. The target often offered itself to a third party, a company whose management was thought to be less undesirable than that of the conglomerate. As Paul explained to the House Ways and Means Committee,

In order to avoid being raped they consummate a legitimate marriage, but in either case they lose their virginity.

If it merged with this third company, the conglomerate lost the battle but still won the war because it made a profit by tendering its shares to the "winner." It also made a profit for its allies. And as a result, it could end up with both more money and wealthier allies for its next takeover attempt. According to Paul, "Grave doubts have been expressed that many of the announced 'takeovers' were ever intended to succeed." And if the target company managed to remain independent, it often did so by adopting extreme measures like taking on too much debt, which could be destabilizing.

If the conglomerate succeeded in acquiring the target company, conflict often arose between the management of the conglomerate, financially motivated and impatient with the plodding strategy of the operating company, and the operating management, dissatisfied with the opportunistic, "get rich quick" style of the predatory conglomerate. Paul supported his argument with quotes from the U.S. Assistant Attorney General, who expressed "serious concern over the severe human and economic dislocations" resulting from "merger mania," and from a *New York Times* story detailing the "human and economic dislocations" resulting from an attempt to take over Allis-Chalmers. Another concern was the depressing impact on business investment resulting from the "winner's" need to service the debt assumed during the course of the takeover.

Paul concluded his testimony by comparing the current problems to past "problems all born of greed and a lust for power," including tulip bulb speculation in Holland, the era of the Robber Barons, the Florida land boom and bust, and the utility holding company scandals, this last highlighting certain similarities between the investment trusts of the twenties and the conglomerates of the sixties.

Clearly, by 1969, he had concluded that when powerful interests, unrestrained by simple decency, preyed upon the weak, or even the slightly less powerful, a change in government policy was needed to preserve the relationships that held society and the economy in balance.[417]

Paul's arguments made logical sense, but he was also following his instincts in trying to prevent those whom he considered speculators from undermining legitimate business enterprise. Just as Paul reacted viscerally against Harvard's proposed spending of endowment principal, he reacted against the conglomerates for reasons of the heart as much as for reasons of the mind. Not only did the conglomerates of the 1960s look like the trusts of the 1920s, but Paul had probably inherited the moralistic point of view that John Brooks outlines in his financial history of the 1960s. Brooks argues that the "Puritan and craft ethic" of the nineteenth century, which survived into the sixties, dictated that "the shoemaker should stick to his last." Diversification was irresponsible, if not immoral.[418]

In the end, B.F. Goodrich turned some of the tactics of the conglomerates against them to thwart the takeover. It used accounting gimmickry to boost its own earnings and stock price. It made acquisitions of its own to make it a less digestible target. It launched a public relations campaign. It instituted staggered terms for its directors so that outsiders could not gain control of the board in one year. And it used its political influence in both Washington and at the state level.[419]

Paul's Years of Pessimism

In his seventies, between 1968 and 1978, Paul, like many of his generation, found himself at odds with much of the society around him—the "Go-Go" stock market with its conglomerates, takeovers, and lax ethical standards; student radicals that brought Harvard to its knees and hastened the retirement of his friend Nathan Pusey; the aggressive spending policies of colleges and charities that, for a time, seemed like they might undermine even Harvard's financial policies. In February 1969, he told *Fortune* magazine that he could "see things brewing right now that could be more troublesome than what we had in 1929." In fact 1969 was not 1929; but whereas in 1929 Paul and his partners were "young and not particularly frightened," by 1969 Paul, at least, had lost his youthful optimism.

And it didn't help that for a while Paul's extreme pessimism seemed justified. The S&P 500, which ended 1968 at 104, fell to 92 by the end of 1969 and to 69 by May of 1970, or a drop of one-third in 17 months. Some stock groups, like the conglomerates, did far worse, falling over 80 percent. Other events of more national importance added to the gloom that Paul and many other people felt. The My Lai massacre, the Bobby Seale trial, race riots, the incursion into Cambodia, the Kent State shootings, high interest rates, and a depressed dollar produced what John Brooks fairly calls "one of the deepest moods of gloom to darken any American April since the Civil War." Things did not get a lot better the following month. Brooks points out that by May, a portfolio consisting of one share of each stock listed on the New York Stock Exchange had fallen by about half since the end of 1968. But by April of 1971, the more established stocks at least, those included in the S&P Index, had recovered to a level above the 1968 close.[420]

In June of 1970, a month after the bottom, *Fortune* asked Paul to update the prediction he had made 16 months before. Even after the market correction, he was scarcely more optimistic.

> **I don't think the worst is over . . . . I'm afraid we're going to see some major scandals, and these are going to shake confidence even further. We may even see some things on the scale of Ivar Kreuger's collapse 50 years back. How's all this business with [Bernard] Cornfeld and [John] King going to end? And these highly pyramided conglomerates? . . . There's got to be more of a purge before we get back to normal again.**

Paul seemed to be looking for a cataclysmic cleansing of the system of nearly biblical proportions, or at least on the scale of the 1929 crash.

He next gave his very pessimistic views on the economy and earnings for the rest of 1970. I suspect that *Fortune* cleaned up his language.

> **I think some of these economists are full of bull with their standard talk about a pickup in the second half . . . . We see report after report for the first quarter with sales up but profits down. Well, what happens when sales go down too? With costs escalating, there's got to be a terrible squeeze on profits . . . .**
>
> **I won't buy stocks until I see at least some hope of an increase in earnings. I can't see it now. Practically every company we look at is bound to earn less. My young men at State Street come in with drastically reduced earnings every time they look. I tell them: "Go back and look again; you haven't reduced the estimates enough."[421]**

Paul was so worried that he endorsed controls on wages and prices, a level of government interference that he never would have endorsed when he was young.

In spite of his hostility to student radicals, he was no fan of the Vietnam War, and blamed it for some of the stock market's difficulties.

> **The best thing the Government could do would be to take the whole damned works out of Asia and go home. Then I think the stock market would go through the roof. But I don't see it doing that.**

Toward the end of the interview, Paul did voice guarded optimism for the longer term.

> **I'm sure that stocks bought today will show a good profit a few years from now, but I'm gambling and waiting to see them go down further.**[422]

They didn't go down further until 1973.

Given that Paul was independent and correct about the outlook for the market in the early twenties and the late forties, one might have expected him to see the seventies, at least 1974, as a buying opportunity as well, or at least to have an unconventional view of the period. But Paul became more pessimistic as the market declined, thus mirroring the pessimism of the era.

John Train captures this best in his generally flattering portrait of Paul in *The Money Masters*, based on an interview conducted in 1978. He began with a description of Paul's office at 225 Franklin Street, which, in contrast to the other offices at State Street Research & Management Co. with their look of modern efficiency, reminded him of his Harvard tutor's study, *circa* 1948. There was the old pencil sharpener, the wooden chairs, a wooden coat rack holding a plain hat and coat, a glass-fronted bookcase, and a large plain desk, behind which sat Paul Cabot in a "grayish tweedy suit with a vest."[423]

Train neglected to mention the pictures on the wall, a half-dozen prints of caged, crazed rats each engaged in a fight to the death for the amusement of an assemblage of equally crazed rat-like men, cheering wildly, betting slips in hand—the very picture of mayhem. These may have merely signified his allegiance to the Wharf Rats Club, a gentlemen's eating club in Boston. But it also probably suggested Paul's enjoyment of chaos and uncertainty and his ability to remove himself from passions of the day.

But this was not so during the 1970s. When asked how he invested his money he answered,

> **I have a big slug of good-grade municipals. Not New York . . . smaller towns with a sense of responsibility. Needham, where I live . . . Newton. I keep them short and roll them over.**[424]

One of the great equity investors of the twentieth century, at a low point in the market, had a "big slug" of his money in municipal bonds, in the town in which he lived and in the adjoining town. It is reminiscent of Philip Dexter who, according to Cleveland Amory, never invested in anything he couldn't see from his office window.[425] But Paul was one of the few who defied the conservatism of the early twenties and late forties. What caused his lack of confidence?

Not counting wars, which have produced sharp but brief drops in the stock market, three more purely financial conditions have sapped the confidence of equity investors at various times since the 1920s—lack of trust in the fairness of markets, depression or recession, and inflation. Wealthy and sophisticated investors always had, or thought they had, the ability and the resources to protect themselves against the first two. They were generally wise to fraud, or at least they were diversified enough to survive it; and their bonds and defensive stocks held up reasonably well in recession and depression. Inflation was always the great leveler, the hardest for the wealthy to guard against. It distorts the ruler used to measure financial transactions and, in particular, it distorts real corporate profits by understating the amount of capital investment required to maintain and grow earnings. They could invest short and roll over their investments, like Paul; and they could buy gold or other natural resources. But gold was more the choice of the European elites with their long memories of broken governments and busted currencies. In the seventies Paul was content to protect himself with a return on municipals that was below the rate of inflation, just to slow his real loss of capital. Train asked Cabot what was the greatest danger to investments.

> **Inflation. It's the biggest problem in the world. I don't think we can do a goddamn thing about it. We'll probably go the way of England and Italy. Look at all these government budget deficits—frightening! I'm pessimistic as hell on that . . . . You've sure built inflation into the system. How are you going to change that?**[426]

Paul concluded that in the future, investors would not be able to earn a real return on capital. Had inflation stayed where it was in the 1970s, he might well have been correct.

George Bennett presents an interesting contrast. While he too was temporarily demoralized during the 1970s by the economic policies of President Jimmy Carter and Federal Reserve Board Chairman G. William Miller, he never lost his faith that things would get better. He came as close to calling the bull market of the 1980s as anyone. In January of 1982, seven months before the market bottom, he told the *Boston Globe* that

> [The stock market] will be much bigger than anyone forecasts. Reagan
> will tough it out through the trouble of the 1982 elections. Then, the
> reductions in government expenditures and the tax bill will pay off. In
> my view the risks are greater being out of stocks than in them.[427]

George, as a political partisan, probably felt that his optimism was a form of loyalty to the President. But he did see that Reagan's policies, along with those of Carter appointee Paul Volcker, would produce lower inflation and an upsurge in innovation and entrepreneurial activity. One day, early in the recovery, he took a poll at lunch, asking all present how long the economic expansion would last. His answer, until 1988, was closest to being correct.

The Final Years of State Street Research

But the economy and the stock market were not the only concerns of the State Street partners in the early 1980s. Throughout his tenure as CEO, George constantly grew and diversified the asset base, first through acquisitions, then exchange funds, and then through other private clients, especially pension funds. Exchange funds allowed wealthy investors with large blocs of low-cost stock to buy in with their stock. The fund assumed the low cost basis for tax purposes, and the investors benefited from diversification, owning a portfolio rather than a single stock. State Street launched the first successful exchange fund, Federal Street Fund, in 1961, aided by Paul's close relationship with Sidney Weinberg and Goldman Sachs, which underwrote it. Goldman had previously had a policy against dealing with mutual funds, dating from the twenties when their name was synonymous with their unsuccessful equity fund; and Eddie Cantor, who had lost a lot of money in it, used them as the butt of his comedy routine. An exchange fund, at least initially, reflected whatever the available pool of investors happened to own in size, but given State Street's connections and those of Goldman Sachs, the stocks offered were overwhelmingly blue-chip. The Internal Revenue Service no longer permits the formation of exchange funds.

After the launch of Federal Street Fund, the Goldman Sachs team came to Boston for a celebratory dinner held at the Wharf Rats Club, or "the Rats," which occupied a series of warehouse-type rooms on one of the upper floors of an old wharf. After many rounds of drinks and Paul's rendition of the club song, more notable for its colorful lyrics than for its aesthetic merits, Sidney rose to speak. He looked around the room and exclaimed, "What a dump! You mean I came all the way from New York for this?"

State Street Research entered the pension fund management business in 1967 with their first client, General Mills, followed closely by Monsanto, Sinclair Oil,

IBM, and Mobil; but the business really took off in 1974 with the passage of the Employee Retirement Income Security Act. ERISA held trustees legally liable for the safety of funds in their care and it therefore encouraged the hiring of the older, more established, more conservative money managers. In other words, it encouraged the hiring of State Street Research & Management Company, among others. While this was lucky, George grabbed this opportunity and ran hard with it. He traveled all over the world to sell State Street's services and he used his personal connections skillfully. Ford, the Hewlett Foundation, and The Billy Graham Foundation, all controlled by George's best friends, became important clients while George ran the firm. Over the decade of the 1970s, State Street's (SSRM's) assets under management grew from under $2 billion to over $10 billion, and revenues and profits grew proportionately, in part because of ERISA, but also because of energetic marketing, and in spite of a mediocre stock market and a friendly divorce in 1974 from the Harvard endowment account.

While George clearly had the ambition needed to build State Street Research, another executive, Peter Vermilye, who joined the company in 1965, had the know-how and contacts required to succeed in the pension fund market. Before the late sixties, the banks controlled that business and Vermilye, who had run the pension operation at J.P. Morgan and had met Paul Cabot there, knew all of the best potential customers. He was the person most responsible for winning the first pension accounts. Even at Ford, where Cabot had known the chairman for decades, Vermilye knew the key decision makers at the fund. State Street's investment expertise and reputation and Vermilye's stature among pension executives were an unbeatable combination, and the continued presence of Paul Cabot, even in semi-retirement, probably didn't hurt. Money poured in the door. Charlie Flather, who worked with Vermilye at both marketing and investing, remembers winning one large account even though the client's chief financial officer snored loudly during the sales presentation.

Vermilye remained with State Street for five years. He had been given a large partnership share upon joining and had hoped to succeed George upon the latter's retirement, which as it turned out was still decades away. After a disagreement, Peter left to become the first chief executive of Alliance Capital Management. When Vermilye left, the remaining portfolio managers had to work hard to reassure the clients whom he had brought to State Street, since Vermilye and Flather had managed these accounts alone. All of the clients agreed to stick with the firm except for General Mills, which felt that they had hired the man more than the company. Vermilye suggested that they split the account and leave half with State Street; but they did not.[428]

The State Street partnership had always changed hands at book value; and it was a people-intensive business with little in the way of assets other than the brains, ability, energy, and courage of its partners and professional employees. A promising young analyst typically received a partnership share from a retiring partner or one beginning to slow down in anticipation of retirement. The new partner, or the somewhat older partner increasing his share, bought at book value; but the assets of the partnership were so minimal compared to revenue and profits that the first year's profits frequently covered the entire cost of the investment. In other words, return on capital exceeded 100 percent, and the older partners were almost giving their business away. As a result of this structure, the caliber of employees was high; turnover was low; and the clients stuck with the employees and the firm. The business remained simple, stable, profitable, and growing.

Paul established and supported this structure. Like many things, it represented a moral imperative for him; and he criticized the old firms, especially the old Boston firms, that had sold out to insurance companies and other financial institutions. In 1971, he recalled the negotiations over the Investment Company Act of 1940.

> **Both the SEC and our industry committee agreed that the management contract between the fund and the management group was something that belonged ... to the fund .... And therefore, the management group had no right to hypothecate it, to sell it, to transfer it, or to make money on the disposition of this contract ...**

> **This was in 1940 and I wake up in 1950 sometime and here is a management company that has incorporated. And there are hundreds of them here in Boston, John Chase's firm [John P. Chase & Co.], Eddy Johnson's [Fidelity] ... who incorporated their management company. Then they turned it all around and at a very big profit and for what I think was ridiculously high prices sold a very large part of their shares mostly to insurance companies at a hell of a profit ....**

> **The fiduciary does not have the right to sell his job to somebody else at a profit.**[429]

One of the managing partners, Bob Lawrence, tells the following story.

> **I was in George's office. Outside his door we could hear Paul arrive, his first day in after vacationing in Maine all of August. Along the hallway we heard a chorus of voices.**

> **"Welcome back Paul!"**

> **"Good vacation Paul?"**

"Good to see you Mr. Cabot."

George looked up at me. "Do you think they'll ever greet me that warmly?"

"Of course they will," I answered. "All you have to do is to let go. When the time comes, reduce your share of the partnership in favor of the next generation, the way Paul did."

Paul, who at one point had owned more than a third of the partnership, had sold all but six percent by the early 1980s. One year, when Bob's share of the partnership increased and Paul's decreased, Bob went into his office to thank him, but noted,

"I see that even though your percentage share goes down every year, your profit in dollars goes up."

"Don't you think I had that all figured out?" he replied, as if he knew his munificence was likely to produce business success.[430]

Paul stood firm on the issue of selling the firm, at least in the 1970s. It was in 1982, however, that his opinion really mattered. During that summer, investment bankers at First Boston Corporation approached another managing partner, Charlie Smith, on behalf of Metropolitan Life, who wanted to purchase an established money manager. Would State Street be interested?

With Paul in Maine for the summer, the four younger managing partners met to consider the proposal. The other twenty partners knew nothing of the offer. Flather spoke last and framed his remarks around three questions. Did they have a right to sell the firm? Was this the right time? Should they sell the firm?

The first question was the easiest, in spite of the doubts Paul had expressed in 1971. It had been done many times since and few questioned the legality or the morality. The managing partners were the entrepreneurs who had built the firm, or at least the survivors among them. Others were talented investors, but the managing partners, especially George, had built it and led it.[431] A senior portfolio manager, Jim Ullman, put it this way to those who questioned the sale.

You young fellows are always griping about George. He sold the firm on you. He dominates the investment process. Let me tell you, without George there wouldn't be any firm. He's the one who in his seventies is flying everywhere from Alaska to Saudi Arabia to sell your services. You're lucky to have him.[432]

George had in fact traveled to Juneau, to Riyadh, and to many places in between to market State Street's investment expertise. Ullman could have added that George's success in marketing allowed him to strengthen the research staff by hiring additional analysts, including some who objected to the sale.

The second question was also an easy one. Flather felt that the timing was wrong. The market was depressed in 1982 and it was likely to rebound. Since the price depended on earnings, earnings depended on assets, and assets, to some extent, tracked the stock market, were they not giving something away by selling their business at the trough in a bear market? The answer was "yes," but the solution was simple. The sales package was structured to include an earn-out provision, a payment in 1988 that tracked the profitability of the 1983-1987 time period. If the market did well, as in fact it did, they would have the opportunity to benefit.

The third question was the most difficult and the most important. Should they sell the firm? At first, only George Bennett and Charlie Smith strongly favored the sale. Charlie Flather remembers that when Paul returned from Maine, his initial reaction was, "I know that for selfish reasons I should favor this, but I'm not at all sure that it is a good idea." Paul felt that it would change the character of the firm. After the sale, a version of events circulated that suggested that Paul, who by age 84 may have begun a long, gradual decline, was not up to understanding the deal and that somehow George had misled him into agreeing to it. Charlie Flather, who was the closest to Paul at the time and the most antagonistic toward George, denies that George misled Paul in any way, or that Paul lacked understanding of the implications of the sale. This writer recalls that Paul's periods of confusion at that time appeared to result more from his refusal to wear a hearing aid than from a decline in his mental acuity.

Charlie tells another story, this from 1983, that demonstrates that Paul's intellectual capacity, as well as his persuasiveness and even his tact, continued almost unimpaired into his mid-eighties. Indeed, his tact may have increased. A dispute arose over the details of the partnership, and the managing partners decided to settle the dispute out of court. George felt that since the decision that created the dispute was the responsibility of the four active managing partners, the four should each contribute 25% to the settlement. Charlie Flather felt that the four should contribute proportionally, relative to their share in the business, since this is how expenses of the entire partnership were handled. This would make George's share of the settlement about 50% and Charlie's about 15%, since the non-Managing Partners and Paul would contribute nothing. George and Charlie were both arguing their own self-interest, but each also had a legitimate principle at stake.

Paul called Charlie Flather at home one Sunday afternoon and told him that George had just spent two hours at his house giving him his side of the dispute. Paul wanted to know where Charlie stood. Charlie told him. Not only did Paul agree that the expenses should be divided proportionately, he insisted on contributing to the settlement himself. Paul, with Flather present, later put the issue to Smith and Lawrence, who felt less strongly than Flather and Bennett on the issue, and did not want to go against Paul's wishes. Charlie Flather and Paul then walked directly to George's office, where George, who had sized up the situation quickly and accurately, smilingly told Charlie, "You know, I think you were right all along."

Charlie Flather explains the issues surrounding the sale of the firm this way. George, who still owned nearly 25%, did not want to sell his share at book value, which was only about one times earnings. He felt that a firm like State Street should be capitalized at a much higher multiple of earnings, ten or fifteen. He kept driving this point home to Paul, who eventually gave in. Charlie felt that George had already capitalized his share by holding onto such a large piece while the number of partners quadrupled. But to Charlie, the important point is that it was George's will and determination that finally won the argument for him, not any obfuscation or misstatements. When he learned that Paul agreed that the firm should change hands at over ten times earnings, sharply limiting the ability of younger professionals to buy in, he gave up his opposition to the sale. Meanwhile, Bob Lawrence, who was also undecided for a while, came to believe that sale to a larger organization was the only way to get around some sticky organizational issues surrounding George's retirement.[433]

So what were the real reasons for the sale of the firm? Many of the younger partners and "not-yet partners" felt that it was all about money. George's 25% share was worth over $25 million, not a great deal to someone whose best friends were named Hewlett and Packard and Ford, and who had been responsible for making the business so valuable. But it looked like a huge amount to anyone in their twenties or thirties in 1982. George wanted to capitalize the company at a higher multiple even if they did not sell to an outside buyer. Certainly money was an issue.

The reasons George gave, and the independent directors gave in the prospectus circulated to the mutual fund shareholders, also had merit.

> **The independent Directors of the Fund believe that after the acquisition the fund will continue to have available the high quality investment advisory services provided for over 54 years by State Street Research & Management Company (SSRM). Management of SSRM and the independent Directors also believe that *the affiliation of SSRM with an organization having the financial and marketing resources of Metropolitan Life will result in the development***

of new products and services which the Fund may determine would be beneficial to its shareholders. (emphasis added) **The Directors of the fund believe that the proposed transaction is in the best interests of the shareholders of the Fund.**[434]

Many believed, correctly, that the financial services business would become increasingly complex in the 1980s, with more products in international investing, asset allocation, and derivatives. Men like Sanford Weil and James Robinson III were already talking about financial supermarkets that would cater to the needs of the affluent. By this reasoning, a firm like State Street had only two ways to go. It could shrink into a specialized niche and become a boutique focusing on what it did best. Or it could join forces with a financial services giant, broaden its product offerings, expand its sales force, and grow. This was not a difficult choice for George. He is not a man to shrink anything. He truly believed that the "merger," as he called it, with the Met was in the best interests of everyone. He did not want to be associated with a firm that had been left behind by history.

In the end, things did not work out as he had hoped. Some firms, like Putnam Investments, arguably achieved their greatest success after being acquired by much larger firms. But State Street was different. Everyone associated with it—partners, analysts, even clients—felt that they were better than the competition, the first to do primary research with an investment record that showed it; founded by an investment legend who still came into the office every day; and the first choice of business school students wanting to work in investment management. The change from a private investment partnership to the subsidiary of a mutual insurance company was so great that, when the sale was announced, some employees felt like they had been fired. Turnover among both employees and clients increased; performance lagged; and the company's position in the industry declined from tops to average.

Throughout the eighties and nineties, the company tried to remake itself several times in several ways. In the mid 1990s, the CEO became convinced that the company's history and heritage were a handicap. White Protestants had always dominated the investment business in Boston, but as the CEO addressed an all-company meeting in 1995, he looked out upon many people from southern and eastern Europe and southern and eastern Asia, or whose families hailed from there, indeed probably more Brahmins from Bombay than from Boston. He wanted to get this largely young, ethnically mixed group energized and on his side, but he attempted this in the most tasteless manner imaginable. "And I had to take down the portraits of those three dead white males," he announced, referring to the portraits of the three founders that had hung in the lobby for decades.

The next CEO returned the portraits. But the luster of the old firm never returned. It continued to be a disappointment to its owner, Metropolitan Life, which sold it in 2005 to a larger New York investment firm, BlackRock Investment Management.

A Man For All Seasons

During the last few years of his life, Paul took the Needham-Boston bus to the office one day a week to keep up with developments at State Street, but mostly to monitor his own investments. In the afternoon, his assistant, Paula Kerrigan, would follow him at a discreet distance, far enough to be lost in the crowd but close enough to make sure he got on the right bus. One day, when she was especially busy and the weather especially cold, she took a chance and let him find the bus on his own. An hour later an anxious, and somewhat angry, Mrs. Cabot called asking why her husband was not on his regular bus. It was the last time he took public transportation to work.

About six months later, August 30, 1994, Paul arrived at State Street Research's building, One Financial Center, this time in his private car driven by a family employee. He stepped out onto the concrete floor of the parking garage, fell, and broke his hip. He died two days later at the local hospital in Needham.[435]

At the memorial service, held a few weeks later on what would have been his ninety-sixth birthday, the celebrants opened with the singing of "America." At the time, it seemed to many a fitting recognition of his service in two world wars and his love of country. But on reflection, it seems like more. Because of his habits, interests, and values, Paul was viewed as a New Englander. But the cliché of the New Englander, at least the twentieth-century parody we recognize from literature, is an ineffective character lacking spirit and spontaneity. Paul resembled an older type of New Englander, the eighteenth-century republican patriot, with his hatred of pretension and corruption. Or as a speaker at a dinner honoring Paul's retirement from the board of National Dairy exclaimed,

> **Well, Paul is Boston all right, and he is a Cabot, but if there is any of the effete easterner in him I have yet to discover it. That fog-horned-voiced, whisky-drinking, cigar-smoking, dirty-story-telling angel of a man could have been born in any state or section of this great country and still be precisely what he is. And what he is, for my money, is truly "A Man For All Seasons."[436]**

Paul remembered his pretentious boss in London as "a horse's ass of the first order, one of those fellows who thought just because he'd been over there a year he was an Englishman." His reaction to the financial corruption of the twenties was, "Unless we avoid these and other errors and false principles we shall inevitably go through a similar period of disaster and disgrace . . . as they did in England forty years" before.

Rather than Marquand, one can imagine Herman Melville, R.W.B. Lewis's "jaunty journalist of the adventures of boys at sea," writing about Paul, a robust, albeit not particularly subtle or nuanced, personality closer to Ahab than to Apley.[437] Or one can imagine Whitman, who "hail[ed] with joy the oceanic, variegated, intense practical energy, the demand for facts, even the business materialism of the current age." It was Whitman, after all, who, like Paul Cabot, saw himself as "no stander above men and women or apart from them." Or perhaps Mark Twain. Paul's resignation from a social club over a slight to Sidney Weinberg is hardly as heroic as Huck Finn's willingness to go to hell rather than send his best friend Jim back into slavery. But Paul was self-directed in the extreme, whether deciding the merits of an investment or choosing his friends. Melville, Twain, and Whitman all had New England connections, but shared a nationalist bent. Melville wanted "no American Goldsmiths; nay we want no American Miltons . . . . Let us boldly condemn all imitation." Whitman believed "Our fundamental want today . . . is of a class . . . of native authors."[438]

Paul's thought, which was revolutionary when he was young, his passion, and his willingness to view matters freshly and consider new ways of doing things are as American as those of the nation's founders. When Paul returned from London in 1923, he

> was still very interested in stocks, common stocks. I wasn't a damn bit interested in bonds and money obligations . . . [The British] investment trusts were very different and a very far cry from anything we started . . . . Stocks were just coming into fashion to be considered respectable moneymaking investments. Up to that time they were just considered wild speculation. People didn't buy common stocks.

Bernard Bailyn writes of the Founding Fathers,

> Refusing to be intimidated by the received traditions and confident of their own integrity and creative capacities, they demanded to know why things must be the way they are; and they had the imagination and energy to conceive of something closer to the grain of everyday reality and more likely to lead to human happiness.[439]

A mutual fund is not as dramatic an innovation as the Constitution, but there is something quintessentially American in Paul's adoption of a British concept, his rejection of many of its received traditions because of his confidence in his own better idea, and his preservation of its clarity and simplicity, through keeping it "close to the grain of everyday reality." It was this "passion for reality" that enabled Paul and his partners and his Boston competitors to make professional money management services available to average investors on a democratic basis, which, even with the troubles and scandals of recent years—in the ninth decade of the open-end fund industry—has made a major contribution to human happiness.

ENDNOTES

NOTES TO INTRODUCTION

1. George Santayana, *The Last Puritan* (Cambridge, MA, 1995), p. 14.
2. *Teaching and Beyond: Nonacademic Career Programs for Ph.D.'s* (Albany, 1984) pp. 21-23.
3. Oscar Handlin, *Truth in History* (Cambridge, MA, 1979) p. 108
4. Reminiscences of Paul C. Cabot (April 9-10, July 11-12, 1980) in the Columbia University Oral History Research Office Collection (hereafter CUOHROC), pp. 7, 12-14
5. CUOHROC, pp. 35-41. Also see Arthur Stone Dewing, *The Financial Policy of Corporations* (New York, 1941) pp. 275-277.
6. CUOHROC, p. 117
7. Hannah Arendt, "Truth and Politics," *The New Yorker* (1967) in David Spitz ed., *Political Theory and Social Change* (New York, 1967) pp. 23, 34.
8. John P. Marquand, *The Late George Apley* (Franklin Center, PA, 1977) p. 1.

NOTES TO CHAPTER I

9. Personal letter from Paul C. Cabot to Anna C. Cabot, December 8, 1918. Emphasis is in the original.
10. Interview with Paul C. Cabot by Rosario J. Tosiello, October 22, 1971, pp. 1-2.
11. CUOHROC, pp. 20, 25, 26, Unsigned memo, June 3, 1918, Unsigned memo, June 15, 1918, Letter from (illegible) to Paul C. Cabot, July 8, 1918, Note from E.R. Hay directed to "the President," June 3, 1918, Letter from Henry Bromfield Cabot to L.S. Mayo, July 10, 1918, P. Cabot '21 Student Folder, Harvard University Archives
12. Letter from Paul C. Cabot to H.A. Yoemans, June 12, 1918, P. Cabot '21 Student Folder
13. The poem is "A Prayer for My Daughter."

[14] CUOHROC, p. 8, Samuel Eliot Morison, *Three Centuries of Harvard* (Cambridge, MA, 1994) p. 440, Interview with George Putnam Jr., January 9, 2001.

[15] CUOHROC, pp. 2,3,7,9. L. Vernon Briggs, *History and Genealogy of the Cabot Family* 1475-1927 (Boston, 1927) Volume II pp. 699-700, 764-769. E. Digby Baltzell, *Puritan Boston and Quaker Philadelphia* (New York, 1979) pp. 366-367. *The Boston Herald*, December 1, 1932, p. 15. *The Chronicle*, Brookline, MA, December 1, 1932, p. 17

[16] CUOHROC, pp. 7, 12

[17] Phoebe Washburn Barnes, *The Pulpit Harbor Cabots* (Cambridge, MA, 1978) p. 134

[18] Ibid pp. 32, 53-54

[19] Ibid p. 124

[20] Ibid p. 130

[21] CUOHROC, pp. 3, 7, 12-14, 181

[22] Conversation with John Thorndike, March 23, 2004

[23] Barnes, *Cabots*, pp. 115-117. *The Boston Herald*, December 1, 1932, p. 15

[24] Barnes, *Cabots*, p. 130.

[25] CUOHROC p.13, Thomas H. Raddall, *Halifax Warden of the North* (Garden City, 1965) pp. 250-255, George Hinckly Lyman, *The Story of the Massachusetts Committee on Public Safety* (Boston, 1919) p. 190.

[26] CUOHROC p.13, *The Boston Herald*, December 1, 1932, p. 15. *The Chronicle*, Brookline, MA, December 1, 1932, p. 17

[27] Leverett Saltonstall and Edward Weeks, *Salty: Recollections of A Yankee in Politics* (Boston, 1976) p.4 Mark I. Gelfand, *Trustee for a City Ralph Lowell of Boston* (Boston, 1998) p. 18

[28] CUOHROC, pp. 2-6, 11, 13-17. Gelfand, *Trustee*, p. 18

[29] Personal letter from Paul C. Cabot (PCC) to Anna C. Cabot (ACC), undated, postmarked December 31, 1918

[30] Morison, pp. 450,451,456,457.

[31] PCC to ACC, October 27, November 3, 15, & 23, 1918

[32] PCC to ACC, November 29, 1918

[33] Personal letter from Paul C. Cabot to Henry B. Cabot, November 17, 1918

[34] PCC to ACC November 23, 1918

[35] PCC to ACC December 31, 1918

[36] CUOHROC, pp. 19-24.

[37] Morison, pp. 441,443.

[38] Paul C. Cabot, Government 1 Examination, May, 30, 1919, Letter from Dean Hay to a Mr. Munro, June 10, 1918, Telephone message June 7, 1918 from H.B. Cabot, Student Folder

[39] Letter from Paul C. Cabot to Dean Chase, April 29, 1919, Student Folder. A student's concentration was his minor. Paul's major was mathematics. CUOHROC, pp. 16, 35-36, 59.

40 Baltzell, pp. 261-262. Melvin T. Copeland, *And Mark an Era: The Story of the Harvard Business School* (Boston, 1958) p. 62

41 Marquand, pp. 11-13, 285.

42 *New York Sunday Times*, October 1, 2000, Sec. 3 p. 18.

43 Putnam Interview, January 9, 2001

44 CUOHROC, pp. 35-36. Copeland, *Business School*, p. 86

45 Copeland, *Business School*, pp. 75-78, 94-95

46 Ibid pp. 98-99

47 Dewing, pp. 275-277

48 Copeland, *Business School*, p. 64

49 Seymour E. Harris, *Economics of Harvard*, (New York, 1970) p. 347

50 CUOHROC, pp. 34-36.

51 Ibid. pp. 36-37

52 Charles D. Ellis, *Capital* (Hoboken, 2004) pp. 17-18, 33-34

53 CUOHROC p. 37

54 Ibid. pp. 41-42, 45, Tosiello, pp. 1-2. Securities and Exchange Commission, "Investment Trust Study," Testimony of Paul C. Cabot, September 23, 1936 (hereafter referred to as SEC Study, Testimony of P. Cabot, 9/23/36) pp. 2709-2711. R.H. Miller, "London Idea Cabot Spur," Boston *Traveler*, October 27, 1958. Memorandum from Charles Flather to M. Yogg, August 18, 2003. (hereafter referred to as Flather Memo)

55 Ron Chernow, *The House of Morgan*, (New York, 1991) p. 53

56 Paul C. Cabot, "The Investment Trust," *Atlantic Monthly*, Vol. 143, March 1929, pp. 401-408.

NOTES TO CHAPTER II

57 Tosiello, p. 14.

58 Tosiello, p. 2, SEC Study, Testimony of P. Cabot, 9/23/36, pp. 2709-2711 Edgar L. Smith, *Common Stocks as Long-Term Investments* (New York, 1924) pp. 3-5, 18-20, 68, 81-82, Warren Buffet, "Warren Buffet on the Stock Market," *Fortune*, December 10, 2001, p. 86. Natalie Grow, "The 'Boston-Type Open-End Fund'—Development of a National Financial Institution: 1924-1940 (Unpublished PhD. dissertation, Harvard University, 1977)", pp. 12-13. Pyramiding could mean different things in different contexts. In this case I believe it simply meant leveraging. In the case of the Anglo-American Debenture Company, mentioned in Chapter IV, the purpose of the pyramiding was to manipulate the price of the securities.

59 Grow, pp. 7-13. John Kenneth Galbraith, *The Great Crash* (Boston, 1961) pp. 48-70.

60 Edward Maitland Campbell, "Some Management Problems of Investment Trusts," *Harvard Business Review*, Vol. II No. 3 (April, 1924), p. 296.

61 Letter from Charles Bennett to Natalie Grow, Oct. 2, 1974, quoted in Grow, p. 15

62 Tosiello, p. 14

63 Ibid. p.2

64 SEC Study, Testimony of P. Cabot, 9/23/36, pp. 2711-2713, 2716-2717, 2719

65 Interview with William Saltonstall and George Lewis, January 15, 2002

66 CUOHROC, pp.114-115.

67 CUOHROC, pp. 117-118.

68 *Harvard College Class of 1917 25th Anniversary Report* (Cambridge, MA, 1942) pp. 726-727. CUOHROC, pp. 47, 117, Briggs, *Genealogy of the Cabot Family* p. 767. Flather Memo.

69 SEC Study, Testimony of P. Cabot, 9/23/36 p. 2712, *Harvard College Class of 1920 25th Anniversary Report* (Cambridge, MA, 1945) p.714. *Harvard College Class of 1921 50th Anniversary Report* (Cambridge, MA, 1971) pp. 66-67. Cleveland Amory, T*he Proper Bostonians*, (Orleans, MA, 1984) pp.231-232. Flather Memo.

70 Interview with Saltonstall and Lewis

71 Saltonstall and Weeks, p. 60

72 *Class of 1920 25th Anniversary* pp. 714-715. *Class of 1921 50th Anniversary* pp. 66-67. *Class of 1917 25th Anniversary* pp. 726-727. *Harvard College Class of 1921 25th Anniversary Report* (Cambridge, MA, 1946) pp. 88-89. *Harvard College Class of 1920 50th Anniversary Report* (Cambridge, MA, 1970) pp. 379-380. Flather Memo.

73 Flather Memo. Amory, *Bostonians*, p. 69

74 In the 1960s when wide ties came back into fashion, Paul showed up at the office with a wide tie from the 1930s. A young analyst asked, "Mr. Cabot you're right in style. Where did you get that wide tie?" He replied, "I didn't get it, I kept it." At an investment committee discussion of a shoe company when Paul was in his fifties, he suddenly lifted his feet, pointed at his shoes, and said, "You see those shoes? I had those shoes in college. Who buys shoes?"

75 *Harvard College v. Amory* (1830), in Charles D. Ellis and James R. Vertin, *Classis II, An Investor's Anthology* (Homewood, Illinois, 1991) pp. 16-17

76 Grow p. 29.

77 Tosiello, p. 13.

78 Tosiello, p. 3.

79 State Street Investment Corporation, By-Laws, Article IX. *Annual Report*, 1926, p.4. *Record Book*, I, p. 72. *Registration Statement* Under Securities Act of 1933, October 30, 1937, p. 19.

80 Max Rottersman and Jason Zweig, "An Early History of Mutual Funds," F*riends of Financial History*, Number 51, Spring 1994, p.12

81 Tosiello, pp. 2, 3, 14

82 Grow p. 64. Courtesy of the Harvard University Archives.

83 SSIC *Annual Report* 1926, p. 3. Almost the exact same language was used in a 1937 SEC Filing, *Registration Statement* Under Securities Act of 1933, October 30, 1937, p. 8b.

84 CUOHROC, p. 46.

85 State Street's performance is taken from the annual reports. The performance of other funds is taken from Grow. S&P performance is taken from *S&P Security Price Index Record*, 2002 edition, p.2

86 SSIC *Annual Report* 1931, p. 4.

87 "State Street Investment Corporation," Memorandum to the SEC, Nov 2, 1933, in SEC Docket File 2-48-3, Records of the SEC, Record Group 266, National Archives.

88 SEC Study, Testimony of P. Cabot, 9/23/36, p. 272

89 Source: SSIC Annual Reports, and SEC Investment Trust Study Questionnaire, SSIC, Part IV p. 5, February 4, 1936

90 Registration Statement Under Securities Act of 1933, October 30, 1937, p. 8c

91 Source: SSIC *Record Book*

92 SEC Investment Trust Study Questionnaire, SSIC, Part VI, February 4, 1936. Turnover is generally defined as the lower of purchases or sales divided by assets, so large purchases that the fund made after the U.S. went off the gold standard in 1933 do not distort the turnover statistics.

93 SSIC *Annual Report* 1936, p. 2.

94 CUOHROC, pp. 106-107.

95 John Train, *The Money Masters: Nine Great Investors: Their Winning Strategies and How You Can Apply Them* (New York, 1980) p. 49.

96 SSIC, *Record Book* I, pp. 84-93.

97 Ibid pp. 14-31.

98 CUOHROC, pp. 48-50, 174-177.

99 Rick Wartzman, "A 1920s Insider Trade Was Ruled by Court To Be Merely a Perk," *The Wall Street Journal*, July 3, 2002, B1.

100 SSIC, *Record Book* I, pp. 91-92.

101 Noam Scheiber, "Wretched Excess," *The New Republic*, December 3, 2001, pp. 19-23. Scheiber's analysis, with which I largely agree, owes much to Joseph Schumpeter, as he acknowledges.

102 SSIC, *Annual Report*, 1927, pp. 6-7. Richard Paine, as President, signed the annual reports; but it is clear that Paul either wrote them or had a major hand in them. They reflect some of his major concerns, including the abuses of the British trusts, on which he alone was expert, similar problems that were arising in the U.S. at that time, and the industry's overemphasis on sales as opposed to investment performance. Some of the language in the reports, particularly the 1928 annual report, is remarkably similar to that of a speech and article that he wrote in 1928 and 1929, which are

covered in Chapter V. And the writing style, on all subjects, resembles Paul's writing style elsewhere—clear, focused, intense, and judicious.

NOTES TO CHAPTER III

[103] CUOHROC, p. 114.

[104] SSIC Letter to shareholders, July 15, 1927

[105] SSIC Letter to shareholders, April 16, 1928

[106] Source: SEC Investment Trust Study Questionnaire, SSIC, February 4, 1936, Part IX.

[107] SSIC Letter to Shareholders, October 15, 1928

[108] The above discussion benefits from readings of Frederick Lewis Allen, *Only Yesterday*, (New York, 1964) pp. 241-281 and John Kenneth Galbraith, *The Great Crash*, (Cambridge, MA, 1961) pp. 93-132.

[109] Studs Terkel, *Hard Times* (New York, 1970) p. 72, CUOHROC pp. 113-115

[110] SSIC *Annual Report 1929* p. 6, CUOHROC p.114.

[111] SSIC *Annual Report 1929* pp.6-7. Emphasis added.

[112] Unpublished Memo from William F. Morton to the SEC, September 2, 1936. The memo was written in connection with the SEC investigation of the mutual fund industry.

[113] SSIC *Annual Report 1930*, p.3. Emphasis added.

[114] SEC Study, Testimony of P. Cabot, 9/23/36, p. 2722-2724

[115] Paul C. Cabot, unpublished typescript beginning, "There were not many warnings," (not dated), p.2, quoted in Grow p. 220. Courtesy of the Harvard University Archives.

[116] SEC Study, Testimony of P. Cabot, 9/23/36, pp. 2722-2724, SSIC *Annual Report 1931*, pp. 3-4, SSIC *Record Book*, p. 118, *Registration Statement* Under Securities Act of 1933, October 30, 1937, p. 16a, SSIC *Certified Financial Schedules to be included in the Registration Statement filed under the Federal Securities Act of 1933*

[117] SSIC *Annual Report* 1931, p. 6

[118] Ibid, p.3

[119] SEC Study, *Testimony of P. Cabot*, 9/23/36, p. 2714

[120] State Street Investment Corporation, *Articles of Amendment*, February 19, 1932

[121] SSIC *Quarterly Report*, Q1, 1932 (emphasis added)

[122] *Registration Statement* under Securities Act of 1933, State Street Investment Corporation, Submitted to the Federal Trade Commission, July 8, 1933, p. 4

[123] SSIC *Annual Report* 1931, p. 4.

[124] Tosiello pp.3-4

[125] SSIC *Annual Report* 1927, p. 3.

[126] SEC Study, Testimony of P. Cabot, 9/23/36, pp. 2721-2722

[127] SSIC *Annual Reports,* 1926 pp. 1-3, 1927 p. 8, 1928 p. 9. Grow pp. 166, 167, 170.

[128] *Registration Statement* Under Securities Act of 1933, October 30, 1937, p. 8b

[129] Open Letter from State Street Investment Corp., February 3, 1932

[130] Tosiello p.11

[131] Max Rottersman and Jason Zweig, "An Early History of Mutual Funds," *Friends of Financial History,* Number 51, Spring 1994, p.12.

[132] State Street did face one problem in trying to maintain its identity, especially after it became a national institution: the similarity between its name and that of the much larger, but wholly unrelated, State Street Bank & Trust. The problem became worse in 1966 when the partnership moved into the State Street Bank Building on Franklin Street. Paul and his partners originally wanted to name the fund Equity or Equitable Investment Trust, but the name was too close to that of an existing trust. The law office where they were drawing up papers of incorporation was on State Street, so on the spur of the moment, they settled on that name, which they saw as synonymous with Wall Street but with more of a Boston feeling.

[133] SSIC, *Quarterly Report,* Q 3, 1932

[134] Grow p. 293

[135] Ibid pp. 49-50

[136] Edward G. Leffler, "Confidential Memo" (typescript, no date) pp. 1-2, quoted in Grow p. 51. Courtesy of the Harvard University Archives.

[137] Grow pp. 50-53, 57 The conclusion on the effect of Edward Leffler's political beliefs on his financial principles rests on Natalie Grow's analysis. Courtesy of the Harvard University Archives.

[138] Leffler, p. 3 in Grow, p. 69. Grow pp. 69-70, 73-77.

[139] Ibid p. 81

[140] Incorporated Investors, *Quarterly Report,* Q 3, 1928, quoted in Grow p. 132. Courtesy of the Harvard University Archives.

[141] Grow, p. 89. Courtesy of the Harvard University Archives.

[142] Grow pp. 90, 191, 292-293, Leffler p. 3 quoted in Grow p. 191. SSIC *Registration Statement* Under Securities Act of 1933, July 8, 1933 pp. 9, 12, 13 and October 30, 1937, p. 19. *Prospectus,* July 17, 1933 p. 15 and October 30, 1937, pp. 14-15. The Blue Sky burden referred to the necessity of registering the fund with regulators in every state the fund was to be sold in and convincing them that the securities in the portfolios had more substance than the blue sky.

[143] SSIC *Quarterly Report,* Q1, 1933

[144] SSIC *Annual Report* 1932 p. 8

[145] SSIC *Annual Report* 1932 p. 4

[146] Train p. 55

[147] SSIC *Interim Report for the Five Months Ended May 31, 1933,* dated June 19, 1933

[148] Letter from management "To the Stockholders of Mohawk Investment Corporation," June 19, 1933

[149] SSIC *Interim* Report, June 19, 1933, SEC Study, Testimony of E. Leffler, 9/23/36, p. 2725

[150] SSIC *Annual Report* 1934, p.2

[151] SSIC *Annual Report* 1933. State Street limited its debt to 50% of assets after November 1932 and 25% of assets after June 1933. And the Revenue Act of 1936 limited their debt to 10% of assets. But in fact, debt never rose much above 25%. SSIC *Interim Report*, June 19, 1933, SSIC *Registration Statement* Under Securities Act of 1933, October 30, 1937 p. 8b, February 16, 1942, p. 2. *Prospectus*, October 30, 1937, p. 5.

[152] SEC Investment Trust Study Questionnaire, SSIC pp. 5-6

[153] SSIC *Prospectus*, February 1942

[154] SSIC *Annual Report* 1932, p. 8

[155] SSIC *Annual Report* 1934, p. 7. Grow pp. 299-300.

[156] Grow, pp. 300-301

[157] Cabot Interview by Grow, April 23, 1974 in Grow pp. 301-302, Courtesy of the Harvard University Archives. SEC Study, Testimony of P. Cabot, 9/23/36, p. 2720

[158] State Street's performance is taken from the Annual Reports. The performance of other funds is taken from Grow. S&P performance is taken from *S&P Security Price Index Record*, 2002 edition, p.2

[159] Grow pp. 578-590, SSIC *Annual Reports* 1926-1940.

NOTES TO CHAPTER IV

[160] Tosiello p. 9

[161] Memo from Marriner Eccles to Franklin D. Roosevelt, May 11, 1936, Memo written by Marriner Eccles May 8, 1936, Undated outline titled "Retention of all present corporation taxes with graduated tax on undistributed adjusted net income superimposed," hereinafter referred to as "Undated outline, 'Retention'" Undated note from Franklin D. Roosevelt to Missy LeHand. These papers are filed together at the Franklin D. Roosevelt Presidential Library

[162] John Morton Blum, *From the Morgenthau Diaries Years of Crisis, 1928-1938* (Boston, 1959) pp 301-305. Grow pp. 452-453.

[163] Blum, *Morgenthau Diaries 1928-1938* p. 305, Grow pp. 557, 559, SSIC *Registration Statement* Under Securities Act of 1933, October 30, 1937, p. 8c, SEC Investment Trust Study Questionnaire, SSIC, Part VI, February 4, 1936 187-14-3. This wealthier group included the partners and their families (owning 22%) and Harvard University among others. Ownership at Massachusetts Investors Trust and Incorporated Investors was more dispersed, with a larger number of smaller holders.

[164] SSIC *Annual Report* 1936, p. 3

[165] Ibid p. 3

[166] Grow pp. 452-455, Merrill Griswold, *Taxation of Investment Companies and Their Shareholders* (18-page typescript labeled 11th Draft," Jan. 6, 1958), p. 14, quoted in Grow, p. 455.

[167] Grow pp. 456-457

[168] Tosiello. p. 9

[169] P. Cabot, W.T. Gardner, M. Griswold, "Memorandum for the Record of the Senate Banking and Currency Committee on Investment Company Bill S.3580, May 2, 1940" in Hearings before a Sub Committee of the Committee on Banking and Currency United States Senate on S. 3580 (Washington, 1940) p. 1077 (hereafter referred to as "Cabot and associates Memo on S.3580"). The best source for events leading up to the Revenue Act of 1936 is the review of these events that took place before that Sub Committee while it was holding hearings on the Investment Company Act of 1940.

[170] CUOHROC pp. 68-69

[171] Grow, pp. 469-470

[172] The House initiates all revenue-raising measures but, in this case, the Senate version ultimately prevailed.

[173] Subscription warrants give existing shareholders the right to purchase new shares on preferential terms.

[174] "Suggestions Regarding Treatment of Mutual Investment Trusts and Corporations Under Revenue Bill of 1936, H.R. 12395 pp. 1079-1081, undated (hereafter referred to as "Cabot and associates Memo on S.3580, Exhibit B")

[175] Cabot and associates Memo on S.3580 pp. 1076-1078

[176] Hereafter referred to as "Cabot and associates Memo on S.3580, Exhibit C"

[177] Grow, pp. 468, 500

[178] Cabot and associates Memo on S.3580 pp. 1076-1078, Cabot and associates Memo on S.3580, Exhibit C pp. 1081-1082 *(emphasis added)*

[179] This is first pointed out by Grow, pp. 461-462. Senate Finance Committee Hearings on H.R. 12395, Revenue Act of 1936, May 26-27, 1936 (Washington, 1936), pp. 58-59.

[180] Grow pp. 463-464, Courtesy of the Harvard University Archives.

[181] *Registration Statement* under Securities Act of 1933, SSIC, February 16, 1942, pp. 5-6, Telegram Allan Forbes to F. D. Roosevelt, June 1, 1936, Memo M. H. McIntyre to F. D. Roosevelt, June 1, 1936.

[182] Griswold, *Taxation of Investment Companies*, p. 12, quoted in Grow, p. 499. Courtesy of the Harvard University Archives.

[183] Tosiello. p. 9, Blum, *Morgenthau Diaries*, 1928-1938 p. 308. Oliphant was a man with a combative spirit. At one point, during a discussion of tactics to be used in the battle over the undistributed earnings tax, he exclaimed, "If we have to fight, we might as well fight the people who are our enemies anyway."

[184] FDR Day by Day—"The Pare Lorentz Chronology" June 3, 1936, Undated outline, "Retention," Roosevelt's notes described the House version of the bill that at that

time seemed more likely to pass. The Senate version ultimately prevailed. The House version, steeper and more progressive, was closer to the Treasury's original thinking.

[185] Letter from M. Griswold, P. C. Cabot, W. T. Gardner, to F.D. Roosevelt, June 4, 1936, Phone message from M. Griswold to M.H. McIntyre, June 4, 1936, Cabot and associates Memo on S.3580, p. 1078

[186] Cabot and associates Memo on S.3580 pp. 1077-1078, Memo from M. Katz to J. Landis, D. Schenker, and P. Gourrich, June 12, 1936, pp. 1078-1079, (Hereinafter referred to as "Cabot and associates Memo on S.3580, Exhibit A."

[187] Tosiello p. 10

[188] Tosiello, pp. 9-10. Emphasis added. *Registration Statement* Under Securities Act of 1933, October 30, 1937, p. 8b.

[189] Tosiello, p. 8

[190] Barnes, *Cabots* pp. 105-106

[191] CUOHROC, p. 121

[192] Tosiello p. 11

[193] Grow p. 501

[194] Ibid p. 476

[195] Ibid pp. 476-477 Courtesy of the Harvard University Archives.

[196] SSIC *Annual Report* 1935, p. 5

[197] Tosiello p. 12

[198] SEC Study, Testimony of P. Cabot, 9/23/36, pp. 2730-2732

[199] Ibid pp. 2732-2733

[200] Ibid pp. 2734-2735, 2738

[201] Ibid pp. 2739-2741

[202] Ibid pp. 2744-2745

[203] Ibid pp. 2746-2747

[204] Ibid pp. 2751-2754, He later amended this testimony to say that the statement appeared in a separate letter, not in the contract itself. Ibid p. 2776

[205] Ibid. 2754-2762

[206] Letter from Paul C. Cabot to John C. Grier, Jr., January 11, 1929, appended to SEC Study Testimony of Paul Cabot, 9/23/36

[207] SEC Study Testimony of Paul Cabot, 9/23/36, pp. 2774-2775

[208] Ibid pp. 2776-2779

[209] Under certain circumstances, individual investors were exempted from capital gains tax on a portion of their investment, if they held their investment long enough. Since the Revenue Act was designed to treat individuals banded together on the same basis as individuals acting alone, mutual fund shareholders should have been given this benefit as well. A second technical item dealt with the application of the surtax to investment income.

[210] Ibid pp. 2782-2796 *The New York Times*, September 24, 1936

[211] Frederick C. Cabot, Remarks at the Memorial Service for Paul C. Cabot, October 21, 1994.

[212] Public Law No. 768 contains three titles. Title I, the Investment Company Act of 1940, deals with investment companies. Title II deals with investment advisors. Title III updates the Securities Act of 1933.

[213] Tosiello p. 12

[214] Hearings before a Subcommittee of the Committee on Banking and Currency United States Senate, 76th Congress, Third Session on S. 3580, A Bill to Provide for the Registration and Regulation of Investment Companies and Investment Advisers, and for other purposes (Washington, 1940) p. 37, (hereinafter referred to as "Senate Hearings on S.3580"

[215] Senate Hearings on S.3580 p. 47

[216] Tosiello p. 12

[217] Senate Hearings on S.3580, p. 476, Grow pp. 510, 512

[218] Senate Hearings on S.3580, pp. 463-468

[219] Ibid pp. 470-476

[220] Ibid pp. 8, 476-477

[221] Ibid pp. 477-478, 482-483

[222] Ibid pp. 10, 478-482

[223] Ibid. pp. 9, 482

[224] Ibid pp. 10, 12-13, 482-484

[225] Ibid pp. 6-7, 483-484

[226] Ibid pp. 10-11, 484, Grow pp. 520-521, 528

[227] Senate Hearings on S.3580 pp. 484-486

[228] Ibid p. 486

[229] Ibid p. 489, Wagner was Chairman of both this Subcommittee and of the Committee on Banking and Currency.

[230] Tosiello p. 12

[231] Grow pp. 516-517 Courtesy of the Harvard University Archives.

[232] Ibid p. 517 Courtesy of the Harvard University Archives.

[233] *Investment Companies 1965 Mutual Funds and Other Types*, (Arthur Wiesenberger & Company: New York, 1966) p. 8

NOTES TO CHAPTER V

[234] Marquand, *Apley*, pp. 186-187.

[235] Interview with Paul C. Cabot by Jessica Holland for Goldman Sachs, December 27, 1979, p.16

[236] In two interviews conducted by Ms. Holland, for Columbia (CUOHROC, p. 101) and for Goldman Sachs (p. 10), Paul used more euphemistic language in relating

this incident, "You can stuff it" in one case and "You can stick your club you know where" in the other. He generally attempted to tone down his language in the presence of women. This writer has heard the story with the rougher language quoted here, though without a recording device in hand. I believe that the earthier version of the story is the more accurate one.

[237] Rose Kennedy, *Times to Remember* (New York: Doubleday, 1974), p. 49.

[238] Marquand, p. 13.

[239] Santayana, *The Last Puritan*, p.553. Irving Singer, *George Santayana, Literary Philosopher* (New Haven: Yale, 2000), p. 50.

[240] Keller and Keller, *Making Harvard Modern* (New York, 2001) p. 14. Gelfand, *Trustee*, p. 235

[241] Gelfand, *Trustee*, pp. 62, 243-244

[242] At least according to the stereotype, Lowells are brainy professionals; Lawrences are known more for warmth, charm, and empathy. Mc George Bundy was a Lowell. Abbott Lawrence ("A smile never hurt anybody.") was the prototypical Lawrence. Henry Aaron Yoemans, *Abbott Lawrence Lowell* 1856-1943 (Cambridge, MA, 1948) p. 15

[243] CUOHROC, pp. 126-129

[244] E.J. Kahn Jr., "Profiles, Director's Director," *The New Yorker*, September 15, 1956, pp. 58-60.

[245] Kahn, "Profiles," September 15, 1956, p. 64. Baltzell, *Puritan Boston*, pp. 266-267.

[246] Kahn, "Profiles," September 15, 1956, p.64.

[247] Ibid, p. 48, September 8, 1956, pp. 38, 62

[248] Kahn, "Profiles," September 8, pp. 40, 50, 52.

[249] Ibid. p. 56.

[250] Ibid. p. 58. CUOHROC, pp. 92-94.

[251] Ibid, pp. 94-97.

[252] Sidney J. Weinberg, "Memorandum re the responsibility of Directors," unpublished memo in Sidney J. Weinberg, "The Corporate Director Looks at his Job," *Harvard Business Review*, Vol. XXVII, No. 5, September 1949.

[253] Holland, Goldman Sachs Interview, p. 4.

[254] Kahn, "Profiles," September 8, pp. 48, 54.

[255] Weinberg, "Corporate Director," p. 589. Lisa Endlich, *Goldman Sachs The Culture of Success* (NY, 1999) p. 56

[256] Cabot, "The Investment Trust,", pp. 401-402.

[257] Tosiello, p.5.

[258] Galbraith, *The Great Crash*, p. 61.

[259] Cabot, "Investment Trust," pp. 402-403.

[260] Ibid, pp. 403-404.

[261] Ibid, pp. 404-405.

262 Roger Lowenstein, *When Genius Failed The Rise and Fall of Long-Term Capital Management* (New York, 2000) p. 181.

263 Galbraith, *The Great Crash*, p. 133

264 Cabot, "Investment Trust," p. 406.

265 Grow, pp.182-183.

266 Cabot, "Investment Trust," p. 408.

267 Galbraith, *The Great Crash*, p.98.

268 CUOHROC, pp. 118-121.

269 Flather Memo

270 James Grant, "Sometimes the Economy Needs A Setback," *New York Sunday Times*, September 9, 2001 Section 4, p. 19.

271 John Train p.51.

272 William S. Knudsen, Administrative Order of the Office of Production Management (number illegible, undated) issued between November 1941 and January 1942.

273 War Production Board, Staff Directory, Spring 1942, "Introduction" accompanying WPB papers at the National Archives. The OPM was established on January 7, 1941, was placed under the authority of the newly created WPB on January 16, 1942, and was abolished on January 24, 1942. The Supply Priorities and Allocations Board was also placed under the WPB in January of 1942.

274 Kahn, "Profiles," Sept. 15, p. 48.

275 Donald M. Nelson, *Arsenal of Democracy, The Story of American War Production* (New York, 1946), p. 343

276 CUOHROC, pp. 124-125.

277 Office of Production Management, memo from Margaret Holmead to William S. Knudsen, June 23, 1941, WPB papers

278 Flather Memo.

279 According to Paul Morgan, a young associate, Paul Cabot had one big advantage in dealing with people of less privileged backgrounds, as he had to at the WPB. "He could use swear words with the worst of them. In fact his vocabulary of swear words was one of the best I have ever run across." Paul Morgan, *Dial "M" for Memories of the Greatest Generation*, (Xlibris, 2001) p. 56

280 Ibid p. 384

281 *Industrial Mobilization For War History of the War Production Board and Predecessor Agencies 1940-1945 Volume I Program and Administration*, (Washington, 1947) pp. 207, 238. Letter from Paul Morgan to M. Yogg, February 14, 2003. Morgan, *Dial "M" for Memories*, p. 384

282 Nelson, *Arsenal*, pp. 329-348.

283 W. T. Hoyt, "History of the Conservation and Salvage Division, War Production Board," unpublished manuscript WPB papers (5 pages)

284 Nelson, *Arsenal of Democracy*, pp. 353-355

285 "A Review of the General Salvage Program (from its inception—Nov. 1941 to Oct. 6, 1942)" unpublished manuscript, WPB papers p. 6

286 Morgan, *Dial "M" for Memories*, pp. 56-57

287 "Junk Will Win The War," Copyright 1942 by Bregman, Vocco, and Conn, Inc., NY

288 Undated note from Leon Henderson to Paul Cabot, WPB papers

289 Letter from Lessing Rosenwald to Carl Adams, January 23, 1942, Memo from Paul C. Cabot to Arthur B. Newhall, March 30, 1942, Memo from PCC to Messrs. Bertch, Gutterson, Murphy, Weymouth, Manuel, April 2, 1942, Memo from Herbert L. Gutterson to "All Members of Staff," June 18, 1942.

290 CUOHROC, pp. 125-135.

291 Letter from Paul Morgan to M. Yogg, February 14, 2003

292 Kahn, "Profiles," Sept. 15, p. 72, Sept. 8, p. 50.

293 Ibid. pp. 40,42.

294 CUOHROC, pp. 110-111.

295 Ibid. p. 190.

296 Kahn, "Profiles," Sept. 8, p. 54.

297 Kahn, "Profiles," Sept. 15, p. 60.

298 After I wrote a brief article comparing the thinking of Oscar Handlin to the thinking, or at least the instincts, of Paul Cabot, Professor Handlin wrote me that "It was good to be linked with Paul Cabot." Otto Eckstein, the Harvard economics professor and economic forecasting consultant was a favorite of Paul for his economic insights, but also his personality and sense of humor.

299 Train, *Money Masters*, p. 56.

300 Kahn, "Profiles," Sept. 8, p. 38.

301 CUOHROC, p. 152.

NOTES TO CHAPTER VI

302 *HARVARD Today*, Spring 1965, pp. 11-12

303 Flather Memo

304 Paul C. Cabot, "Chasing the Budget, My Twelve Years as Treasurer," *Harvard Alumni Bulletin*, May 25, 1963, p. 637

305 CUOHROC, p. 186

306 Paul C. Cabot and Leonard C. Larrabee, "Investing Harvard Money," *Harvard Alumni Bulletin*, May 12, 1951, p. 630

307 CUOHROC, pp. 181-184, Registration Statement under Securities Act of 1933, State Street Investment Corporation, February 16, 1942, pp. 2, 16.

308 Boston *Post*, February 26, 1929, p. 1 Boston *Transcript*, February 26, 1929 p.1

309 Keller and Keller, *Making Harvard Modern*, pp. 143-145

310 Ibid p. 144. He was in fact prescient in anticipating a decline in the relative importance of "receipts from accumulated wealth." From 1930 to 1955, the contribution of endowment to the cost of operating the college fell from 47% to 27%. Seymour E. Harris, *The Economics of Harvard* (New York, 1970) p. 335.

311 Keller and Keller, *Making Harvard Modern*, pp. 19-20. See Gelfand, *Trustee* pp. 178-181 for a more detailed account.

312 CUOHROC, pp. 85-88, 170

313 Telephone conversation, Edward M. Lamont with M. Yogg, December 30, 2003

314 Edward M. Lamont, *The Ambassador from Wall Street* (Lanham, MD, 1994) pp. 215, 505-507. Chernow, *House of Morgan*, pp. 277-284

315 Personal letter from Peter Vermilye to M. Yogg, November 18, 2003

316 CUOHROC, pp. 87-88

317 Lamont, *Ambassador*, pp. 291, 478 Chernow, *House of Morgan*, p. 277

318 Keller and Keller, *Making Harvard Modern*, pp. 84, 257

319 Boston *Herald*, October 19, 1948

320 Cabot, "Chasing the Budget," p. 637. CUOHROC, pp. 185-186

321 Letter from Paul C. Cabot to James Conant, September 27, 1948 (emphasis added).

322 Interview with John Thorndike, March 23, 2004. Interview with George Bennett, January 14, 2004.

323 *HARVARD Today*, Spring 1965, p.11

324 CUOHROC, p. 186

325 Interview with George Putnam, Jr. November 6, 2002

326 *HARVARD Today*, p. 11, A. Theodore Lyman, Jr. "The Harvard Endowment Fund 'Blue-Chip' Investing Pays Off," Research Report of the Putnam Management Company, Summer 1954, George Putnam, Jr. "The Harvard Endowment Fund Forging Ahead," Research Report of The Putnam Management Company, Summer 1955.

327 "Educated Money," *TIME*, October 29, 1962, p. 76

328 *HARVARD Today*, pp. 11-12

329 "Degrees Granted to 2301 at Yale," *The New York Times*, June 15, 1965

330 Lyman, "Harvard Endowment," Putnam, "Endowment Fund Forging Ahead," Seymour E. Harris *The Economics of Harvard* (New York, 1970) pp. 370-371. Using a different methodology, one that gave Paul credit for the reinvested money saved due to his reduced payout to the faculties (which was the result of his fiscal, not his investment, prowess), H. Bradlee Perry concludes that Paul is "responsible for at least $2 billion of the Harvard endowment's present (in 1999) $13 billion market value!" H. Bradlee Perry, *Winning the Investment Marathon* (Upton, MA: 1999) p. 213.

331 *HARVARD Today*, pp. 11-12

332 The term "religious opposition to borrowing," comes from a memo, McGeorge Bundy to Nathan M. Pusey, June 28, 1957. Letter from Paul C. Cabot to Sherwin C. Badger,

February 15, 1957. Paul C. Cabot, "Should Harvard Borrow? The Treasurer Thinks No.," *Harvard Alumni Bulletin*, October 8, 1960, pp. 65-67. Richard N. Cooper, "On the Other Hand—A Summary of Discussion," *Harvard Alumni Bulletin*, October 8, 1960, p. 67. Keller and Keller, *Making Harvard Modern*, p. 185

333 *Harvard Alumni Bulletin*, October 27, 1956, p. 107, Keller and Keller, *Making Harvard Modern*, p. 184.

334 Flather Memo

335 Keller and Keller, *Making Harvard Modern*, p. 191

336 CUOHROC, p. 195

337 Ibid, pp. 194-197

338 Keller and Keller, *Making Harvard Modern*, pp. 174-175 (emphasis added).

339 Ibid, p. 203

340 Boston, *Post*, June 12, 1953

341 Keller and Keller, *Making Harvard Modern*, p. 202

342 Ibid, pp. 315-318

343 Ibid, p. 336

344 Ibid, p. 337

345 CUOHROC, p. 193

346 Keller and Keller, *Making Harvard Modern*, p. 316

347 Ibid p. 315, Presumably the Harvard President.

348 Personal Letter from Nathan M. Pusey to Charles Mortimer, October 15, 1964. (Emphasis in original)

349 CUOHROC, pp. 197-198

350 Advisory Committee on Investment Management, *Managing Educational Endowments, Report to the Ford Foundation*, (New York, 1972) pp. x, 16-21.

351 CUOHROC, pp. 202-203

352 Ibid, p. 200

353 Ibid. p.200

354 Letter, Paul Cabot to Derek Bok, June 28, 1972

355 CUOHROC pp. 204-205

356 Keller and Keller, *Making Harvard Modern*, p.179

357 "THE TALK OF THE TOWN, Harvard's Cabot," *The New Yorker*, April 27, 1957, pp. 23-25.

358 Personal letter from Arden Yinkey Jr. to Paul C. Cabot, April 29, 1957

359 The Kellers identify the Kennedy administration as the high point of Harvard's confidence, or as they say in Cambridge, *hubris.*

360 Keller and Keller, *Making Harvard Modern*, p. 210

361 CUOHROC, pp. 73-74

362 Interview with John Thorndike, November 18, 2002. Flather, Memo.

363 CUOHROC, p. 74

364 Gelfand, *Trustee*, p. 192 John Kenneth Galbraith, *A Life in Our Times*, (Boston: Houghton Mifflin, 1981) p. 226

365 Galbraith, *A Life*, pp. 274-275

366 John Kenneth Galbraith, "Reflections A Visit to Russia," *The New Yorker*, September 3, 1984, p. 60.

367 CUOHROC, pp. 75-76

368 Ibid p. 75

369 Galbraith, *A Life*, pp. 276-277

NOTES TO CHAPTER VII

370 Frederick C. Cabot, Memorial Service Remarks

371 Barnes, *Cabots*, pp. 50-51

372 Barnes, *Cabots*, pp. 57-59

373 Amory, *Bostonians*, p. 200

374 Flather Memo.

375 Barnes, *Cabots*, pp. 60, 132

376 Ibid pp. 61, 77-78.

377 Ibid pp. 5, 46, 61-63, 86-87.

378 *NY Times*, July 11, 1936

379 *NY Times*, July 10, 1936

380 Tosiello p.7

381 Barnes, *Cabots*, pp. 44, 71

382 *The New Yorker*, April 27, 1957. Gelfand, Trustee, pp. 1-4

383 Barnes, *Cabots*, p. 97

384 Ibid pp. 121-122

385 "Paul Cabot for Harvard Treasurer?" Boston *Transcript*, February 26, 1929, p. 1

386 *Class of 1921 50th Anniversary*, p. 66

387 Holland, Goldman Sachs Interview, p. 12.

388 Ibid, p. 24.

389 Memorial Service Remarks

390 Personal note from Frederick C. Cabot to M. Yogg, May 23, 2003

391 Memorial Service Remarks

392 Robert J. Garofalo, *Frederick Shepherd Converse (1870-1940) His Life and Music*, (Metuchen, NJ: 1994) pp. 75-77. CUOHROC pp. 138-139

393 CUOHROC, pp. 160-162

394 Barnes, *Cabots*, p. 140

NOTES TO CHAPTER VIII

[395] Paul Cabot, "Testimony to the House Committee on Ways and Means," March 12, 1969

[396] SSIC, *Annual Report*, 1940, p. 2, 1941 p. 2

[397] SSIC, *Annual Report*, 1943, p. 2

[398] SSIC, *Annual Report*, 1944, p. 3

[399] Interview with George F. Bennett by David Joy, c. 1990, p 3

[400] Registration Statement under Securities Act of 1933, State Street Investment Corporation, February 16, 1942, p. 2

[401] SSIC, *Annual Report*, 1944, p. 3

[402] "The Decay of a Myth," *Fortune* Magazine, June 1, 1974, p. 48

[403] Joy, Bennett Interview, p. 3

[404] Lee Iacocca with William Novak, *Iacocca: An Autobiography* (New York: 1984) p. 151

[405] Flather Memo

[406] *Fortune*, June 1, 1974, p. 48

[407] Interview with George F. Bennett, January 14, 2004

[408] "Businessmen in the News "The Faces of Friends," *Fortune* Magazine, July 15, 1966, pp. 71-72.

[409] CUOHROC, pp. 147-148.

[410] Ibid, pp. 139-140, 146-148.

[411] Jean Edward Smith, *Lucius D. Clay* (New York, 1990) pp. 13, 158, CUOHROC, pp. 171-172

[412] Smith, *Clay*, pp. 653-654, 666-667

[413] CUOHROC, pp. 177-180

[414] Ibid pp. 156-157

[415] Ibid pp. 176-177

[416] George Soros, "Why the Stock Market Can't Fix Itself," *The New Republic*, Issue 4,572, Sep. 2, 2002, pp. 18-21

[417] Paul Cabot, "Testimony to the House Committee on Ways and Means," March 12, 1969

[418] John Brooks, *The Go-Go Years* (NY, 1999) p. 154

[419] Ibid p. 176

[420] Ibid p. 3

[421] While Paul was divorced from the management of the firm, he remained close to the research and investment process until the late 1980s.

[422] "Faces Behind the Figures," *Fortune* Magazine, June 15, 1970, p. 80

[423] Train p. 48

[424] Ibid p. 54

[425] Amory, *Bostonians*, p. 66

[426] Train, p. 53

[427] Robert Lenzer, "A Proper Boston Investment House," *Boston Globe*, January 12, 1982, p. 57

[428] Flather Memo. Interview with Peter Vermilye, October 2, 2003

[429] Tosiello, pp. 12-13

[430] Interview with Bob Lawrence, July 23, 2002

[431] Interview with Charles Flather, February 19, 2003. Flather Memo.

[432] Conversation with James Ullman, 1983. This a paraphrase rather than a direct quote.

[433] Lawrence interview, July 23, 2002, Flather interview, February 19, 2003, Flather Memo

[434] State Street Investment Corp. proxy statement, December 14, 1982

[435] Interview with Paula Kerrigan, June 19, 2005

[436] Anonymous, "PAUL C. CABOT A Man For All Seasons," National Dairy Products Corp. Directors' Dinner, Chicago, April 16, 1969

[437] R.W.B. Lewis, *American Adam* (Chicago, 1959) p. 130. Ahab never said, "First you've got to get the whale, then you've got to face the whale." But he might have.

[438] Lewis, pp. 134-135, Mark Van Doren, ed. *The Portable Whitman*, (NY, 1977) pp. 56, 320, 374

[439] Bernard Bailyn, *To Begin the World Anew* (New York: 2003) pp. 35-36

Index

A

W